Branded by Spirits

A Life Between Worlds

Kenneth Drake

BEYOND
THE TRAY PUBLISHING

Contents

Preface

"Black."

Even now, after all this time, I can think of no other word that adequately describes it. But even that term, as a descriptor, does very little justice. To call the form merely a "shadow figure" fails to illustrate the immense darkness of it. After all, even a shadow, by definition, implies the existence of some light, somewhere.

But there was no hint of light. There was only sheer dark—the absence of any light. It was as if *void* had taken shape before my eyes, materializing into an obvious human form. It was a darkness I had never seen before. I have not seen such darkness since.

"Black."

It was the stuff of nightmares—though it was not a dream. I was awake. Fully and consciously alert. I *know* that I was awake. Even in a darkened bedroom, I could clearly see a figure so dark it cast a stark silhouette, even against shadows.

There was a time when I wondered often if it had been *sleep paralysis*—one of those moments when we feel trapped, suspended between the realm of sleep and waking, conscious thought. One of those many times when our most nightmarish visions take shape and seem to peer at us, leaving us helpless to resist.

But it was not that. There is no question I was awake. There was a literal eternity encapsulated in those passing moments.

I know I was awake and alert because I had been awakened not by the rustlings of some intruder, but by the sound of my *own* voice. In fact, it was my voice I noticed first. I was speaking—loudly. I have no sense of time having passed, and even now I don't know how long I had been speaking.

All I know is that when I awoke, I awoke to the sound of a language I did not know. Someone—something—was speaking through me.

Before I turned to notice the darkness peering up at me, I paused, struggling to collect my bearings. My tongue moved quickly and violently. The sounds were not gibberish, nor the mumblings of someone half-asleep. No. It was a distinguishable dialect—tones and complete phrases.

I had awoken to the sound of myself speaking in unknown tongues. And once I gained full awareness—that sharp alertness that distinguishes sleep from wakefulness—I struggled to stop. Even then, the words kept coming.

I also found my arms suspended above me, contorted in a way that brought no comfort. My hands moved violently, uncontrollably, forming gestures and indecipherable poses—*mudras*, as I would later come to know them.

Much, much later I would recognize that the movements and postures had meaning. That the violent gesturing signified something.

"*Mudra*," in ancient Sanskrit, means "seal" or "sign."

After what seemed like an eternity, I regained control of my body—though not easily. I stopped gesturing. I lowered my arms. I closed my mouth and ceased speaking.

Everything returned to normal.

And only then did I turn.

And as I turned my head, I saw it.

"Black."

A sheer, pitch-black silhouette in human form. Someone—something—had been watching me the entire time. The *watcher* had been kneeling beside my bed, looking on curiously and intently.

Had I unknowingly, unconsciously *summoned* something in my sleep? Even the idea sounds absurd. After all, summoning requires conscious, willful intent.

I had regained my sense of control—my ability to speak my own words, in my own voice, under my own power. I looked at the dark figure and noticed how curious it seemed—how intrigued it was by everything that had occurred.

Then I screamed.

It was then—and only then—that I screamed. A blood-curdling, soul-crushing scream of sheer horror.

The kind of horror that can only come from complete helplessness. A scream born of hopelessness.

Preface

Not a single day has passed since that moment that I haven't heard the voice of the dead.

Introduction

"And I will give thee the treasures of darkness, and hidden riches of secret places..." – Isaiah 45:3

The most beautiful things often come in the most horrifying, darkest of ways. Even now—some twenty-five years later—I often wish I could have known then the beauty that would emerge from my greatest horror. But life rarely works that way.

Today, in my soul, I understand that the greatest, most beautiful things can only come from darkness if—only if—we continue the journey, moving forward. I never would have chosen this life, quite frankly. I never would have wanted these experiences. And if I'm to be fully candid with you, I spent the better part of my life trying to run from them as far and as fast as I could.

"Treasures of darkness." "Hidden riches." Even now, those phrases carry immense meaning for me. The ancients, the spiritual seekers of long ago, had a poetic way of describing the spiritual awakening experience. "Treasures of darkness" feels most fitting. The words ring true, not just because of their poetic beauty, but because, back then, I was deeply religious. I had just begun seminary.

I think often of the beliefs I held during that time—the sincerity, the passionate pursuit of the unseen. "Treasures of darkness" resonates deeply because, as a young kid raised in the religion of the rural South—a world of revivals and fiery Pentecostal preaching—I never could have imagined that the most horrifying moments of my life would yield the kind of beauty I now live.

There were no stage lights then. This was long before all that. Before Hollywood came calling. Before sold-out tours or celebrity clientele. I was just a strange kid, alone in the world, desperate for something more. And I found it—in the most horrifying of ways.

Across history, cultures, and faiths, angelic encounters often begin the same way—not with awe, but terror. That's why angels in sacred texts so often begin with "Fear not." The transcendence comes later. But in the beginning? It's horror.

Now, years later, I often joke on stage, "You never forget your first time," when it comes to angelic or otherworldly encounters. I share it lightheartedly, to reflect just how terrifying my first encounter was—and just how routine these encounters have now become. As "Hollywood's Psychic," it's part of my daily life. I no longer hide that chapter; I embrace it. I try to use it to encourage others—seekers and sensitives—who feel alone in the horror of their own awakenings.

I was marked by the spirit world all those years ago. Not a day has passed without being reminded of that mark—etched deeply in my soul. And maybe it's cynicism, but I smile when I hear others describe their awakenings with words like "love," "light," or "peaceful." I don't diminish those experiences—who am I to judge? But for me, this "treasure" arrived like a violent force. It was a mental and spiritual assault. A ripping away of any normalcy I had imagined for myself.

Looking back, though, I feel an immense gratitude. I'm thankful it happened the way it did. I was stubborn. An immovable force. People ask me often—students, clients, even audience members—"Did you abandon your faith after it happened?" It's an understandable question. A psychic who's spent two decades in entertainment seems a far cry from the young man who once dreamed of becoming a preacher.

Without hesitation, my answer is always no. "It was my faith that led to this," I tell them. "And I'm still being led." That's why I end every performance—onstage or on camera—by blowing a kiss to the sky, then to the audience. It's become a trademark. I say, "Thank you to the spirits. And thanks to you."

In remembering those formative years, I am thankful. First and foremost, to my family—without their love, I wouldn't have survived. In my early twenties, I waged war on myself. I tried to sabotage everything. I didn't want this life. This persona. The "I see dead people" identity.

I remember watching that film and thinking, "At least that kid could see his visions clearly." At least his ghosts were human. With human stories. I envied that. He had no religious dogma to wrestle with. No demons or angels or Heaven or Hell to complicate the narrative. Just spirits, wanting to be heard.

For me, clarity didn't come for many years. After addiction. After public scandals. After trying desperately to silence the voices. After falling from the stages of revival into the arms of an entertainment world drenched in excess. Especially in the South, where even the word "psychic" still sparks outrage.

Introduction

I've always related more to Tangina Barrons than to the boy in *The Sixth Sense*. The eccentric, flamboyant medium from *Poltergeist*—played brilliantly by Zelda Rubinstein—felt familiar. *Poltergeist* always felt more real to me than *The Sixth Sense*. I'm still not entirely sure why.

While we're on the subject of psychic depictions, I should say: to me, the dead have always felt more like Nicole Kidman in *The Others* than like Patrick Swayze in *Ghost*. It's subtle. Nuanced. Complicated. Not all mediums see the same way. And I would never suggest mine is the only right way.

The spirit world speaks a universal language. So does horror, if you think about it. In horror, especially film, it's what we *don't* see that terrifies us most. As a lifelong horror fan, I've always found the knife-wielding maniac trope almost comical. But unseen forces? Entities that possess the soul? That's terrifying.

To this day, *The Exorcist* remains the most horrifying film I've ever seen. Interviewing Eileen Dietz, who played Pazuzu, for the 50th anniversary of the film on *Voices of the Dead*, was unforgettable. And somehow, she hasn't aged a day.

At conventions now, I always remind audiences: horror speaks a language we all understand. And when I look into those crowds of fans and seekers, I see myself. A once wide-eyed kid with a passion for the unseen. A kid who was branded for life. And no, that's not hyperbole.

Does that surprise you? My darling, there's a reason you've always been drawn to the dark. To the unseen. A reason you're holding this book right now. The spirit world has been calling you, too.

I'll never forget a woman who contacted me years ago, terrified by events in her home. "The voices are everywhere," she said through tears—not internal voices, but disembodied ones.

Introduction

Others heard them too. Her home had been blessed repeatedly by priests. "I sleep with a crucifix under my pillow," she confessed. Then she asked: "Why would God let this happen?"

Her question struck a nerve in me. Her story mirrored my own. And as clearly as I've ever heard the spirits, I heard the answer. "You are being called. When you stop fighting this, this will stop." Then I added something I almost never say: "I promise you."

Three weeks later, she called again. "That same night," she said, "the voices stopped." Peace had finally come.

You see, the reason we encounter such things is because the reason itself is hidden within the experience. *Treasures in darkness*, indeed.

I share my story candidly—not to make light of the horror, but to say: yes, the terror is real. But terror was never the spirit world's intent. It doesn't want to frighten us. It simply wants acknowledgment. Once seen, it no longer needs to scream. The war has never been with the dead. The war has always been within us.

"If it's your calling, it will keep calling." And it won't stop—until you surrender to the truth that we are never alone.

Let me leave you with a thought at the start of this book. Even now, every time I recall this memory, I feel the spirit world all around me. It still takes my breath away.

It happened decades ago, on vacation in Miramar Beach, Florida. I remember every detail.

Walking the shoreline, sandals in hand, I noticed how clear the water was. Like glass. Every grain of sand visible. Every shell. Every detail of my feet beneath the water. Shallow, pristine waters.

Later, on a dinner cruise, I stood at the railing with a glass of Cabernet. The sun reflected brilliantly on the water's surface. Blindingly bright. Then I looked down. And beneath the boat, there was no light. Just blackness.

We had drifted into deeper waters.

Darling, *depth* can look like *darkness*. Depth, at first glance, is terrifying. A void. But if you keep looking, if you really focus—you'll see that even in the dark, something exists. Something hidden. Something rare. Treasures, buried deep.

Too often we flee the dark, never realizing it's trying to show us something.

I don't consider myself nihilistic. I now identify as a Spiritualist. Though I cherish friends of every faith—and none at all. Some still call what I do "witchcraft." That's fine. I own that too.

Nietzsche wrote: "He who fights with monsters might take care lest he thereby become a monster. And if you gaze long into an abyss, the abyss also gazes into you."

For me, monsters are of our own making. Ghosts are not monsters.

So much has changed in twenty-five years. I barely recognize the scared kid I once was. But some things haven't changed. I still love a good ghost story. A good horror film. And I'm still captivated by the world that called out to me all those years ago.

Twenty sold-out tours later. Thousands of readings. Countless moments—beautiful and horrifying—I think back to the early days in rural Alabama. The roots of everything.

Every success I've known is because of those encounters—and the people who loved me through them.

My life changed in the most terrifying, most horrific of ways. And not a day has passed without the voice of the dead. I still hear them. I still see them. And I'm still called to share their stories.

More than two decades later, the journey continues. There are no endings, my darling. As you'll see in these pages—we'll be around for quite some time.

Thank you for being part of this strange, wild, often horrifying ride with me.

"Thank you to the spirits. And thanks to you."

Part One

Foundations of Spiritualism and the Occult

Chapter 1

The Birth of Spiritualism

He was called a madman by some. By others, a "prophet." Some claimed to have been miraculously healed by his unconventional methods and teachings. To some, he was regarded as a man of God—a man of great faith. To others, he was a servant of the Devil, calling upon dark forces to do his bidding. But he regarded himself as "The Poughkeepsie Seer."

A "John the Baptist" of sorts, he would unwittingly become the forerunner of one of the greatest spiritual revivals in history—a literal revival of spirit activity. Andrew Jackson Davis heard voices in the wind, calling out to him. He recounted the experience in his own words:

"About daylight this morning, a warm breathing passed over my face, and I heard a voice, tender and strong, saying, 'Brother, the good work has begun—behold, a living demonstration is born.'"

The date was March 31, 1848.

Unknown to him at the time, on that exact day and not far from where he lived, strange and bizarre events began to unfold in a small cottage in Hydesville—events that would single-hand-edly propel mediumship and spirit communication into the spotlight, igniting a newfound passion for the occult.

The event? "The Rochester Knockings."

The unwitting participants? Two young girls—Kate and Maggie Fox, the Fox Sisters.

The horrifying and unusual paranormal happenings at Hydesville sparked the advent of Modern Spiritualism. Though history continues to judge the claims of the Fox Sisters as either famous or infamous—and though they would eventually recant their claims of spirit communication, even publicly—the undeniable truth remains: what transpired in their family home forever changed the course of human interaction with the paranormal.

In fact, Sir Arthur Conan Doyle, the famed author who gave the world Sherlock Holmes, once remarked that the Fox Sisters were the greatest gift America had ever given to the common-wealth of the world. Doyle, himself an ardent Spiritualist, would spend the later part of his life chronicling psychic phenomena and participating in numerous séances.

The wind howled, rattling the windows of the Fox family home —a small, creaking cottage in Hydesville, New York. A bitter winter had wrapped the land in an icy grip. It was on nights like these that the walls always seemed to whisper, filling the house with the unsettling uneasiness of something unseen, yet undeniably present.

Margaret and Kate Fox, just fifteen and eleven years old, had grown accustomed to the haunting sounds that echoed through their home. There were knocks in the walls, dragging noises beneath the floorboards, and distant tapping that pulsed with unnatural, otherworldly rhythms. Their parents, anxious and nearing the end of their wits, often dismissed the disturbances as tricks of the wind or the typical groans of an old house settling in the cold. But the girls always seemed to know better. They were mediums.

It was on a night much like this—when the sounds became nearly unbearable—that Kate decided to challenge the unseen forces at work. Sensing there was more than wind at play, she put her instincts to the test.

"Do as I do," she said, clapping her hands loudly three times.

Three knocks answered in return.

Margaret gasped, pressing her hands to her mouth. "It is listening to us, Sister!"

Contact had been made.

The girls continued their strange communication with the otherworldly presence, asking it specific questions and commanding it to respond with knocks. It claimed to be the spirit of a murdered peddler, buried beneath the very floorboards they stood upon. They began to refer to the entity as "Mr. Splitfoot," a nickname commonly associated with the Devil.

Their mother, horrified and shaken to her core, summoned neighbors. Upon witnessing the phenomenon firsthand, the neighbors quickly spread word of the Fox Sisters' eerie and inexplicable abilities.

But as their fame grew, so too did the presence in their home.

The knocks became violent. Doors were flung open in the dead of night. Whispers floated through the air like unseen fingers brushing their ears. One evening, as Margaret lay in bed, she felt something cold and skeletal clutch her ankle and pull her abruptly, jolting her from sleep. Kate awoke to find her sister hovering an inch above the mattress, eyes wide, lips parted in a scream that would not come.

They fled the house soon after, their parents too terrified to remain. But the spirits followed. The girls had been marked.

Wherever they went, the knocking followed. Sometimes it came softly, like a secret conversation. Other times, it struck with the fury of the damned. They sought solace in séances, surrounded by crowds of believers and skeptics alike. But with every performance—every audience held breathless by their spectral communion—something darker clung more tightly to them. It followed them, always.

By the time they reached adulthood, their eerie talents had made them icons of the burgeoning Spiritualist movement. But they had also become prisoners of their own dark gift. Strong drink became their only reprieve, dulling the ever-present whispers clawing at their consciousness in the quiet hours of the night.

When Margaret eventually denounced their abilities—calling them nothing but trickery and charlatanism—she did so with trembling hands and hollow eyes, as if something unseen was watching from the shadows, waiting for her to return.

Perhaps this is a grossly exaggerated account of the happenings at Hydesville, told with great liberty. And perhaps it is not. Perhaps it is simply the horror enthusiast in me that envisions these events in such a way. Or perhaps it is something deeper— a medium seeking to validate other mediums and their mediumship.

What cannot be denied, and what cannot be dismissed, is that the events that transpired in that small cottage branded the Fox Sisters for the rest of their lives.

Had it all truly happened as they claimed? Had genuine contact been made with the Other Side? Or had it all been an elaborate hoax, carefully crafted and expertly performed?

Perhaps the most shocking truth of all is this: within five years, Spiritualism had swept the globe—not only as a practice, but as a burgeoning new religion. Mediumship had been thrust onto the world stage. Seekers from all walks of life, across countless belief systems, found within themselves a renewed hunger for communion with the dearly departed.

Perhaps to understand how and why Spiritualism spread so rapidly—faster, even, than the growth of more traditional religions like Christianity—it is essential to look at the broader context of the nineteenth century.

In many ways, it was the perfect storm.

The Pentecostal resurgence within Christianity—a movement marked by its emphasis on speaking in tongues, ecstatic visions, and angelic visitations—would not arrive until later in the century. Spiritualism, however, predated it by nearly fifty years.

I often tell clients and audiences at my shows that, even after all this time, I still consider myself a student of the spirit world. I am always the first to admit I'm still learning. The journey is never-ending. In fact, the best way to describe the Spiritualist revival of the nineteenth century—which continues to resonate globally today—is to see it not as a beginning, but as merely another leg of a much longer journey.

You see, communion with the Other Side was nothing new—not even then. For as long as humankind has walked the earth, there has been a fascination with what lies beyond the veil. Is this physical, waking reality all there is? Is this life the end-all, be-all of existence? Or, as so many quietly suspect, is it merely one brief part of a tapestry much, much larger?

The question has lingered as long as humanity has possessed the ability to reason.

By the mid-nineteenth century, many long-held beliefs were being challenged. People were searching for deeper spiritual fulfillment—fulfillment that often transcended the dogma of organized religion. I often refer to this innate longing as an "experiential passion." Belief, in and of itself, is a beautiful thing. But as our understanding evolves, so too does our desire to experience what those beliefs truly mean.

Mediumship offered more than abstract theology. It promised tangible, seemingly physical proof of a world beyond. Séances were no longer confined to dimly lit backrooms and shadowy parlors. Instead, public demonstrations of spirit communication took center stage in theaters around the world.

The Spiritualist revival emerged during a time of profound cultural transformation in Western society. Industrialization, scientific progress, and sweeping social change reshaped the collective mindset. Traditional religious institutions struggled to address these rapid developments, and into that void stepped alternative spiritual movements—chief among them, Spiritualism.

The climate was ripe for its rise. The spirit world, it seemed, was waiting.

By this time, many faithful individuals had already begun questioning the authority of organized religion. The rationalism and intellectualism of the Enlightenment had paved the way for scientific discoveries that challenged longstanding theological doctrines. Meanwhile, Romanticism—especially in art and literature—reintroduced emotional and mystical elements to spiritual life.

Even Protestantism was splintering. Denominations were breaking apart, with some groups emphasizing personal, experience-based faith over rigid doctrine. This broader cultural shift created fertile ground for alternative paths to thrive.

Spiritualism, with its unapologetic emphasis on personal proof of the afterlife, appealed deeply to those disillusioned by institutional religion. Unlike traditional faiths that relied on scripture and belief, Spiritualism offered direct, often dramatic evidence of life beyond death. Séances, spirit writings, ghostly raps, levitations—these were not metaphors or myths. They were, to believers, firsthand demonstrations of the afterlife breaking through.

The nineteenth century was also a period of tremendous scientific advancement. When Charles Darwin published *On the Origin of Species* in 1859, it challenged traditional views on creation and human purpose. For many, this prompted a search for alternative explanations—new ways to understand the soul's journey and the mysteries of existence itself.

It was during this same era that mesmerism—an early form of hypnosis—and phrenology—the study of skull shapes to determine personality—captivated the public. Both disciplines reinforced the idea that unseen, often spiritual forces governed human behavior and consciousness. Spiritualism thrived in this intellectual and cultural stew, claiming to offer direct, observable evidence of life beyond death: raps on tables, levitating furniture, automatic writing, and even spirit art.

As the movement grew, it evolved into an organized religious and social force. Spiritualist churches and societies sprang up across the world. Unlike traditional religious institutions of the time, these groups often welcomed women into leadership roles, recognizing their perceived natural sensitivity to spiritual forces. This progressive openness made Spiritualism one of the few religious movements of the nineteenth century to provide women with a prominent public platform.

In fact, it could be argued that the modern feminist movement owes much to early Spiritualists. Figures such as Cora L. V. Scott and Emma Hardinge Britten electrified audiences with their powerful oratory and psychic demonstrations. Scott would go on to co-found the National Spiritualist Association of Churches in the United States.

Personally, the work of these two remarkable women—and many others—profoundly shaped my own development as a psychic and medium. One of my most cherished possessions is a first-edition 1875 printing of *Discourses Through the Mediumship of Mrs. Cora L. V. Tappan* (Tappan being her married name). The book is a collection of "orations" delivered by Scott during a two-year stay in London.

I've always been drawn to old books, especially those exploring the occult. After a long day of readings or returning from tour, I love stepping into my study and feeling the power in those volumes. As a medium, I know all too well that spiritual energy is transferable—and the legacy of these extraordinary pioneers still pulses through the pages.

But Spiritualism wasn't just about individual development or metaphysical philosophy. It intersected deeply with the progressive movements of its time. Many Spiritualists were abolitionists, suffragists, and social reformers. The movement's core message—that spirit communication offered divine insight—gave moral weight to causes like women's rights and racial equality.

Victoria Woodhull, for example, was both a medium and a vocal advocate for gender equality. She argued that her spirit guides had called her to the cause of women's suffrage. Frederick Douglass and other influential reformers also engaged with Spiritualist circles, recognizing their commitment to justice and change.

This alignment with progressive causes helped cement Spiritualism's place in nineteenth-century cultural life. It opened doors for seekers from all backgrounds—skeptics and believers, reformers and mystics—to find community and purpose. The movement had become more than a religious curiosity. It was a force.

The rise of Spiritualism in the nineteenth century was no accident. Whatever one chooses to believe about the Fox Sisters and their original claims, the movement took on a life uniquely its own. It emerged at a time when traditional beliefs were being questioned, science was expanding human understanding, and society was yearning for something deeper—something experiential. And with that yearning came a need for education.

As many of the great pioneers of Spiritualism began to pass into what is called the Summerland, it became essential that their work be documented, preserved, and taught to others. Mediums of the time began training future generations, passing down not just technique, but philosophy.

Even today, long after the height of the movement, these institutions of learning still exist. Though not always well publicized and often overlooked by the casual observer, they remain. I owe a deep debt to Spiritualist education. As a child in the rural South, experiencing unexplained phenomena and feeling completely isolated, I didn't even know there were others—many others—who had endured similar things. I had so much to learn. I still do.

But it was through the Spiritualist movement that I realized something profound: the spirits *are* speaking—and they always have been. I had never truly been alone. None of us are. I simply needed to find my tribe.

I was deeply honored to become a member of the Spiritualists' National Union of Great Britain—the governing body that oversees the world-renowned Arthur Findlay College. For those who are fans of *Harry Potter*, imagine a kind of "Hogwarts" for mediums. That's Arthur Findlay.

Not only did it transform my life and development, but it has also inspired countless thousands of seekers around the globe. In fact, after surviving some of the darkest experiences of my own life, it was British mediumship and the support of that community that helped me reclaim my footing. To this day, I still have handwritten notes and messages of encouragement from prominent U.K. mediums—many of whom are now dear friends—reminding me, during my hardest times, that I was never alone.

Spirits lead us to where we're meant to be. I firmly believe that.

One dear friend and mentor who teaches at Arthur Findlay once sent me a message:

"This will take over your life if you let it."

At the time, I found the message a bit ominous. But it wasn't meant to be. What I didn't say in return—but deeply understood—was that it already *had*. I had long since surrendered to the pull of the Other Side. I had tried to run, tried to escape.

And yet, in my soul, I knew: there's no need to run. There never was.

These days, when I have rare time off from the road and readings, I do everything I can to support the Spiritualist movement here in the United States. And believe it or not, one doesn't need to travel abroad to find magic. Right here at home, there are "hidden gems" for the spiritually curious—if you know where to look.

In Wisconsin, we have our very own Spiritualist college.

At the peak of the movement in the late nineteenth century—when séances, spirit photography, and paranormal investigation captivated the public imagination—one man dared to envision something extraordinary. His name was Morris Pratt. A businessman and devout Spiritualist, Pratt believed so deeply in the importance of mediumship and spirit communication that he invested a large portion of his personal wealth into building a school dedicated to those teachings.

In 1902, the Morris Pratt Institute was born. Nicknamed "Spooks' College," the school offered education in mediumship, healing, metaphysics, and Spiritualist philosophy. It was the first of its kind.

Though the original physical campus no longer bustles with students, the mission of the Morris Pratt Institute lives on. Over a century later, its legacy endures—a testament to humanity's enduring curiosity about the afterlife.

And it's not alone.

There is Cassadaga, Florida. There is Lily Dale, New York. And nestled in the heart of Indiana, there is Camp Chesterfield—one of the most celebrated and enduring Spiritualist camps in the country.

Founded in 1891 by the Indiana Association of Spiritualists, Camp Chesterfield has long served as a sanctuary for seekers, mediums, and anyone drawn to the mysteries of the spirit world. To this day, it offers classes, events, and healing services that continue to inspire and challenge.

Visitors are often struck by its unique architecture and the palpable sense of energy that surrounds the camp. It is also home to the Hett Art Gallery & Museum, which houses an incredible collection of spirit art, automatic writing, and historical artifacts related to mediumship. One need not even be a medium to feel the *power* there.

I was once part of a rare paranormal investigation inside the museum. It was one of the only times in my entire life I had to step outside—overwhelmed by the intensity of the spirit activity within. It was dizzying, electric, unforgettable.

Places like Camp Chesterfield are treasures in my life. They came to me at a time when I needed them most. And when the opportunity arises, I return—not as a performer, not as a public figure, but simply as a soul making pilgrimage to sacred ground.

In these places, the spirits still whisper. And for those of us who listen, the call continues.

By now, darling, you may be wondering why I've chosen to share so much about the history of the Spiritualist movement at the very outset of our time together.

Does one need to subscribe to Spiritualist philosophy or principles in order to experience the Other Side?

Does one need to adopt Spiritualism as a religion to unlock their own psychic abilities?

Absolutely not.

The spirit world speaks a universal language. So too, I believe, does the horror that so often accompanies it.

I share this backstory for one simple reason: when I first found myself consumed by terrifying encounters—those that marked the beginning of this strange and unusual journey—I felt utterly alone. As a young, odd kid who believed he was cursed, discovering a sense of community was nothing short of a godsend.

Over the years, I've been incredibly fortunate—blessed, really —to meet so many others who share a deep passion for the otherworldly. People who, in their own way, have heard the call of the shadows.

As of this writing, I've completed over twenty sold-out national tours, demonstrating mediumship and sharing messages from the dead. I've given more psychic readings than I can even count—though I've been credited with over fifty thousand.

And yet, there is never enough time. Onstage, there are always more hands raised, more hearts waiting, more spirits eager to speak. When the curtain closes, the next city awaits.

More recently, I've begun accepting invitations to speak at horror and paranormal conventions across the United States— something I never imagined I'd do. But within those conventions, I've discovered a family all its own. The horror and paranormal genres have a fandom unlike any other: passionate, expressive, fiercely loyal.

From ghost lovers to cinephiles, what I've found at these events is a community I wish had existed for me when I was young. I often say during my talks, "The reason we are drawn to these things is because, in some way, these things have always been calling out to us." That message lands deeply every time.

For many young people—those who've always felt like outsiders, whether due to their love of the macabre, their interest in the supernatural, or simply because they never quite fit in—horror and paranormal conventions offer far more than a weekend of frights. They offer belonging.

Horror, as a genre, has always spoken to the misunderstood. Classic monsters like Frankenstein's creature or spectral beings trapped between worlds are metaphors for those rejected by society. It's no surprise, then, that these conventions become havens for young misfits seeking connection.

Walking into a horror or paranormal convention feels like stepping into another world—a world where the weird is celebrated and the unusual is embraced. Every corner is buzzing with excitement. For me, it feels like home.

For many attendees, especially those who've endured bullying, alienation, or judgment, these gatherings are more than an escape. They're a lifeline. A safe haven. A tribe. No one questions why you wear all black, love ghost stories, or can quote *The Exorcist* line by line. It's simply understood—and welcomed.

Friendships are formed instantly. The bond is effortless, born of shared passion and the deep relief of being seen. There is no need to explain why you believe in spirits or why you crave the eerie. At these conventions, it just *is*.

Being branded as "Hollywood's Psychic" has given me a unique opportunity to bridge two worlds—horror and the paranormal. And when you stop to think about it, those two worlds are more alike than different. They are, in many ways, synonymous.

Whether I'm recounting terrifying experiences from my own life, sharing documented accounts from actual case files, or discussing how horror themes have shaped pop culture and our collective fascination with the unknown—I feel most at home among fellow enthusiasts. These events, these fans, these conversations... they're sacred to me.

At conventions, I speak on panels, host workshops, and meet attendees one-on-one. We talk about the latest horror releases, share personal ghost stories, and debate which cryptid is truly the most terrifying. These aren't just casual conversations—they're connections. The kind that linger long after the weekend ends.

And here's something I need to make clear: I never charge for these appearances. As much as I can control my schedule, I will always attend these events free of charge. I tell my management plainly—if an invitation comes and I'm available, I will be there. No invoice. No expectation.

Why?

Because this is the community I needed when I was young. The one I longed for. And for every seeker attending today—many of whom never had the chance to come to one of my live shows—I want them to know they are *not* alone.

Beyond the deep sense of belonging, there's also an unmistakable joy that pulses through these events. Haunted houses, horror-themed escape rooms, immersive experiences, ghost-hunting panels—these aren't just thrills. They're portals. They give us permission to play with the unknown, to explore our fear safely and with curiosity.

Horror isn't just about being scared. It's about being *transformed*.

And what better way to explore the unknown than surrounded by friends who feel the same pull? Friends who don't just tolerate your weirdness, but celebrate it.

For many attendees, these weekends are life-changing. The guests, the panels, the haunted attractions—they're all wonderful. But what keeps people coming back year after year are the relationships. The tribe. The *family*.

I was recently honored to be a featured speaker at Evansville Horror Con in Indiana. I left that event feeling humbled and grateful—like I had been part of something so much bigger than myself. My presentation, titled *"Beyond the Grave: Exploring the Paranormal Theme in Horror with Hollywood's Psychic,"* focused on how films like *Rosemary's Baby* and *The Exorcist* helped open a gateway—not just for horror as a genre, but for real-world interest in the paranormal.

Those films—and countless others—sparked phenomena in people's lives. They awakened something. That's the power of horror. It asks the unspoken questions. It dares to look beyond the veil.

In a world that too often demands conformity, horror and paranormal conventions offer something radical: permission to be *exactly* who you are. For young people who've spent their lives feeling like outcasts, these spaces aren't just fun. They're sacred. They're home.

At these conventions—and in every city, every venue, every whispered message from beyond—I've come to realize something powerful:

This work was never just about me.

It's about *them*. The seekers. The curious. The frightened. The misfits. The ones who have felt something brush past them in the dark and wondered if they were crazy—or if they were being called.

It's about the spirits, too. About their persistence, their longing to speak, and their desire to be heard.

And so, I continue to show up. Whether on stage or in a darkened museum gallery filled with spirit art. Whether at a séance, a sold-out tour, or a horror convention buzzing with excitement. I show up because, once, I needed someone to show up for me.

Throughout my journey, I've met thousands—people who, like me, have lived with the inexplicable. People who were told their experiences were imaginary, delusional, or even dangerous. But deep down, they knew better. They knew what they had seen, what they had felt.

And when we gather—whether in auditoriums or on the convention floor—there is an undeniable energy that moves through the room. It is ancient. It is sacred. It is *home*.

To this day, I still consider myself a student of the spirit world. The learning never stops. The mystery never fully reveals itself. And, in truth, I don't want it to. That's part of the beauty. The wonder. The terror.

I believe the spirit world is still calling out to us. I believe horror—when seen for what it truly is—isn't about glorifying fear. It's about confronting it. Transcending it. Learning from it. And yes, finding *community* through it.

There's a reason horror resonates with those who feel like outsiders. Because monsters and ghosts, demons and shadows—they all reflect something we know inside ourselves. That we are not what the world says we are. That we are *more* than what we seem.

So whether I'm giving a reading, stepping on stage, or simply standing among friends in a crowd of black-clad fans trading ghost stories and horror trivia, I carry this with me:

We are never alone.

The spirits are still speaking.

And the shadows?

They've always been a place some of us call home.

Chapter 2

Finding Grace

"If you ask me whether I support Brother Drake, I do not. And furthermore, this church will not support Brother Drake."

To this day, I often wonder if I only imagined the audible gasp that swept across the auditorium in that moment. But I know I heard it—a gasp of shock and disbelief. What had been merely a difference of belief among friends had, with those words, become a very public excommunication.

"As for the future I had long envisioned for myself, it may as well have been a public execution. Had it been another time in history—three hundred years earlier, in fact—it would have been a literal one. I would have been drowned or burned at the stake for even entertaining such heresy. Or hanged. Or drawn and quartered, perhaps. Something fabulous, I hope."

I often jokingly say to audiences, "Live the sort of life that, three hundred years ago, would've gotten you burned at the stake." I say it in jest, of course—but there's truth in it. What I really mean is that one should never fear nonconformity—not for its own sake, but because we shouldn't be afraid to step into the unknown, especially when the path ahead has already begun to reveal itself.

So yes, the audible gasp was very real. It happened. Brittania— a dear, dear friend and confidant at the time—just so happened to be seated beside me in the congregation. She placed her hand over mine and said with a gentle smile, "I'm sorry." I glanced at her briefly, then looked straight ahead. I knew, in that moment, all eyes were on me. I was determined to smile, though I felt like crying under the weight of it all.

Was I sorry?

Was I sorry for choosing to no longer publicly deny the experiences and visions that had, even up to that very moment, seemingly overtaken my life?

No.

No, I was not.

I never imagined I would find myself standing at the crossroads —cast out by old friends, whispered about in hushed voices, and treated as though I had turned my back on everything I once believed in. Had I truly abandoned my faith, as most seemed to believe? Had I consciously made the decision to sabotage a life that, up until only a month before, had seemed to be a literal "calling?" If you had told me a decade earlier that my faith journey would lead me to what most in the rural South considered the throes of heresy, I would have called you a liar. And yet, I found myself caught between the world of the religion that once consumed me and the world of psychics, spiritual seekers, and Spiritualism that felt like "home."

I found myself forced to experience firsthand a truth that I would soon share with the world in a very public way through countless readings: "You can only deny the voice of your soul for so long, until your soul will force you to make a choice." I was a minister—someone who stood before a congregation each Sunday, delivering messages that I genuinely believed would inspire others in their faith and belief. My faith was genuine. It was real. I believed in the power of my faith. But then something happened that I never saw coming: my faith shifted.

It didn't happen overnight. It was slow and subtle—questions bubbling beneath the surface, doubts that I had tried to push away. It felt like a season of loss I had never experienced before. It was as if there had been a literal death of a loved one, and I found myself mourning the loss. The loss of what I had once known, coupled with a feeling of uncertainty regarding my own future, brought about what felt like a soul-crushing numbness. Grief hit me in a way that made traditional answers feel hollow. I prayed, as I had been taught. But even in my times of fervent prayer, it felt as if there were other voices speaking—voices beckoning my attention to them.

I surrendered my credentials of ordination and resigned from my position within the church. Little did I realize, it was my first step toward a life more authentic to the language of my own soul.

It was Shakespeare who so famously wrote, "All the world's a stage." All this time later, I believe that more than ever before. What so often goes unnoticed, though, is that there is much more to be said about those beautiful words. They are attributed to the character Jaques in Act II of *As You Like It*. The passage continues: "All the world's a stage, and all the men and women merely players; they have their exits and their entrances; and one man in his time plays many parts."

An obvious metaphor comparing the experiences of life to a stage performance, what most often goes unsaid is that, while waiting for the next role, the feeling of uncertainty can resemble a final curtain call—particularly when you find yourself removed from the only stage you've ever known. And especially when you feel as though you've been booed by the only audience you ever really knew. Little did I know that other stages would come calling in time.

Through the years, I have often imagined what might have been if I had been able to return to my much younger self to offer words of encouragement—reminding him that, in the span of the following twenty-five years, his life would become unrecognizable. That the uncertainty of the moment would serve to catapult him to stages he never could have dreamed of or imagined. But that, my darling, is the beauty of uncertainty.

Uncertainty beckons us to take a step of faith into the unknown, only to leave us pleasantly surprised by the beauty we find awaiting us just on the other side of fear. Uncertainty primes us to enjoy the adventures that await us.

I am an explorer. I always have been, really. Even now, all this time later, I view myself as merely a seeker, always awaiting the next adventure. Perhaps it is the nature of a Sagittarius. Perhaps it is something else entirely. What I find, though, is that in the journeys on the Other Side, there really are no points of arrival—no moments at which one can safely say, "This is all there is." Because there is always, always more. More to see and more to experience.

In that small, rural town where everyone knows everyone else, I had become a sort of social pariah. And it was all the result of my own doing. But I could not deny my experiences, although I had yet to truly understand them or make sense of them. There was nothing rational about those visions and encounters. Yet I knew that to deny them would be to deny my very self. That denial, for me, was a sacrifice I was no longer willing to make—especially when it felt like I had already sacrificed so much.

Something I find myself sharing with audiences more often as I grow older is that there is power in sharing your ghost stories with the world—especially when otherworldly experiences can cause some to feel so alone and so isolated in the world around them. To put it another way, quite frankly, there is power in owning the story of your life. I found myself determined, regardless of what the road ahead might bring, to own the story of my life. With this sense of resolve, the feeling of uncertainty quickly began to give way to a sense of otherworldly audacity. I was determined to navigate the unseen world, no matter the cost.

There is a lot to be said, I find, for having a simple belief—a simple, childlike wonder and curiosity, if you will. Most often, this simple sense of wonder opens the doorway to questioning. "Can this be?" "Could it be that there really is no death?" "Could it be that we are never alone?" I find it is within this simple questioning that the doorway to the Other Side becomes opened all the more. I found myself doing what, for years prior, I had been far too fearful to do: I began to question my experiences.

I began to immerse myself in the study of psychic phenomena, looking for answers wherever possible. And where there were no answers, I became determined to, at the very least, surround myself with like-minded individuals who, like me, possessed the same sense of curiosity about such things. What I soon began to realize was that there were others who had also questioned. There were those who, like me, had faced otherworldly encounters all their own.

Yes, there truly is power in sharing your ghost story with the world. When you do, what you will begin to find is that there have always been other seekers all along—simply waiting to step from the shadows.

Then, in what I can only describe as a moment of desperation, I visited a psychic. Not out of rebellion, not out of some desire to betray my faith, but because I was searching for something—anything—that could help me make sense of what I was going through. I expected skepticism. I expected theatrics. What I didn't expect was the feeling of being seen in a way I never had before.

When I began exploring the spiritual world outside the boundaries of traditional belief, I told myself I could do it privately. I tried for weeks to convince myself that the horrifying experiences I faced each day could simply be kept to myself. First came the side glances that I tried to ignore. Then came the questioning—questioning that arose not out of curiosity, but out of suspicion. Soon, the whispers turned to outright accusations: "Have you turned away from God?" "Are you dabbling in the occult?" "Do you realize you're leading people astray?"

I had spent years offering insight to my congregants, but now they saw me as "lost." The strange irony is that I understood completely. I held no animosity. Had it been a different time, I would have openly criticized such curiosity and self-questioning. Friends I had known for years—people who had once embraced me—suddenly began to keep their distance. Some of them tried to "save" me, passionately urging me to renounce what they saw as dangerous "witchcraft." Others simply cut ties altogether. The community, overall, simply could not, in good conscience, allow themselves to accept a former minister who was now "flirting with the darkness."

I had spent months quietly studying energy work, intuition, and Spiritualist energy healing, testing the waters in private sessions with a handful of people who, like me, were searching for something beyond the walls of traditional, mainstream belief. When I finally made the decision to go public, I did so with a deep sense of conviction. It became clear to me that I was in no way abandoning my faith. I was exploring it. I was putting it to the test. Still, such things are often frowned upon. My life had become the storyline of some Southern Gothic.

Looking back all this time later, I view that season of my life as one of awestruck wonder—and one filled with literal miracles. New and lasting connections were made with people who, only weeks earlier, had been total strangers to me. In what seemed like a season of deep isolation, a few like-minded seekers and explorers began to become lifelong friends. To this day, I reflect on that time not only with fondness but also with a deep sense of nostalgia, because of the unexpected friendships that were forged—friendships that came when I truly needed them most.

It was around this time that I noticed an advertisement in the local paper for a new coffee shop coming to the area. It might as well have been news of a luxury resort being built—because anything new generated quite a buzz in my small hometown. The location was inconspicuous and fairly nondescript. It was to be opened in a former storefront on Main Street that had been abandoned for decades. The building, at least as I recall it, had been in a state of disrepair for as long as I could remember. To even pass inspection and safely open as a new business, the out-of-town investors would certainly have their work cut out for them.

I can still see it so vividly, even now.

"Open late."

"Everyone welcome."

"Live music every Saturday night."

"Poetry night every Monday."

I remember thinking this new "coffee shop" would be much, much more than just a place to enjoy a casual cup of espresso. Little did I know it would become not only a hub for artists, seekers, and explorers of the Other Side—but that it would soon set the stage for one of the most beloved periods of my life.

I was there on opening night. Where else would a young, single loner be on a Friday night in a small, rural town? The place had sprung up quickly in what used to be an old hardware store— one of those dusty, forgotten storefronts that had sat empty for years, its windows ghosted with grime and old sale signs faded by time.

But now, it was something else entirely.

The heavy wooden door groaned slightly on its hinges as I pushed it open, and I was met by a wave of cozy warmth and the low hum of quiet conversation. Jazz guitar played faintly in the background. The interior was a blend of the old and the intentional. It was as if someone had carefully peeled back layers of time and decided what to keep.

Exposed brick walls and rustic wood lined the space, their surfaces uneven and flaked in places, but somehow beautiful in their rawness. Edison bulbs hung low from black iron pipes across the ceiling, casting a soft, faint amber glow that made the place feel like it was suspended somewhere between now and more than a century ago. The counter was made from reclaimed wood, sanded smooth but left with its imperfections. A hand-lettered chalkboard menu hung above it—charmingly imperfect. Behind the bar, glass jars held loose-leaf teas and spices, and the young baristas moved with a kind of easy rhythm that made it seem as if they had been there forever, even though the new establishment had only just opened.

I found a seat near the back, where an old church pew had been repurposed into bench seating along the back wall, cushions tossed casually over it in muted earth tones. The table was small, with metal legs and a weathered top that might have once lived in a school cafeteria or been forgotten in the back of some garage long ago. I ran my fingers across it, feeling the slight dip in the center where time had worn it down. Every detail in the shop seemed like it had a story. And so, too, did every person there.

As I sipped the dark, rich pour-over I had ordered—served in a thick ceramic mug that in no way matched any others I could see—I let myself sink into the atmosphere. Those timeless words uttered by Judy Garland in *The Wizard of Oz* about not being in her hometown anymore came to mind. There was something quietly magical about the place, like it had been waiting for someone to breathe life into it again. It was rustic, yes, but not in a way that felt manufactured. It was warm, real, grounded. Was I even in my own hometown any longer? And who were all these magical, fabulous people?

The longer I sat there, the more I noticed that the place served more than just coffee. It also offered a certain kind of refuge. It was as if the heavens had opened, and for the first time in a long, long while, I felt the sensation of coming "home." Psychically, I could feel the intense energy encapsulated within the walls. The building pulsed with tales of its own, as did the vibrant, captivating souls within. The music changed, easing into a slow, sultry blues melody. I reclined, sipping the final drops of my drink, trying to soak it all in. On the back wall, hanging just over my right shoulder, was a hand-written sign—the kind up-and-coming independent bands use to advertise upcoming shows in the area:

"Coffee and philosophy every Sunday afternoon."

What did those words even mean? Would anyone really be interested in such events? What would even be discussed? Would this just be more of the same traditional religion, masquerading as edgy, trendy, new thought?

I admit, I still had much to learn when it came to my own preconceived judgments and biases. Still, I was determined to be there—regardless. And I had no way of fully understanding just how much my life would be changed because of it.

I stood from the table and quietly walked out, as the magic of Ella Fitzgerald played faintly behind me.

That first Sunday, I arrived early—more determined than ever to immerse myself in this newfound community. But I was just as determined to remain merely a spectator. After all, what could a shunned, seemingly disgraced former Pentecostal minister possibly offer to such an environment?

The crowd was small that day, unlike what I had witnessed on opening night. Only eight people. Quite a motley crew, as I recall. One musician from an up-and-coming band. One woman who worked in accounting in a neighboring town. A few younger individuals employed in the local fast-food scene. A truck driver. And yours truly. Given my recent experiences, I believed myself to be the only one out of place.

A man I'd never seen before stood up and walked to the corner of the room, approaching an old, antiquated microphone. Oddly, the sound system seemed much different this time—

nothing like the seamless audio that had funneled music just days before.

"Today, I want to talk to you about dreams," he said, his voice soft and quiet, interrupted at seemingly random moments by the crackling of a microphone that had clearly seen better days.

"Dreams?"

I sat intently, determined to observe and listen—but not participate.

For more than two hours, he expounded on the topic of dream symbolism, sharing how dreams speak the language of the soul. More than once, he even used the term "vision."

"Our souls are always speaking to us," he said in a dry, almost whispered tone.

As I sat there, completely captivated and enthralled, I began to hear other voices speaking to me as well.

"Follow us," they said gently, almost in faint whispers. "Follow us, and we will show you the way."

Although I still found it hard to believe that such a place could truly exist in my own hometown, I had never felt more at home.

But then it happened—the words that seemed to change everything.

"Kenneth, I'd like to invite you to share with us next week, if you'd be willing."

I was speechless. The look of shock and bewilderment on my face must have been obvious to everyone in the room.

"I'm familiar with your story," he continued, "and I think you have a lot to share with us."

I imagine that look never left my face for even a moment. But I had already learned to recognize the feeling of being watched.

All eyes were on me.

I struggled to find words—until I heard my own voice whisper:

"I would be honored."

Little did I know I had just stepped onto what would soon become the most monumental stage of my entire life. That, as Shakespeare had so famously spoken of, I was about to take on a brand new role. Though the audience seemed much smaller than the one I had become accustomed to seeing, something about this audience fulfilled my soul. I had never felt more at home—or more at ease with a response. It was destiny calling.

After the presentation ended, I nervously hurried home without staying for what had already become my usual espresso. I thought, *What just happened?* But I felt there was really no time to analyze. I had to prepare. What would I share? What even *could* I share? Dream symbolism was one thing; however, talk of encountering ghostly, shadowy apparitions was another matter entirely. Did I even need to share such things? Would I even have a say at all?

That night, returning home, I turned on the evening news and heard a story that has haunted me ever since. I remember I was just trying to settle into the quiet rhythm of the evening, attempting to clear my mind of what had only hours before been asked of me—lights dimmed, a glass of wine beside me. Then I heard her name: Grace Garner. An elderly woman, 87 years old, murdered just miles away in the neighboring city. I froze. Something in the anchor's voice—it seemed to tremble under the weight of what they were reporting. Grace had been killed outside her own home, over twenty-three dollars.

Twenty-three dollars.

That number sat heavy in my chest like a brick. How could a life be taken for something so small and so meaningless? But as the segment unfolded, it became painfully clear just how deeply meaningful Grace Garner's life had been. She was not merely a face flashing across a television screen. She had spent decades working in food pantries and teaching literacy classes at the community center. People in the neighborhood described her as the kind of woman who never forgot a birthday. She had never had much, but what she had, she gave freely to others.

It was a tragic story, I admit. Unfortunately, though, I must also admit that the story itself was not altogether shocking. There were other stories of tragedy reported that evening, too. Day after day, we find ourselves bombarded with stories of horror and sadness when watching the evening news. Stories of tragedy and hurt are never truly far away from us. We hear stories of suffering so often that we can become desensitized to the pain of others.

I felt the sadness of the story—but, admittedly, I tried to put it out of my mind. After all, I had a presentation to prepare.

I had decided, for my upcoming presentation, to share a few thoughts that had always intrigued me throughout my own philosophical journey. A few years earlier, I had stumbled—quite unexpectedly—upon a book by Elaine Pagels titled *The Gnostic Gospels*, which completely upended much of what I had always believed about the historical origins of my faith. In the book, Pagels offers insight into the ancient manuscripts found at Nag Hammadi, which seem to suggest that early Christianity was far more mystical and "psychic" than much of what mainstream thinking proposes.

I would not be sharing religious views with the audience at the coffeehouse, as I no longer participate in traditional religion. But I did want to propose the idea that, though often unpopular, reassessing our beliefs can be a healthy and enlightening process. To allude, in some way, that questioning the supposed norms can lead to profound spiritual experiences. I adore the work of Elaine Pagels to this very day.

When the time finally came for the presentation, I was ready. I had my notes neatly prepared and felt confident in what I planned to share. I even arrived early enough to purchase an espresso, which had quickly become my staple at the new coffeehouse. Surprisingly, a much larger audience had gathered that day. It seemed word of the new lecture series had finally spread and sparked interest. Like me, everyone appeared to adore the town's new venue. In many ways, the coffeehouse represented what could only be described as the region's "counterculture," as people from all backgrounds, beliefs, and persuasions found themselves drawn to the community of fellow seekers.

When the time came, I walked toward the old, antiquated microphone and began to speak.

But then I heard it. The voices of others—speaking.

It started as a whisper, barely audible in the silence of the room. A dry, rasping sound, like dead leaves scraping against stone. At first, I thought it was simply the wind slipping through the cracks of the old building. But then I heard it again. Much closer this time.

My breath caught in my throat. The room was dark, save for the dim glow of faint lights filtering through the space, casting long, spindly shadows that clawed at the walls. I tried to speak, but I couldn't.

It was as if my voice had vanished, even as I opened my mouth with the full intention of speaking. An overwhelming, crippling anxiety immediately set in—the sort that always accompanies the body's fight-or-flight response.

I looked to the faces in the crowd and saw only confusion and bewilderment. Everyone seemed to wonder what was happening to the speaker. As someone who had always prided himself on his ability to present—even up until that point in my life—the looks of concern and perplexity in the crowd only deepened my anxiety.

Then, quite unexpectedly, I was overcome with emotion. Intense emotion, in fact—so intense that it felt otherworldly. As if I were suddenly experiencing feelings that were not my own.

I felt a sadness that defied logic and reason.

I began to sob uncontrollably—violently, even. To the onlookers, I have no doubt now that what they witnessed must have resembled a complete and total mental breakdown. It felt like a breakdown, to be quite honest with you. My thoughts, my words, and my emotions were not my own. Through tears and sobbing, I then heard these words in my own voice: "I'm sorry, Grace."

I stood there, trying desperately to regain my composure and dismiss the unease creeping up my spine. But as my eyes adjusted to the room, looking through my own tears, I saw her. She stood in the corner of the room, half-shrouded in shadow, her frail, brittle frame barely more than a silhouette. But then she became clearer to me. Her clothes were tattered, stained, and worn, the fabric clinging to her in decayed layers. Her skin —if you could call it that—was stretched tight over a skeletal frame, gray and lifeless. The most terrifying part was the expression on her face: hollowed-out eyes, deep and empty, black pits of nothingness that seemed to drink in the faint light of the room.

It was Grace Garner.

Then she moved. Just a twitch at first—a slight jerk of her arm. And then she lifted one long, bony finger and pointed. She was pointing at me. The audience no longer seemed to matter. It was as if the entire world around me had stopped and ceased to exist.

A scream tangled in my throat, thick and suffocating. I wanted to move, to run from the room, but my limbs had turned to lead. My heartbeat pounded in my ears, drowning out all else. The voice came again, curling around me like icy tendrils, but now I could make out the words. A single sentence, repeated over and over in a cracked, aged, brittle voice soaked in sorrow: "He killed me. He killed me. He killed me."

The air turned frigid, and a stench filled the room. It was the scent of damp earth and decay—the unmistakable smell of a grave left open too long. My breath came only in gasps as she took a step forward, her bare feet dragging against the wooden floor of the coffeehouse. My mind screamed at me to run, to do anything but stand there, frozen in terror. But I was caught in her gaze—in those empty sockets that saw everything and nothing all at once.

Beginning to come to my natural senses again, I suddenly remembered that I was standing in front of a crowded room, in front of actual, living, breathing humans who had come to hear me speak. I apologized—profusely, in fact. Any sense of dignity I felt I had was stripped away by the experience, and I realized I owed my audience an explanation.

I began to share how, only a week earlier, I had heard a tragic story on the evening news about a wonderful, beloved woman named Grace Garner. I shared her story with the audience. And the greatest miracle of all? As soon as I shared her story, I finally felt like myself again.

It was that night that changed everything. I had always heard strange noises, felt cold spots in empty rooms, caught glimpses of movement just beyond my peripheral vision. I had always been aware that the dead were not truly *dead*. But I had always convinced myself it was simply my imagination—tricks of the mind. That night proved otherwise.

I could see the dead.

And worse, I could hear them speaking clearly.

The realization settled over me like a heavy, dark shroud. The whispers I had ignored for years, the shadows that seemed to breathe in my presence—now, they all made sense. I had not been imagining things. I had simply been denying the truth. I was a medium. I was a conduit for both the living and the dead.

Sleep never came to me that night. I sat in the dim light of my bedside lamp, my hands trembling, my mind racing with questions. *Why me? Was I cursed? Was this a gift or a burden?* The ghostly woman's words still clawed at my thoughts, insistent and desperate: *He killed me.* But who was he? What did she want me to do? What even could I do? I shared her story and, seemingly, that was enough—at least for the time being.

I had spent my entire life avoiding the unseen and pretending that the strange occurrences around me were nothing more than mere coincidence. But there was no denying it now. The dead could see me just as clearly as I could see them. And for the first time, I understood what that meant. They would never leave me alone. And they wanted their stories told to the world of the living.

This revelation branded me. The mark of the dead is not something seen by the living, but I felt it seared into my very soul. It created a scar that would never fade. It was in the way my skin prickled at unseen presences, the way my breath caught in my throat when I passed through a cold spot no one else ever seemed to notice. It was in the way the world seemed to shift around me with the weight of unseen eyes pressing against my back—always watching me.

I had stepped beyond the threshold of normal existence, into a realm where death did not mean silence, where shadows whispered, and the walls bore witness to horrors untold. The spirits knew me now, and they would come. Not just the lost ones like her, but the others, too. The restless, the vengeful, the things that lurked in the darkness—simply waiting for someone like me to see them.

There would be no peace. No return to ignorance. No escape. I had been marked. And now, I belonged to the dead.

Part Two

The Author's Awakening

Chapter 3

A Haunted Childhood

I was five years old the first time I saw him: the man with the scar on his face. A man with a deep, gnarled scar that twisted from the corner of his mouth up to his temple, as if something had slashed through his face with deliberate cruelty and intent. He stood outside my childhood bedroom, always seeming to peer through the window with curiosity, bathed in the sickly yellow glow of the nightlight. I remember the way his eyes gleamed—dark pits in the dimness—watching me with an intensity that froze the breath in my young lungs.

"Who is that man with the scar on his face?" I asked my mother one night, my small fingers rubbing the sleep from my eyes. My mother turned toward the window, a look of confusion on her face. But when she looked, the man was gone. She told me it was just my imagination. Children see things, she said. But it felt like something more.

He came to me often after that. At first, he only lingered in the periphery of my vision—just outside the doorway, or at the foot of my bed, reflected in the glass of my bedroom window when there was nothing but empty night behind it.

But then, he got bolder.

I would wake to the feeling of breath on my face and the scent of something foul and rotting filling my nostrils. My blankets would be pulled back slightly, as if someone had been peeling them away inch by inch as I slept. I stopped sleeping for a while. The weight of exhaustion pressed on my bones, but every time I closed my eyes, I would hear the creak of the floorboards, the whisper of something shifting in the darkness around me.

Was it all in my imagination? If so, why was it that his whispers seemed so evident?

"You're mine," he rasped.

I would hear it repeatedly, like a record replaying over and over again in my mind. Was it audible? It seemed so—at least to me. But the experiences of children, we are told, can be easily explained away as little more than a fear of the dark.

But I had no fear of the dark. I never did. Instead, I always seemed to have a certain sense that I was being watched. In fact, when I think back over the course of my life, that is the only way I know to adequately describe the feeling of unease.

I know I'm always being watched.

Years passed, but the memories never faded. The fear lay dormant, buried beneath the surface of my mind—until one night, in my twenties, I awoke to a familiar sensation. My room —my new apartment in a different city—was suffocatingly still. The air was heavy, thick with an unseen presence.

Then, the unmistakable creak of floorboards.

I turned over, dread pooling in my stomach.

And there he was. The same scar. The same dead eyes. Standing at the foot of my bed. His mouth twisted into that ruined, broken smile.

My breath hitched as he leaned closer, his voice slithering through the dark.

"You thought you could leave me?" he whispered. "You are mine."

I scrambled back, my heart hammering against my ribs. But before I could scream—before I could move—the darkness enveloped him again. The room was empty once more. Yet, the smell of decay lingered, thick and heavy. I never saw him again —not with my eyes. But I still feel him at times, lurking in the shadows, watching from just beyond the veil to the Other Side. And some nights, when the air is too still and the silence too deep, I feel the sense that he is still watching. And waiting.

Then, the whispers started. They seemed so very faint at first, but I could hear them clearly. Even as a child, it seemed the whispers were never far away—always near and always present, as if others were constantly looking on, wanting me to be aware of their conversations.

Today, when I hear the accounts of other psychics and mediums recounting the experiences of their childhoods, I find myself relating. "I thought everyone could hear it," most seem to say. "I thought it was normal." I relate, because when the whispers are part of the only norm one has ever known, what would a life without the noise even be like? I have never known a life without the sound of whispers.

I grew up in a small town in the rural hills of the Deep South, tucked into a valley where the hills were stained red with iron dust and the sky always seemed a little too quiet. It was the kind of place where time felt heavy, as if the earth itself was pressing down on you. Everyone knew everyone else. There were no traffic lights—only one stop sign. It was the sort of community that even now one might struggle to find on a map. We knew who had lost someone in the mines, who had ghosts in their family history, and who kept secrets close to their chest. My family lived on the edge of that town, where the dirt roads turned to gravel and corn-fields stretched out like a golden ocean in the summer.

This is where it all started. Where I first began to hear them and sense them. Growing up, days passed in a haze in my sleepy little town. My childhood home—the last house on the right, just before the hill leading to the coal mines—had once been part of an old mining camp. My father was a coal miner, as was his father, and his father's father before him. It was a world far removed from the lights of Hollywood and a life very different from the world of the entertainment industry. The only stages that existed were in small, dilapidated church buildings. I still miss those hot summer nights in the South. I miss the smell of honeysuckle.

My parents married shortly after high school. They purchased the home from an older, flamboyant Pentecostal woman named Loni. For young lovers just starting out in life and hoping to raise a family, it was the deal of the century. "Just make monthly payments to me and y'all can be homeowners," she promised. To my knowledge, there was never even a contract in place— just a spoken agreement. I still vividly recall sitting in the passenger seat of an old truck, accompanying my father as he went to make the "house payment." Now, looking back as an adult, it truly must have seemed like the deal of the century, because the home—at least to my young mind—seemed to be the largest in the community. At least it felt that way to me.

At the end of the road leading to our home, where the pavement began, was a small convenience store where coal miners would stop for gas before heading into the mines. It was called "Beaulah's." She was always larger than life, as I recall. She provided not only refreshments and lunch supplies for passersby but, for many of us, also a sort of escape from the mundane. Many miners in the community went there on their lunch break for her fried bologna and cheese sandwiches. I walked to "Beaulah's" countless times to get a cold cola—more times than I can even count, in fact. I always had to leave the glass bottle behind before I left.

Late one night when I was five years old, I remember hearing the sound of commotion and police sirens from the county police. Noise like that was a rarity in our community. Our next-door neighbor, an elderly man named Alvie, knocked on our door and asked if we had heard what had happened. A robber had attempted to rob the convenience store when Beaulah—being the feisty, no-nonsense firebrand that she was—reached for her gun behind the counter in an attempt to defend herself. She was shot in the head and died instantly. It was my very first encounter with something so horrifically tragic. We still talk about it on occasion to this very day.

One afternoon, while playing outdoors in the early evening, when the light was low and syrupy—at that golden hour when everything in the South looks a little more haunted than it should—I was walking along the edge of the field behind our house when I looked up and saw a man standing perfectly still between the rows. He wore an old miner's helmet, covered in dust, the kind with a lamp still attached—although it didn't glow. His eyes were hollow. Not out of malice, but like he had seen too much. I blinked, and he was gone.

They started coming more often after that—men and women, sometimes children—all with that same faraway, distant, expressionless look, standing among the corn as though waiting for someone to call them home. I never heard them speak. They never moved. They just stared. Not at me, but through me, like I was a window into some place they could no longer reach. In towns like ours, death wasn't a stranger. It was a neighbor. A shadow that sat at your kitchen table with you, listening intently to your conversations.

Sometimes I think the land remembers. Those mines are mostly closed now, sealed up with rusted gates and faded warning signs. But I still see them, even now, years later and a thousand miles away—especially in the summer, when the corn grows high in rural areas and the wind makes it sound like whispers. I've come to believe they have no intention of frightening me. Maybe they find themselves drawn to me simply because I'm willing to look. Maybe because I never ran. Because I carry their stories, even when I never seem to know their names.

Looking back, all these decades later, I now realize those moments marked the first of many such occurrences. I would continue to say things that a child my age simply should not have known. Sometimes it was a prediction. Sometimes a feeling. Sometimes a word from someone who had passed on. At first, my mother tried to dismiss it, thinking I was just parroting something I had heard, or maybe it was just an overactive imagination. But then the things I said began to come true, and there was no denying that something was happening.

As a child, I never knew how to explain what I was experiencing. And I never felt the need to. I didn't have the language, the maturity, or the context to understand that I was channeling. The idea of being "psychic" wasn't even in my thoughts. It was never something I could have explained, even if I had wanted to. It just *was*. It felt as natural to me as breathing. Fear began to dissipate, leaving only a quiet certainty that these messages were not my own. That they came from somewhere else—from a realm beyond this one.

I feel I have always known I was different. Even as a child, I would sit in a room full of people and sometimes feel overwhelmed—not by noise, but by emotions. It was as if every feeling around me seeped into my skin, making me feel things that were not my own. I didn't understand it then, but I could sense sadness hiding beneath a smile, anger tucked away behind clenched fists, or deep love unspoken yet pulsating in the air.

My mother was always the first to notice. She would speak to me, and before she could finish her sentence, I would say exactly what she was about to. At first, she laughed it off, calling it a lucky guess. But as it kept happening, she grew quiet, watching me with eyes that flickered with curiosity. It wasn't only her sentences I finished—it was her thoughts. I knew when she was worried before she said a word. I could feel her stress pressing against my chest like a weight. If she had a bad day, I knew before she walked through the door. We still share that bond to this very day.

Years later, when I gave my very first public demonstration of mediumship, she was there in the front row. And when my more than twenty years of sold-out national tours ended on a stage in Boston, Halloween weekend of 2022, she was there. Her unwavering, unyielding support—for longer than I can even remember—has helped make this life possible. In fact, she has psychic premonitions of her own. I often wonder if these abilities are passed through blood, presenting themselves as gifts from familial seekers of long ago.

At school, I often struggled to understand why I felt the way I did. A classmate would sit next to me, looking perfectly fine, but I would be hit with a wave of sadness so strong it felt dizzying. I'd ask if they were okay, only for them to insist they were. Hours later, they would break down crying. I never seemed to know what to do—or how to fit in and relate socially—because this strange ability caused me to feel others so deeply, to predict emotions before they were revealed. It wasn't until much later, when the experiences began to consume me entirely, that I realized the callings served a purpose.

The otherworldly rarely made an already desperate attempt to fit in any easier—especially in high school. I often sensed things were about to happen, felt the emotions of others around me as if those emotions were my own, and dreamed of events that would later come to pass. At the time, I never questioned it much. It was merely part of how I experienced the world. But somewhere along the way, I began to doubt it. I tried to talk myself out of what I knew deep down to be a very real reality. I fought to repress it. After all, high school in those formative years is already a difficult road to navigate for us all—especially in small towns.

I think most of us go through that season of searching for normality. As children, we are so open and unfiltered, so naturally connected to things we can never quite put into words. Intuitive. But the world teaches us what is "normal" and what is "real." Anything that refuses to fit neatly into that mold is quickly dismissed. I remember desperately not wanting to be different. I no longer wanted the strange dreams, those gut feelings that always turned out to be true, or the way I could feel the emotions of others. I just wanted to fit in. So I tried to bury it. But now, looking back, I realize how much I lost by doing that. That part of me was never something to fear or hide. It was merely a calling I had yet to recognize.

I still remember that morning of my sophomore year like it was yesterday. As soon as I walked through the front doors of the high school, I knew something was terribly wrong. The air felt heavier than usual, and a strange stillness hung in the hallways. I hadn't taken more than a few steps before I saw clusters of students standing silently near their lockers—some crying, others hugging each other, trying to offer comfort but looking just as broken. At first, I didn't understand what was happening. I thought maybe there had been a fight or some kind of announcement I'd missed. But then I overheard a boy whisper through his tears that someone had died.

It didn't seem real until I heard the name. A classmate. "Lauren." A girl I admit I never knew well but had seen every day for years. Sometimes laughing with her friends in the cafeteria, sometimes just sitting in class with that gorgeous half-smirk she always wore. She had been killed in a car accident the night before. She was leaving church when she lost control of her vehicle in the rain. I remember the way the words hit me —it was as if the hallway suddenly tilted sideways and I lost my breath. It wasn't just that someone our age had died. It was that it had happened so suddenly, out of nowhere, in the middle of what should have been just another normal week. For the first time I could ever remember, I felt nothing but numbness.

We were never best friends, but she was always there. She was just familiar enough to feel like part of the background of my life—like a beautiful, ornate wallpaper you never truly appreciate until it's suddenly stripped away. Her father was a close friend of my father. The two had worked together for years in the coal mines. Her face was one I had seen almost every day of my life since first grade. I still see those big, brown, curious eyes and her long, flowing black hair, which always seemed to be worn down, falling over her shoulders.

It would later be revealed that in the accident, she had been decapitated.

The rest of the day blurred into something surreal. Some teachers tried to hold class like usual; others gave up and let us sit in silence. Counselors and local ministers came into classrooms and offered to talk, but most of us just stared at the floor or out the window. I do not remember learning anything that day. I only remember the aching quiet and the sound of someone sobbing a few rows behind me. I remember the dull throb of disbelief. It was the first time I truly understood how fragile life is—and how fast a life can be taken away.

Up until that point, though the dead had surrounded me, death had always seemed distant and impersonal. It was something that happened in movies or to older people who had already lived such full lives. But that day, it walked into our school with us. High school was never really the same again after that.

In the days that immediately followed, the school shifted into a kind of collective mourning. Posters went up in the hallways with her picture on them—candid shots from the yearbook and photos with friends. Memories frozen in time. Students brought flowers, left handwritten notes at her locker, and lit candles during a vigil that Friday night on the football field. I stood there among hundreds of classmates and parents, watching the flickering candlelight dance against tear-streaked faces. I remember thinking how strange it was that we were all brought together by the absence of someone who, only days before, had been just like us.

What struck me most of all, though, was seeing her closest friends. These were girls I had seen laughing every day— always loud, always full of life. Now they were quiet, pale, and seemed to carry a heavy weight that had aged them overnight. One of them spoke during the vigil, her voice cracking as she tried to say something meaningful—something to honor the one who was no longer there. I could not imagine the pain of losing someone that close. Though I did not know her well, the grief was contagious.

It was also the first time I ever saw my teachers cry. That shook me to my core. There is something overwhelming about seeing the adults you've always assumed were unshakable suddenly break down in front of you. It changes the way you see the world. They were not just educators that week—they were human. They shared stories about her and let us share our own. And for once, it felt like school wasn't just a place for learning facts and figures. It was a place where we also had to learn how to mourn.

I remember the air felt heavy the morning of her funeral. It was as if the sky itself knew something had gone terribly wrong. The church was overflowing. I sat toward the back, half listening to the pastor and half drifting into my own memories —school dances, passing notes, her laughter at some dumb jokes. I found myself suddenly beginning to appreciate the fact that she had been part of so many moments. Moments I had never really recognized or appreciated before.

Then something happened that I still, to this very day, cannot fully explain.

I remember closing my eyes, just for a second, overwhelmed by the weight of it all.

And then I saw her.

She was standing at the front of the church, just off to the right side of the casket. She wasn't looking at the crowd, and she wasn't looking at me. She was staring at her own former body, lying so still inside that box. Her expression was unreadable—not afraid, not sad. Just curious. Curious, as if she was trying to make sense of something that still didn't quite feel real to her either. She was wearing the same dress I remembered from eighth-grade graduation—pale blue with tiny flowers.

It made no sense. My mind told me it couldn't possibly be real, although I already knew it was.

She looked more solid than any dream or premonition I had ever had.

I opened my eyes and saw her standing there. I wanted to look away, but I simply could not. I was transfixed. I watched her watching herself, as if we were both caught in some transcendent moment outside of time. Then she turned her head, just slightly, her big brown eyes meeting mine. Not for long—maybe a second, maybe two. But it hit me like a wave.

She didn't say anything, but I felt it, like a wordless whisper in my mind: *I see you. It's okay.*

Then she flashed that gorgeous smile of hers.

And then she was gone. I blinked, and everything was back as it was—back to the church, the casket, and the silence.

I never told anyone about it. Not for years. Who would believe me? I barely believed it myself. But something shifted in me that day. In some strange, inexplicable way, it gave me peace—and a new understanding of a part of my own life I had wrestled with and fought to suppress.

I had a greater peace than ever before. Not just about Lauren, but about life, and how thin the veil really is between here and the hereafter.

After that day, life moved on, as it always seems to. The seasons changed. Classes resumed, and her name stopped being spoken quite so often. But I carried that moment with me, tucked deeply inside my mind, like a secret.

I would walk down the same hallways where we used to pass each other, now painfully aware of how ghostly everything feels after loss. You begin to notice the negative spaces people leave behind—an empty seat in the cafeteria, a locker left untouched, a silence in a conversation where her laugh once echoed.

I became much quieter after that—more observant. And I had always been quiet.

I would find myself staring at the corners of rooms, wondering if someone unseen might be standing there, watching, just as she had.

Sometimes I would dream about her. Not in the terrifying, twisted way people sometimes fear the dead will appear, but in calm, soft dreams. Always somewhere quiet, like a field or a dim hallway, with her just standing there.

She would never speak. She would just smile. And I would wake up with this hollow warmth, like the feeling that always seems to accompany hearing a favorite song.

The week of Lauren's funeral was also the week I first fell in love with Fleetwood Mac—and began my lifelong love affair with Stevie Nicks.

My father gifted me an album on cassette: *The Dance*.

To say I was smitten would be the understatement of a lifetime.

I had never been familiar with Fleetwood Mac prior to that haunted week of my life, and in many ways, the band provided not only the soundtrack to a week of otherworldly encounter, but seemingly the soundtrack to my entire life.

It was the night before Lauren's funeral when I first heard the live version of *Rhiannon*. To this very day, the piano intro remains the most hauntingly beautiful sound I have ever heard:

> *"Rhiannon rings like a bell through the night, and wouldn't you love to love her? Takes to the sky like a bird in flight, and who will be her lover?"*

And shortly after that came *Silver Springs*.

> *"Time cast a spell on you, but you won't forget me. I know I could've loved you, but you would not let me. I'll follow you down 'til the sound of my voice will haunt you. You'll never get away from the sound of the woman that loves you."*

My love for Stevie Nicks immediately became a sort of personal religion.

For a young kid consumed by the otherworldly all his life, lyrics of dreams and visions, and of time "casting spells," seemed to offer a deep solace.

I was utterly, painfully entranced. Her voice—raspy, ethereal, otherworldly—felt as if she were singing directly to the part of me I didn't yet have words for.

Her lyrics spoke of dreams, visions, shadows, witches. She sang about the kind of magic I felt pulsing in my bones but never dared to name.

When she sang, it never felt like just music. It felt like prophecy.

Like someone in the world finally understood the haunted feeling that lived in my chest—putting my own experiences into words in a way so deeply personal, it felt like possession. Though not even an exorcism could have satisfied it.

Throughout the years, I've been privileged to see her perform live more times than I can even count.

But never will I forget the first time.

Fleetwood Mac had recently been inducted into the Rock & Roll Hall of Fame, and it felt as though the timing couldn't have coincided more perfectly with my final days as a high school student. In the summer and fall of '97, they seemed to be everywhere I turned—gracing the covers of magazines and appearing in interviews on my television screen. Their album *Rumours*, still regarded as one of the best-selling albums of all time, was celebrating its twentieth anniversary that year. They had aged like fine wine and only gotten better with time.

But when it was announced that Stevie Nicks would embark on a nationwide solo tour, called the *Enchanted Tour*, I was elated. And when I heard she would be performing a mere fifty miles from my home, it felt as if I had left my body.

In the mid-nineties, the experience of buying concert tickets was a completely different world from what we know today. There were no sleek apps or online platforms to scroll through —no instant purchases with the tap of a finger. Instead, getting your hands on concert tickets often meant planning, persistence, and physically being in the right place at the right time. One of the most common methods was heading to a local record store. For me, that meant a shop in the neighboring city. Even smaller, independent stores often had ticket counters, and fans would stand in line—sometimes for hours, even overnight.

You had to be organized and proactive. You read local newspapers, listened to radio announcements, or called venue hotlines to find out when tickets would go on sale. Missing the date might mean missing the show altogether, as scalping and reselling were mostly limited to word-of-mouth or classified ads. In retrospect, the process was much more inconvenient, but it also made seeing a band live feel like an earned reward. There was a kind of magic in the ritual of it—a tactile thrill that today's digital convenience can never quite replicate.

I've been to more concerts in my life than I can even count, but nothing could have prepared me for seeing Stevie Nicks under the stars at Oak Mountain Amphitheater in Birmingham, Alabama, when I was seventeen years old. It was a spellbinding night—like stepping through a portal into some dreamy, velvet-draped realm where time softened and music became a magic all its own. The moment I stepped into the venue, I felt the energy shift. The air was thick with anticipation—almost electric—like the crowd collectively knew we were about to witness something rare and mystical. There was a certain sort of psychic power that was palpable. The amphitheater, nestled in the trees, felt like the perfect sanctuary for a woman who's always danced between the realms of the earthly and the ethereal.

Back then, Oak Mountain Amphitheater offered inexpensive tickets—sometimes as low as twelve dollars—allowing patrons to bring lawn chairs and watch from the surrounding hills. Far removed from the stage, the music still coursed through the trees, but for these particular tickets, actually seeing the performer typically required a pair of binoculars. Suffice it to say, this was the ticket I had. I sat on the grass, without a lawn chair and without a blanket. I somehow knew I would never be the same again.

The opening act on that tour was the brilliant Boz Scaggs.

When the lights finally dimmed and that first haunting chord echoed across the night, it was as if the moon leaned in a little closer to listen. Stevie emerged from the shadows like a ghost from a dream—flowing black chiffon, silver chains catching the light, her tambourine in hand. The crowd erupted, but I found myself breathless, unable to speak or cheer. Her voice—raw, gravelly, unmistakably hers—cut through the Alabama night like some ancient, witchy incantation. I swear, I felt the wind stir, even though the air had been still all evening.

She gave herself fully to that stage. Between songs, she told stories—about old friends, about dreams, about learning to survive the impossible while keeping your spirit intact. Her words were offerings. It was a spiritual experience. She shared how Birmingham had been instrumental in giving airplay to *Buckingham Nicks* shortly before she and Lindsey Buckingham joined Fleetwood Mac, cementing their place in rock & roll history.

I watched couples sway. Strangers held hands. People wiped tears they never expected to shed. And all the while, the stars hung above us like sequins on a black shawl—silent witnesses to the spell we were under.

By the time she sang *Landslide*, I could feel my heart cracking open in the best way. I also felt a sense of wonder that quickly began to turn into a feeling of anxiety. Panic, even. *Is there a way to get closer to the stage?* I couldn't help but wonder. I looked. I pondered. And then I took my chance.

Concert venues were different in those days. In fact, the entire music industry itself was much different. There never seemed to be as many barriers or barricades separating the stage from the audience—at least not at this particular venue. I quickly walked down the grassy hill, going as far as I possibly could until my feet reached pavement. To the right of the stage, a narrow walkway led to what appeared to be the only railing in sight—the only barrier separating the audience in theater seating from the stage just in front of them.

To this day, I will readily, happily admit that I climbed over the railing when no one was looking. All eyes were transfixed on her and her closing encore.

It seemed that by this time, others had discovered the same idea I had. There was now a line of people behind me, struggling to make it toward the stage. Some behind me also made it over the railing. Some did not. But where there had only moments before been a narrow, empty walkway, there was now a throng of people. Some in the front row reached up to hand her bouquets of flowers. I still vividly remember someone attempting to gift her a stuffed penguin, though she couldn't accept it because her hands were full. She was so very close.

An assistant came to the stage to take the bouquets as she said her goodbyes to the crowd, reaching down to shake the hands of audience members in the front row. If only I could have gotten closer. If only I could have afforded one of those tickets. It all felt like a dream—and it still does to this very day as I recall it. But premonitions, dreams, and longings always seem to have a way of coming to pass.

What I did not realize was that the walkway just to the right of the stage was mere steps away from where she would exit, just behind the thick, hanging curtain. Suddenly, in what already seemed to be a dream, she became even closer.

Making her exit, she walked toward me. Our eyes met. She reached out her hand, and her hand met mine. It was brief—so, so very brief—but the entire world around me stopped. And for a strange, outcast kid who had for so long wrestled with his own magic and mysticism, it was a saving grace I had needed.

No religion in my life had ever provided such a meaningful, transcendent instance of time.

Time, I have since learned, really does cast spells.

I was always the outcast in high school. The strange, quiet, socially awkward kid in the back of the classroom, wearing darker colors, my hairstyles always refusing to conform. While other kids talked about sports, I was reading poetry, watching horror films on repeat, and sketching.

Horror, for me, was not simply entertainment; it was a language I fully understood. Monsters made sense to me. They were honest. Genuine. They never pretended to fit in.

Loving horror films was always effortless for me. They reflected the world the way I experienced it—so unpredictable, dark, and layered with symbols and meanings most others missed. But Stevie? She helped me *feel*. She helped give shape to the psychic fog I lived in. For the first time, I didn't feel like I had to explain myself.

I was not crazy. I was not broken. I was just tapped into something ancient and mystical and wild. Her music made me feel less like a freak and more like an experiencer.

Now, I look back at that lonely kid and wish I could tell him what I know now: that the things that made him an outcast were actually his greatest power. That being sensitive is a gift. That seeing beyond the veil is never something to hide, but something to nurture. And that there are always, always others —artists, witches, dreamers—who see the world through the same strange lens.

I was never as alone as I had imagined.

Chapter 4

The First Possession

I t was around the time I found myself wrestling to come to terms with my very public excommunication—only mere months before my seemingly divinely appointed meeting at the new coffee house—that I leased my first apartment. It was my first opportunity to have a space all my own. The motive, at least initially, had been simply to live within walking distance of the church I had given much of my life to. But with the world of traditional religion stripped away, it also served as a sort of rite of passage. A time to explore. A time to taste the proverbial forbidden fruit I had long denied myself the pleasure of.

Living on your own for the first time is one of those monumental moments in life—a personal sort of rite of passage that often slips by without fanfare but leaves an indelible mark. For me, it was more than just signing a lease or buying my first furniture. It was about standing in a space that was entirely my own, where every detail reflected no one's tastes, routines, or beliefs but my own. This newfound independence became a kind of mirror, reflecting back parts of myself I had never had the chance—or the need—to meet before. In that first, small, one-bedroom apartment came a raw kind of self-discovery. Little did I realize, though, that it would also serve as the backdrop to many of my most transformative encounters beyond the veil.

It was there that I learned the value of my own company. I began to notice the small habits that brought me peace, the routines that grounded me, and the hobbies and passions that lit up my life. That season of life—often full of uncertainty and trial-and-error—was also a chance to rewrite the rules of how I wanted to live. I got to experiment and explore my beliefs and interests without the noise of others' opinions clouding my judgment. But I was never truly alone. To this day, I still never really am.

To my great shock and surprise, the very public spectacle that had taken place at the coffee house in no way added to my feeling of being a social pariah. Quite the opposite, in fact. To my amazement, not only did those attending the presentation that day welcome the otherworldly, but they continued to welcome me. So much so that I began to become a regular weekly speaker for the Sunday philosophy presentations. And the crowds began to grow. They grew to the extent that, before long, I had replaced the income I had lost by resigning from my church. Lecturing was becoming more and more a part of my life.

I was determined to fully own the narrative of my life and experiences—even as I continued to struggle to make sense of them. All these years later, I look back to those times inside my first apartment and consider them a sort of training. I had no teacher or instructor any longer, save the voices of the spirit world, who always seemed so content to instill in me images, mental pictures, and ideas worthy of exploration. The world of psychic phenomena was beginning to open to me in real time

—and in very real ways. And at the local coffee house, I had found in that audience a hungry, motley crew of fellow explorers who were more than happy to entertain my experiences. They say that when one door closes, another opens. What's so often omitted, though, is that most often the new door opens to something even more satisfying than what we could have imagined or dreamed.

It was in that first apartment that something quietly profound began to shift inside me—something that, at the time, I could only sense in fragments, like glimpses of movement behind a curtain. The apartment itself was small and unremarkable. A simple one-bedroom tucked on the second floor of an aging brick building—the kind with creaky floors and windows that whistled in the winter. But what it lacked in luxury, it made up for in solitude, and it was that solitude that always seemed to crack open doorways I hadn't even realized had been locked. For the first time in my life, I had space to think without interruption and without any sense of expectancy. With no one telling me what to believe, no weekly sermons, and no inherited dogma wrapped in guilt, there was only silence. And in that silence, a strange kind of invitation.

I started reading more than I ever had before. Not just flipping through articles, but devouring books, journals, and accounts on all the topics I had once dismissed without a second thought —psychic phenomena, energy healing, near-death experiences, astral projection, and all the wonderful things that would have been scoffed at in the religious circles of my youth. And yet, something about them called to me, resonating in a way that the rigid, rule-bound religion of my upbringing never had. I wasn't searching for a new dogma to replace the old. I was searching for something that felt true—something alive. Slowly, I began to understand that belief doesn't need to be confined to pews or parables. I realized that spirituality is meant to be expansive, exploratory, and deeply, deeply personal.

Meditation became my anchor. Not the kind of meditation and prayer I had been taught at youth group retreats, where prayer felt like a script performed for distant gods. This was different. I began experimenting with guided meditations that took me far beyond breath and stillness—journeys that led inward, deeper than I had ever gone before. I found myself practicing meditative techniques that left me feeling more connected to my experiences than any church service from my more traditional past ever had. In those moments of quiet awareness, I could feel something vast and benevolent watching me back. I was no longer sensing the spirit world. I was blending with it.

Looking back, that first apartment was more than just a place to live and more than just the backdrop for a much-needed reset in my younger life. It was a kind of sanctuary—a threshold between lives lived. It was where I began to unravel the tightly wound threads of who I was told to be and started weaving a brand-new tapestry of meaning. One that was stitched together from curiosity, experience, and a newfound reverence for the mystery of it all. I did not have all the answers then. I still do not. But for the first time, I stopped being afraid to ask the questions. And it was in the deeper questioning, I think, that the real beginning was discovered.

It was in that same cramped, dimly lit apartment that I began to come to terms with something far stranger and far older than I had words for. As I peeled back the layers of my traditional beliefs and replaced them with the sprawling, mysterious tapestry of psychic exploration, something in me began to unearth itself. Perhaps it had always been there, waiting for me to be still enough—quiet enough—to finally listen. That was when I realized that the whispers I had been hearing for years weren't figments of imagination, or echoes of anxiety, or dreams mistaken for memory. They were real. And they were not coming from the living.

"Your calling will keep on calling you." I began to make peace with the simple fact that my experiences had always served some far greater purpose. I gradually came to understand this truth more profoundly in the stillness and quiet of my dimly lit bedroom. At first, I told myself it was the isolation playing tricks on me—the late nights, the incense smoke curling in strange shapes, the static hum of an old radiator. Maybe my mind was inventing things to fill the silence. But deep down, I knew better.

I remembered being a child, hearing those soft murmurs in the dark, feeling presences in the room when no one was there. Back then, in the fear-based mindset of my youth, I had been taught to rebuke it, to pray it away, to call it demonic, and to slam spiritual doorways shut. But now, without those old frameworks to cast shame over the experiences, I started to see it all so differently. I began to understand that this ability had never been a curse. Looking back, it was a season of exploration.

The more I read about mediumship and psychic intuition, the more everything began to make sense. I had never been broken, or possessed, or "too sensitive." I was open. And in that openness, the voices grew clearer and louder—not always threatening or terrifying, but often gentle, inquisitive, and even sorrowful at times. Some were mere fragments—names, emotions, images that flickered across my mind like brief transmissions. Others were more insistent, speaking in whispers just behind my ear, seemingly nudging me awake in the early hours of morning with memories that were not my own.

Accepting it was a slow process. There was fear, of course—fear that I was losing touch with reality, and fear that others would see me differently if they knew the full extent of my exploration. But there was also relief. Relief that I no longer had to keep pretending I didn't hear what I heard or feel what I felt. That apartment, though small and imperfect, became my testing ground—my proving place. I lit candles not for ritual, but for comfort. I kept journals beside my bed, scribbling down messages, symbols, and sensations. I learned to ground myself, to discern which energies were truly mine and which came drifting in from elsewhere. I learned, most of all, to listen—and to experience without my own self-judgment.

And as I embraced this part of myself—the part that could feel beyond the veil—I began to change. Not only in how I saw the world, but in how I saw myself. I began to realize that I was not just seeking spiritual truth in books or practices, but that I was beginning to actually live my experiences. It was flowing through me, in every flicker of intuition, every whisper at the edge of sleep. It was both strange and beautiful and, at times, overwhelming. But it was mine. And in the quiet corners of that old apartment, I stopped trying to silence the voices. Instead, I started answering them.

Being aware of the voices of the dead is one thing. Believing in their ability to speak is another. But something altogether different begins to happen the moment you start to answer. Suddenly, where there were once only faint whispers and subtle silhouettes, there comes terrifying clarity—clarity that is unmistakable. The kind of clarity that can never again be questioned or avoided.

It was in that cramped one-bedroom apartment on the edge of town that I started noticing things. Small things at first—the air would feel dense at odd times, and shadows in the corners seemed just a little too deep. It wasn't until the night the banging started that I realized something unnatural had taken notice of me. That something else had become aware of my newfound sense of openness.

I had just drifted off when a sharp, steady, rhythmic pounding echoed through the walls. It came from the other side of my bedroom, where there was nothing but an empty hall leading to the kitchen. At first, I thought someone next door was being noisy, but the sound was too precise and far too deliberate. Three loud bangs. Silence. Then three more. My heart pounded in response. I sat up in bed, listening, waiting. The silence stretched unbearably, and just as I started to relax, the banging resumed—this time on the wall beside my bed.

That was the first night I became aware of it.

Over the next week, the activity escalated. I would hear drawers in the dresser scraping open in the dead of night, only to find them shut tightly again by morning. The refrigerator door creaked open on its own, and the lights would flicker in slow, pulsating patterns—as if breathing. I told myself it was faulty wiring, or my exhausted mind playing tricks on me, but deep down, I knew something was wrong.

Then came the out-of-body experiences. Ones I could no longer control.

It started subtly. At first, it felt like I was dreaming. I would wake up to find myself hovering above my own body, staring down at my motionless form in the dim moonlight. I would panic, struggling to move, fighting to wake up, but my body remained still and unresponsive. The first few times, I would snap back into myself like a rubber band recoiling, often gasping for breath as if I had just emerged from deep, dark water.

But then, one night, I noticed something else in the room with me.

I floated near the ceiling, watching as my bedroom door slowly creaked open. My body lay still on the bed below, but I—whatever "I" was in that moment—felt an unnatural chill seep into the air. A shadow shifted near the doorway, darker than the surrounding night, twisting and writhing as if aware of my presence. It was watching me. It stepped inside, though it had no discernible form. No feet that I could see. Yet the floor creaked beneath its weight. It had no voice, and yet it had physical presence.

I tried to scream, to move, to do anything, but I was a helpless observer. The shadow crept closer to my bed, and as it reached toward my motionless form, I felt a violent, forceful tug—as though something had seized my spirit and yanked me back into my body. I awoke with a desperate, shuddering gasp, my chest heaving as the residual cold of that presence lingered in the air around me.

After that, the entity made itself known in my apartment even more aggressively.

The banging on the walls became constant, unpredictable, echoing through the rooms at all hours. The dresser drawers no longer slid open—they slammed shut violently, rattling their contents. The worst part was that I could feel it now, hovering just behind me, whispering just beyond the threshold of hearing. I could never understand the words, but they slithered into my ears as if not of this realm.

Sleep became impossible.

Every night, I would find myself floating—unmoored from my body—just watching as the thing in the shadows loomed closer. It never touched me, but it always lingered, watching, waiting. And every time I returned to myself, I felt less whole, as if pieces of me were being shaved away, taken bit by bit.

Little did I realize then the importance of protective boundaries.

Had I become too open? Had I summoned something altogether different?

I knew I had to leave. I packed in a frenzy, shoving clothes and essentials into a suitcase. But as I reached for the front door, every light in the apartment flickered out. The oppressive darkness swallowed me whole. The air thickened, pressing against me like unseen hands.

Then came the final sound.

I heard a deep, guttural breath only inches from my ear.

To this day, I can barely remember how I got out. I only recall running—stumbling into the cold night air, my skin crawling with the sensation of something unseen still reaching for me. I left everything behind that night and went to stay with family.

I know it followed me. I know it sensed and fed on my fear.

When I returned to my apartment the following day, fully expecting to find furniture thrown about and items in disarray, I found only a quiet, cramped one-bedroom unit. It was as if nothing had happened at all.

But in the days that followed, I heard it again. The rhythmic banging—softer this time—like a gentle reminder that it was still there. My dresser drawers remained closed, but I began to find small objects out of place. Items I was certain I'd left in one spot appeared somewhere else entirely. The whispers returned —distant and unintelligible—but they grew clearer with each passing night.

Then the dreams began.

Or, at least, I prayed they were dreams.

I'd find myself floating again, staring down at my sleeping body. But now the shadow stood at the foot of my bed, its shape shifting and writhing, as though composed of a hundred grasping hands. It never moved toward me, but I knew it was always waiting—biding its time.

I tried to ignore it. I filled my days with noise, distractions, anything to keep my mind occupied. But the nights were inescapable. The boundary between dreams and waking life blurred, and I started to see it even when I was awake—flickering at the edge of my vision, lurking in the reflection of my bathroom mirror, standing silent and patient in the corner of my room.

All this time later, even when recounting these experiences to clients, to audiences, to fellow seekers at conventions, or to students coming into their own mediumistic development, I share this truth:

Once the doorway to the spirit world is fully opened, it can never be closed. Not entirely. Not really.

Something happens when the spirit world recognizes your willingness and openness. You become branded in a way no words can truly describe.

But I've come to understand something else in the stillness of those nights. The voices—the whispers—were not just from the entity. There were always others. Many others, in fact. They murmur from beyond the veil, their presence pressing against my mind like an ocean against a fragile dam. They call for me, plead with me, seek me out—as though I have been branded.

I realize now, in that apartment, I was opened. Changed. My openness and my questioning caused my mind to become a beacon—and my body, a doorway.

I can never truly escape that.

Because they will always find me.

The dead do not rest. And now, neither do I.

As time passed, the fear transformed into something else—understanding. I began speaking of my experiences, cautiously at first. Then more openly. Word spread. Soon, invitations came from libraries, universities, paranormal societies, Spiritualist churches—they all wanted to hear my story.

At first, I thought I was merely recounting a nightmare. But as I spoke, I realized I was teaching—guiding others who had heard the same whispers in the dark.

Though the encounters felt like they spanned an eternity, in only a few months, I was no longer speaking at just the local coffeehouse.

This is the call of mediumship, in a sense. A seemingly dark gift I've never been able to truly escape, though I've tried many times.

In the depths of my terror, I began to understand that I was never meant to escape. Perhaps, all along, I was meant to hear them—to speak for them.

The weight of the dead is unbearable at times. Especially for untrained, unvetted senses.

But I began to slowly learn that this is not a curse—but a calling.

It was also in that place—during that suffocating yet extraordinary season of awakening—that I met Miriam.

We met at the bookstore down the street, both reaching for the same tattered copy of a philosophy book. She was beautiful in a quiet, haunting way. Deep brown eyes. A slow, knowing smile. The air of someone who had seen too much, but never spoken of it.

We started talking, and I felt an instant connection, as if we had known each other in another life.

It was inevitable that I would invite her back to my place, even though I knew—deep down—it would be a mistake.

The apartment did not like her. That was apparent from the very beginning of our summer romance. The first night she stayed over, the temperature plummeted. I woke to see my breath curling into the air, and beside me, Miriam shivered violently, even though the blankets were pulled up to her chin. A shadowed shape stood in the corner, just outside the reach of the streetlamp's glow. It had no eyes and no features, but I felt its anger seeping into the room like a thick, poisonous fog. I could see it clearly.

Miriam woke up gasping, clutching her beautiful chest as though unseen fingers had tightened around her ribs.

"Something doesn't want me here," she whispered.

I knew she was right, but I wasn't ready to let her go. Even though she couldn't see the details, she sensed it.

As the weeks of summer passed—between evenings out, music festivals, passion, and memories—the disturbances grew worse. The whispers turned to moans. And the moans turned to wails. The cabinets slammed shut if she tried to cook, and the water in the shower ran scalding whenever she stepped inside. More than once, I woke to find the shadow standing over her, its amorphous shape quivering with rage. Then came the scratches.

One morning, I woke to find long, red welts down her back, as though something had raked its claws against her skin in the night. She didn't remember anything, but I could see the fear in her eyes.

"What's happening?"

I can still see the look of concern and worry in those beautiful brown eyes. I didn't have a complete answer to give. And even if I did—could that answer have even been shared?

I tried to help as best I could. I researched protective sigils, burned sage, and even delved into the study of "energy clearing." I kept protective crystals near the bedside, without even fully understanding their meaning. Honestly, deep down I seemed to know I was only grasping at straws. I had so much yet to learn. Even now, I still do.

The experiences had become commonplace for me, but I didn't want those experiences to include her. It's human nature, I suppose, to hope for the best while anticipating the worst.

"I don't know how much longer I can do this," Miriam told me one night, her voice trembling but her tone laced with resolve. "I can't live like this."

My whole life, it seemed, I had carried this apparent curse—always tethered to things that lurked beyond the realm of understanding. To reject that fact would be to reject a part of myself. And yet, if I did nothing, I knew I was potentially putting her at risk.

One night, I woke to the sound of her screaming. The room was suffocatingly dark, with the shadows pressing in on all sides.

She was on the floor, writhing, clawing at something I couldn't see. I reached for her, trying to wake her from what I prayed was only a dream.

When she opened her eyes, it was as if nothing had happened.

A little more time passed, and I finally brought myself to say the words I never wanted to say.

"I think we should stop seeing each other."

The words came out, though I felt the weight of them crush me as I spoke. I can still clearly see the expression on her face—it was almost one of peaceful relief, as if I had finally said what she had hoped I would eventually say.

In my own naivety and pride, I used the excuse that my upcoming lectures would soon keep me away for longer periods of time. It was a valid reason—I had begun to receive more invitations to lecture than ever before—but we both knew that wasn't the real reason.

I still think of her to this day.

Today, she's happily married and the mother of three beautiful children. I find myself grateful to have known her, looking back with fondness and nostalgia on that summer that marked both of our lives.

I stayed in that apartment for three more months, struggling to cope with the effects of consciously opening a doorway to the realm of the dead.

What had I gotten myself into by responding to the voices?

I had no way of knowing.

But, quite frankly, that is the burden of exploration, is it not?

The constant, burning desire to keep traveling.

The shadows, though, had begun to watch me with something like satisfaction. Their whispers turning gentle, almost loving at times. I had made my choice—whether I meant to or not.

Opening the psychic and mediumistic senses is a journey into very subtle realms—an awakening that draws the veil between the seen and unseen world ever thinner. And, mind you, it is already quite thin to begin with. As the senses stretch beyond the familiar five, the mind becomes a vessel for impressions, energies, and messages that often defy logic or language.

But this expansion is rarely linear or serene. Instead, it moves like an ever-changing tide, rising and receding between fear and faith.

Change through ebb and flow is both profound and paradoxical.

In the early stages—and sometimes even years in—fear often arrives first. Fear, after all, is a primal and immediate response to horror. It can manifest as the dread of encountering something malevolent, the terror of being watched by unseen forces, or the anxiety of losing touch with three-dimensional, physical reality. The psychic world doesn't always introduce itself with soft light and angelic voices, as some teachers seem to imply. No—sometimes quite the opposite. Sometimes the veil lifts just enough to glimpse shadows, or to feel presences that challenge the illusion of safety and control. Nightmares intensify. Sensations grow sharper.

There may be unexplained noises, flickers of movement at the edge of vision, or sudden drops in temperature. These experiences can unsettle even the most open-minded of seekers, especially when the line between internal intuition and external influence feels impossibly, inescapably thin.

But then, my darling, faith enters—not the blind sort of belief, but a quiet, anchoring trust. A sort of knowing. It's the knowing that even the most disorienting messages are never random. A knowing that the experiences serve some purpose, always. A knowing that beneath the fear, there is a deeper current carrying the soul toward something meaningful. Faith shows itself in those moments of horror.

I found myself praying again—praying prayers that, at least to me at the time, seemed very religious in nature. I did so not only in an attempt to make peace with my own horrifying encounters, but even more so, to make peace with my own personal faith—a faith that had, at times, seemed so contradictory to the life I lived. In that early season of my life, everything I thought I understood about the world—both seen and unseen—began to shift. I found myself praying again, not out of duty or ritual, but from a deep, almost unexplainable longing.

For a season, I had distanced myself from even the notion of such things, wary of the contradictions and disillusionments that often come with traditional faith. But as I stood in the middle of a life that felt both fragile and mysteriously guided, I started to make my peace—not just with the idea of a higher power, but with the parts of my own story that defied logic. The strange things I had seen and the unexplainable encounters I had tucked away in the corners of my memory suddenly felt less like burdens and more like invitations. More like "callings," if you will.

I remembered something from my short time in seminary. There was this incredible passage from the ancient texts, where, during an exorcism, the spirits sneered, "Jesus I know, and Paul I know about, but who are you?" That line never left me. It became emblazoned on my soul. At the time, it felt ominous—much like some dark warning. But in this new season, it echoed differently.

It struck me that the spirit world, for all its mystery and menace, recognized people who were rooted in something deeper than fear or performance. "Who are you?" The question began to sound more like a challenge—to know myself and to be known, not just by those around me, but by the very forces that move beneath the surface of reality. I started to believe that maybe the spirits actually wanted to know me—not just as a name, but as a soul who had finally decided to show up.

I didn't always have the right words. Often, I didn't say anything at all. I just sat with the silence, letting it speak back to me in ways I had never expected. I stopped looking for certainty. What I found instead was something more enduring: a strange kind of peace in not having to explain everything away. A sort of quiet confidence that maybe faith has never been about controlling the unknown, but instead, being willing to walk with it.

The veil between the physical and the spiritual had always been thin to me. I just had never been ready to acknowledge how much it had already shaped me. But now, with open hands and a curious heart, I was finally beginning to listen.

It slowly began to dawn on me that the spirits—whatever their nature, whatever their alignments—weren't merely passive observers of my life. They were paying attention. And more than that, they wanted to engage. For me, this was a humbling realization that changed everything. For so long, I had assumed that if anything in the spirit world noticed me at all, it was either to test me or torment me. But in that quiet season, I started to understand something deeper: they wanted to work with me. Not in some transactional way I had once feared, where deals are struck in desperation, but in a more mysterious, purposeful collaboration. As if they had been waiting for me to wake up to who I really was—and to who I was becoming.

As the days blurred into nights, and the chilling whispers grew louder in the shadows, I began to understand that what I had been experiencing was not some curse or haunting, but something much more profound. It had been a calling. A summons that had been waiting for me long before I ever stumbled into it. And with each vision, each voice that echoed through the silence, I could no longer deny the truth that had slowly woven itself into the fabric of my daily life. The dead were not just lingering souls, lost in time or trapped in the spaces between worlds. No. Instead, they were reaching out in desperation for something—for me to hear them, for me to become involved in some way. And in that moment of revelation, I realized the connection to the words Andrew Jackson Davis had spoken so long ago: the "good work."

The voices and the terrifying visions—they were not simply random or malicious. They were part of something greater. A purpose that stretched beyond fear and confusion. The dead were calling to me, urging me to step into the role that had been waiting for me. I wasn't just hearing them—I was meant to help them, to aid in their passage, and in doing so, to fulfill a destiny I hadn't known I had. The dead, my darling, truly have no interest in frightening us. At least, that is never their true intent. Instead, they desire communion.

Even now, as I sit here recounting these experiences, I feel their presence around me. Not as terrifying specters, but as guides— as mentors, even. They are no longer mere whispers in the dark, but instead voices that show me the way forward. And I, still with a heart as filled with wonder as ever, am so grateful for their companionship.

By the end of that year, things had changed drastically. What began as a solitary, fearful existence within the confines of that creaking old apartment had transformed into something entirely different—something I couldn't have foreseen, even in my wildest dreams. The spirits, once shadows that whispered in the dark, had become my companions, my teachers. Through them, I learned not only that the messages serve a purpose, but that the purpose is for both the realm of the dead as well as the realm of the living. I realized that the dead have quite a lot to say about life. In fact, all this time later, I still believe that much of what I've learned about life, I've learned from the dead.

Word of my "gifts" began to spread. Quietly, at first—a hushed rumor here, a whisper there. Friends and acquaintances, drawn by the strange and unexplainable occurrences that seemed to surround me, would visit, seeking answers. They came with broken hearts, troubled minds, and questions they couldn't ask anyone else. And I, with the guidance of the spirits, found myself able to offer not just words, but clarity, solace, and even, at times, a sense of peace.

Ironically, even local ministers and members of the faith community who had once shunned me began to reach out, asking what I was sensing for their lives and for their churches. The predictions, at first vague, began to sharpen. People would come to me with questions about their lives, their relationships, and their futures, and I would speak with an eerie precision. I never intended to predict anything. I never considered myself a "fortune teller." I never have. I was simply relaying what I was shown by the spirits—relaying to seekers what the spirits whispered into my mind. But the accuracy with which my words unfolded was nothing short of astonishing. Relationships were healed. Jobs were found. Paths were cleared. Those who had come to me in desperation began to leave with the answers they sought.

What began in horror quickly began to feel good. Still, even now, I often find myself saying that feeling good is the message. I truly believe that. In fact, there's quite a lot to be said about the spirituality of *feeling good*—as simple and elementary as that might seem.

As the weeks passed, my reputation spread like wildfire. I was no longer a mere experiencer; I had become a sought-after speaker, a lecturer even, finding myself standing before crowds of people eager to hear what I had to say. Invitations to spiritual gatherings, conferences, and private events flooded in.

In the surrounding areas, I became known as someone who could see the future—someone whose predictions held an almost supernatural weight. Even skeptics—those who once mocked the very idea of psychic abilities—soon found themselves lining up at events, often out of sheer curiosity. Unsure of what they believed, they were nonetheless unwilling to dismiss what they had witnessed with their own eyes. It was no longer just about the dead reaching out to me; it was about the living finding answers and healing in the unlikeliest of places.

But it wasn't just the predictions that set me apart. There were the healings—another facet of Spiritualism I hadn't fully understood in the beginning. People came to me not just for advice, but for relief from physical ailments, mental anguish, and emotional scars. And again, I was able to help.

Well, not me. Not really.

To regard myself as a *healer* is something I still refuse to do. What I *can* claim is that on more occasions than I can even count, I have watched as people received physical healings of symptoms due solely to the intervention of the spirits.

I never claimed to be a doctor, nor did I pretend to understand the intricacies of the human body. But what I seemed to become keenly able to do was channel the energy I had been given—relaying the power the spirits wanted to share, to heal. I could feel the dark energies that clung to the people who came to me, and with the right focus and intent, I watched them get pulled away, allowing the light to enter.

The transformations I witnessed in others were nothing short of miraculous. Pain disappeared. Old wounds were healed. And most of all, once-burdened hearts were lifted. Experiencing the power of the spirit world in those moments was remarkable.

As the following year wore on, I found myself standing before larger crowds. My once-small apartment was now replaced by venues filled with people seeking answers, healing, and insight into what lay beyond the veil. They called me a *healer*, a *psychic*, and even a *prophet* in some circles. But to me, I was simply a man who had answered the call of the spirit world. To this very day, all this time later, I still see myself as simply that.

Each lecture, prediction, and healing confirmed I was on the right path. It was never easy—not even in the beginning. The pressure to perform and to meet expectations was immense. But with every success, with every breakthrough, I felt more certain that I had found my true calling—and that I was experiencing, in real time, the "good work" Andrew Jackson Davis had spoken of long, long ago. The good work of bridging the worlds.

Looking back, even then, I scarcely recognized the person I had been when I first entered that apartment. I had been a man terrified of his own visions. A man who had questioned whether he was losing his sanity. But I had become someone much different. Someone stronger. Someone who spoke with more confidence. And, above all, someone who understood the weight of the responsibility that had been placed upon him.

And though the whispers of the spirits had quieted somewhat, their presence was always with me—even to a greater degree than before. The whispers were replaced, instead, by a sort of inner knowing.

As the leaves began to turn and the first chill of autumn settled in, I knew this was only the beginning of a much larger journey. A journey that would continue to unfold, so long as I was willing to listen, to answer, and to serve the purpose for which I had been chosen.

The world around me seemed to be watching, and I was ready.

Part Three

Journeys Through the Veil

Chapter 5

Séance

"What does mediumship mean to you?"

Throughout the years, I've been asked that question more times than I can count. What mediumship meant to me then, I've since learned, was only a portion of all that it is—of all that it can be.

In those early days, mediumship was a long and winding series of experiences I could never quite put into words. But mediumship now? I've come to realize it is the most beautiful ache that can never fully be relieved, and the most haunting longing that can never properly be expressed in human language.

There is a sorrow that walks in silence. Not loud like grief or sharp like fear, but a soft, haunting ache that tugs at the hem of the soul. "Mediumship," as we call it, is not just hearing the unheard or seeing the unseen, but feeling what was never meant to be fully touched again. It's the whisper of a name you don't personally know but somehow already love. The echo of laughter trapped in a memory that isn't your own.

And the veil—that gossamer-thin fabric between now and not-now—always beckons me to feel a longing for something I can never fully articulate. It is the ache of unfinished goodbyes.

The medium is not a prophet or a priest, but a carrier of borrowed heartbeats, standing in the middle—never belonging fully to the living, never fully welcomed among the dead.

The medium feels what others have let go. The medium listens to voices that plead not to be forgotten. Always, there is this dull ache—not pain, but a pull of emotion that can never fully be expressed. A sadness too deep to speak aloud, too familiar to be strange, and yet never truly her own.

To be a medium is to be haunted not by ghosts, but by yearning itself. By a love that outlived the lips that spoke it. By dreams that faded before the dreamer awoke. And by the shape of a touch that was never meant for your skin, but still presses into your skin in the dark.

It is living with the feelings—the pleasures and the pains—of others, never fully able to share every message.

Throughout the years, especially after the glamour of Hollywood came calling, I've been credited with thousands upon thousands of readings. My life changed beyond my wildest dreams because of these feelings.

But to a young seeker just starting out, just beginning his journey into the unseen world, I longed for closeness to the spirit world. I needed it—desperately. Though I had begun to trust it fully and wholeheartedly, and though I knew without question I was never alone, I still wanted more.

Every moment, even in those early days, I searched for ways to put the spirits to the test. Not because I didn't believe their words, but because I wanted them even closer.

When I surrendered, I surrendered completely. Of course, there were times my surrender was far from graceful—moments of regret and questioning, as we all have from time to time.

But when I gave my life to this work, I gave it away completely. I would come to give it not only to the dead, but to the living—to countless beautiful audiences, to every client, to every moment in which the spirit world asked for my attention.

Suffice it to say, when you agree to give so much of yourself away, you long for constant assurance that you are not alone.

Mediumship, for me, began to become a kind of communion—a religion all its own. I spent countless hours communing with the spirits. Where I once saw them as enemies or tormentors, I came to see them as dear friends. Not merely guides or teachers, but companions. Helpers. Individuals concerned with every detail of my life.

And just as clients came seeking guidance from the spirit world, I did the same—every single day.

I often tell fellow seekers and students developing their mediumship: it's not really about what you do on a stage in front of an audience under bright lights.

Yes, that is the outward manifestation of the gift. The performance. The demonstration.

But mediumship is not what you do on a stage.

Mediumship is the communion with the spirit world when no one else is watching. After the stage lights have dimmed. In the quiet of your personal, private life.

When you establish that connection and give your life to that element, rest assured—the spirits will support you every single time you stand before an audience.

In my season of surrender—my season of reckoning—I was left with no doubt that the dead can and do interact daily with the realm of the living. There was no question of that. For me, it was already a proven, established fact based on my experiences of encounter. But to what extent, exactly, could the worlds blend? I continued to wonder. Did the dead speak to the living merely through impressions of thoughts and emotions, or through seemingly random sounds that awaken us in the dead of night? Certainly, there had to be more, I thought. The realm of the dead, after all, is a realm of intelligence.

I had heard and read accounts of the dead interacting with the living in physical, tangible ways. The religious part of me recalled passages of ancient text recounting instances in which spirits interacted so perfectly with this world that they seemed very much alive. The passage about entertaining angels "unaware" comes to mind. Could it truly be so? I was more eager for experience than ever before.

The Spiritualist movement, which surged in popularity in both the United States and Britain in the nineteenth century, was far more than a fringe fascination with ghosts or an esoteric form of entertainment for audiences. It was a cultural phenomenon and a very real religion that wove together faith, science, psychology, and belief into a complex web of ideas about life, death, and the afterlife. Among its most dramatic and controversial practices were materialization séances, in which mediums claimed to bring spirits not just into contact with the living, but into full, physical manifestation. Through these extraordinary events, the dead were said to walk, speak, and even leave behind tangible, physical objects.

In these séances, phenomena such as apports, spirit-precipitated portraits, and even fully materialized figures were understood by believers not just as signs of the continuity of life, but
as proof that the boundary between the spiritual and physical
worlds could be breached—or that there was no true boundary
in place to begin with. Unlike traditional ghost sightings or
psychic impressions, materialization in Spiritualism referred to
the actual creation of a visible, physical form of a spirit—often
appearing as a full-bodied figure or a disembodied part, such as
a hand or face. This was typically accomplished in a darkened
séance room, with a medium acting as the bridge between the
worlds.

The process, at least then, often involved a mysterious
substance known as ectoplasm, said to emanate from the medium's body and be used by spirits to construct temporary physical forms. Observers of the period described this ectoplasm as
luminous, vaporous, or "gauze-like," and in some accounts, it
would gradually coalesce into a human figure resembling a
deceased loved one. One of the most famous mediums to
conduct materialization séances was Florence Cook, whose
spirit guide, "Katie King," was said to appear in full form and
interact with attendees—sometimes even allowing herself to be
touched. These events were viewed with awe by believers and,
understandably, greeted with deep skepticism by critics, especially after several exposures of fraud.

Another startling phenomenon reported in Spiritualist séances
was the apport—an object that would allegedly materialize in
the séance room, often falling from the ceiling, emerging from
seemingly nowhere, or even appearing inside a closed
container. These objects ranged from flowers and jewelry to
coins and stones, and they were said to be gifts from the spirit
world, brought through the mediumship of the séance leader.

Apports were seen as concrete evidence of spiritual interaction —signifying that spirits could not only communicate but actually manipulate matter. Their sudden appearance, sometimes accompanied by strange and haunting flashes of light or mysterious breezes, added a dramatic and theatrical air to the séances.

And then there was the art. One of the more visually compelling aspects of Spiritualism at the time was the phenomenon of spirit-precipitated portraits—images said to have been created by spirits without any human intervention. These portraits would often appear on canvases or photographic plates during séances, seemingly without the use of paint or brushes.

In many cases, the faces depicted in these portraits were claimed to be those of deceased relatives of séance participants —completely unknown to the medium and sometimes even unidentified until after the session. Some mediums and spirit artists, such as the Bangs Sisters of Chicago, gained fame for their ability to "precipitate" lifelike portraits that seemed to appear before the sitter's eyes, without direct human touch. The Hett Art Gallery on the grounds of Camp Chesterfield now houses many of these portraits, and the power within the room is still palpable to this very day.

In these instances—regardless of whether you view such things through the lens of belief or understandable skepticism—there is no doubt that these events often blurred the lines between faith and spectacle. Materialization séances occupied a curious position between religious ritual, scientific experiment, and stage performance. The Spiritualist movement itself often emphasized scientific investigation of the paranormal, with societies of researchers and investigators, like the Society for

Psychical Research, seeking to verify—or debunk—the extraordinary claims being made.

Photographs were taken, measurements were made, and eyewitness accounts were painstakingly recorded. At the same time, fraud was admittedly rampant. Many mediums were exposed using sleight of hand, puppets, muslin cloth, or accomplices to fake "manifestations." But despite these exposures, belief in genuine materializations persisted. For the devout Spiritualist, the occasional presence of deception in no way invalidated the entirety of the movement. Instead, it was seen as the unfortunate cost of venturing into the spiritual unknown.

At its core, the appeal of materialization séances was the promise of tangible proof that the dead could not only communicate but physically return. And in a Victorian world increasingly shaped by scientific discovery and religious doubt, these séances offered a mystical counter-narrative. They provided physical interactions with the afterlife: a kiss from a departed spouse, a lock of hair from a deceased child, a written message in a familiar hand. In an era wracked by war, disease, and high mortality rates, such encounters brought peace and comfort—and understandably so.

Spiritualism, through its theatrical and often deeply emotional displays of showmanship, reshaped how people thought about death. The dead, it suggested, were not really gone. They were just a veil away. Whether one views materialization séances as literal spiritual phenomena or elaborate social theater, they remain a fascinating window into the human desire to touch the untouchable and to bridge the unbridgeable. In the flickering candlelight of a séance room, believers saw not only spirits, but a certain kind of hope—a hope that death was not the end, but simply another room in the house of existence.

I believed in the possibility of these things, wholeheartedly. Even in the stories and accounts that seemed far too extreme to be possible. Or, at least, I wanted desperately to believe. I was of the mind that though there had been moments of supposed fraud in the movement, the movement itself represented a belief in endless possibilities. If communion with the dead was already an established fact, just how far could the dead go in interacting with the land of the living? I had to know in my own personal life.

It was around this time that I began to read the accounts of Aleister Crowley and how his interactions with spirits inspired him to begin his practice of channeling. His encounters—mere sounds and whispers at first—became very physical, as his own spirit guides made themselves known to him. Could it all have been true? Could it truly be that there is no boundary between the worlds at all? His writings inspire me to this day.

At the turn of the twentieth century, nestled on the mist-shrouded shores of Loch Ness in Scotland, Aleister Crowley undertook one of the most ambitious and arcane magical rituals of his life within the walls of Boleskine House. His aim was to perform the Sacred Magic of Abramelin the Mage—an intense, months-long operation that sought to invoke his Holy Guardian Angel, a deeply personal spiritual entity believed to bestow enlightenment and divine, occult knowledge. Boleskine, isolated and brooding, provided the perfect backdrop for this ancient ritual. But as the days turned into weeks, the house itself seemed to begin to respond in terrifying ways. The perceived line between the physical and spiritual began to fade away.

Crowley, always meticulous in his preparation for rituals, had sprinkled flour around his doorway as a means to detect the movement of spirits or intruders—a centuries-old technique rooted in folk magic. One morning, to his astonishment and dread, he awoke to find footprints leading across the powdery trail. Prints that neither began nor ended. It was as though they had materialized out of thin air. There were also strange knocking sounds echoing through the halls—deliberate, insistent, and with no earthly source. The boundaries between the material and the spiritual worlds were thinning, and Boleskine became a crucible of paranormal phenomena.

These harrowing, awe-inspiring experiences were more than just hauntings for Crowley. They were affirmations that he was breaching the veil of the invisible realms. Though he never completed the Abramelin ritual in full at Boleskine House, the moments of spectral contact left a profound imprint on him for the remainder of his life. He came to believe that he was being guided by higher intelligences, preparing him for something greater. A few years later, in 1904, during his fateful stay in Cairo, Crowley claimed to receive a dictation from a non-corporeal entity named Aiwass, who delivered *Liber AL vel Legis* to him. *The Book of the Law*, as it came to be called, would become the foundational text of the religion of Thelema.

"Do what thou wilt shall be the whole of the Law." This guiding mantra, given to Crowley by his spirit guides, would go on to become a central tenet in various other religions, even inspiring the formation of Wicca. The occult knowledge formed much of Crowley's spiritual and philosophical worldview. Looking back, it is difficult not to see the eerie occurrences at Boleskine House as the opening act of his transformative journey. The footprints in the flour, the knocking at the door—these were not simply ghost stories, but moments in which Crowley felt the cosmos itself was speaking to him. They cemented his belief that ritual was not superstition, but an unacknowledged science. That spirits not only seek to commune—but to lead.

The ripple effects of Boleskine never truly left Crowley. Though he would go on to travel extensively—scaling the Himalayan peaks, conducting rituals in the deserts of Egypt, and establishing the Abbey of Thelema in Sicily—the doorways opened at Boleskine House remained a fixed point in his spiritual evolution. He often spoke of the house with a mixture of reverence and fear, always seeming to acknowledge that something ancient and powerful had been stirred there. The unfinished Abramelin ritual haunted him, both metaphorically and perhaps literally. He believed that by failing to complete the intricate rite, he had left portals open and spirits unbound.

According to local legend and the accounts of later occupants, Boleskine House became a place of unsettling events. There were unexplained fires, tragic deaths, and persistent feelings of dread. Crowley's own writings hinted that the veil torn there was never fully mended.

Even decades later, as Crowley reflected on his life and writings, he often returned to the days of those early summonings. He described himself as a "beast" in the Biblical sense—an adversary of conformity and religious stagnation. The unsettling events at Boleskine House, far from deterring him, only deepened his certainty that he had tapped into something real—something dangerous, and something sacred. The spirits he called, the footprints they left behind, and the cosmic voice that would eventually dictate to him *The Book of the Law*—all of it wove together into the story of a man who believed he stood at the edge of a new spiritual age.

I remember those weeks in my own life when I realized just how present the spirit world actually is. That it is not some distant, far-off realm. That it is as close as the breath we breathe. I realized that séance was not merely a practice relegated to the darkened corners of parlors, but that it could be a way of life. I began to understand that even the physicality of this realm is laced with the presence of spirits.

I had moved to a much larger city. It started small, in the beginning—like a radio signal tuning in and out, barely perceptible at first. But as I acknowledged them, the phenomena around me escalated. One night, as I lay in bed, I idly thought to myself that I wished the door would close. It was only a thought. I never expected anything to happen, honestly. But then, with an almost deliberate slowness, the door creaked shut. My breath caught in my throat. I sat up, heart pounding, unsure if I had imagined it. Testing the limits of what I had stumbled into, I whispered, "Open." And the door obeyed.

From that night forward, my surroundings seemed charged, as if alive with an unseen, almost electric force. The air itself began to feel much different—heavier, thick with a kind of static that raised the hairs on my arms. I could feel the energy pulsing around me, as if an invisible current ran through the walls. Lights flickered when I entered a room, and sometimes, they turned off completely. Windows that had been latched shut would suddenly pop open, as if in response to my thoughts. And the more I embraced it, the stronger it became.

It was equal parts thrilling and terrifying. I was immersed in this newfound sense of communion. Whatever barrier had once kept it at bay was now paper-thin, and I had no choice but to navigate this new reality. I could still hear them, too—some calling my name, while others murmured indistinctly, their voices blending into the hum of existence around me.

Watching the door open and close on command, I can still remember my very first thought: "Why me?" It wasn't a thought of fear, but rather a sense of simple, childlike wonder. I remember the feeling of elation, of gratitude—that the spirit world is not only capable of giving such offerings of confirmation, but that they seem to take great delight in even being asked to provide them. Though I didn't know why I had been "graced" with such a partnership, what I did know, immediately, was that life would never again be the same. I knew that once I had opened the door to this level of communion, it would never close. And I was certain I would never want it to.

At first, I told no one. Not even fellow seekers or clients who came to me. How could I? Who would believe me if I admitted that doors and windows shifted at my command? It felt too strange—too impossible—even as I lived it. But the more I tried to ignore it, the more the spirits made their presence known. It seemed they were enjoying it just as much as I was.

One evening, as I sat alone in my living room, I felt a distinct change in the air—a change I had come to recognize immediately as confirmation of the presence of spirits. The temperature dropped suddenly, an icy breath sweeping across my skin. Then that familiar electric hum filled the space, crackling in the silence. I could feel someone standing just beyond my sight.

"Who are you?" I asked aloud, my voice barely above a whisper. For a moment, there was nothing—just the stillness of the room and the sound of my own heartbeat pounding in my ears. A sensation I had become quite familiar with. But then, from somewhere near the doorway, came the unmistakable sound of a reply. A whisper. It was faint—almost too soft to catch—but I knew I hadn't imagined it.

I wasn't alone.

The encounters became more frequent after that. Shadows moved where no one stood. Objects shifted places without rhyme or reason. I would hear voices calling my name in empty rooms, and sometimes, I could feel a presence brush past me—light touches against my arm, whispers of movement against my skin. The more I acknowledged them, the more they responded.

There were nights when I could barely sleep, my senses overwhelmed. Not by the dread or fear that had once been there before my surrender, but by the electric energy in the air. At times, it was overpowering—the constant hum of voices, the sudden movements of objects, the unmistakable feeling of eyes watching from the dark. But strangely, I felt no fear. Instead, I felt something else entirely. A connection. An exhilaration.

I had been given a window into something most might never experience—or even want to. I could no longer ignore the undeniable proof that the spirit world was not some distant, ethereal place reserved for the sweet hereafter. It was here, intertwined with our own reality, invisible to most but impossible to ignore. It was as if I had stumbled upon my own personal validation that the things I had read about and studied for so long were not merely the results of nineteenth-century showmanship. That physical contact with the spirit world could be a deeply personal experience.

And so, I listened. I learned. And I accepted that my life had changed forever. I couldn't ignore what was happening, but I also refused to accept it blindly. If this was real—if the spirits were truly aware of my intent to interact with them physically —then I had to test it. I had to know if they could respond in a way that left no room for doubt. Perhaps it wasn't merely testing, though. Perhaps it was my desire to prove my willingness to them.

So, I continued to test even my own limits of belief. At first, it was simple. I would ask yes-or-no questions aloud, watching and waiting for a response. One night, I sat at my kitchen table, the only light coming from a flickering candle. The air around me was still, heavy with that strange charge I had come to recognize.

"If someone is here, make a sound."

For a long moment, there was nothing. I almost laughed at myself, feeling ridiculous for speaking to an empty room. But just as I exhaled, there was a distinct knock—sharp and deliberate—against the wooden surface of the table. My stomach tightened.

I swallowed hard and asked again, this time specifying, "Knock once for yes, twice for no. Do you understand?"

A single knock echoed through the room. My breath caught in my throat. This wasn't random. This wasn't my imagination. I was communicating. It was a form of communion.

The more I tested, the more undeniable it became. I would place objects in specific positions—like keys on the table or a chair pulled slightly away from the wall—and ask for them to be moved. Sometimes, nothing would happen immediately. But hours later, I would return to find the chair shifted, or the keys now resting on the floor.

It wasn't just movement, either. I began to sense very distinct personalities. Some spirits felt passive, as if merely observing me, while others were more eager to interact. There were nights when I would hear whispers so clear I could almost make out the words, but just as I focused, they would slip away, leaving me grasping at echoes.

One of the most startling moments came when I issued a direct challenge. I stood in my dimly lit hallway, staring at the door to my bedroom.

"If you can hear me, open the door."

I felt the electricity in the air intensify, a current seeming to buzz around me in excited anticipation. Then, as I held my breath, the doorknob turned—not violently, as if pushed by the wind, but with a slow, intentional motion. The door creaked open a few inches, then stopped.

I stepped forward cautiously, my pulse hammering in my ears.

"Thank you," I said. "I see you, and you're welcome here."

It felt as if I were speaking to a lifelong friend.

"Close it, please."

The door obeyed.

It was then that I knew, without a doubt, that this was not some trick of my mind. The spirits were aware. They were listening. And they were responding. It was as if they were as desperate to get to know me as I was to know them. These were not the mere parlor tricks I had often heard of and studied. This was a different level of communion entirely—a special sort of intimacy, even. The kind of secrets shared only between the most trusted companions.

But with this realization came an even greater question: Who were they? And why had they chosen to speak with me?

I became obsessed with finding answers. If spirits could hear me—if they could respond to my commands—then surely they had stories of their own to tell. I needed to know who they were and why they lingered with me. But most of all, I needed to know their intent. Why had they chosen to reveal themselves to me?

Soon, I began asking for names. "Tell me who you are," I would whisper into the silence, straining to catch even the faintest response. "Can you tell me more?" Sometimes I would hear nothing. Other times, there would be a soft murmur, just below the threshold of understanding—like voices carried on the wind. There were always subtle impressions in my mind's eye, but I craved something more.

Then, one night, I received my first clear answer.

It was just past midnight. I sat in my bedroom with a notepad and a recorder, determined to capture anything that might come through. The air was thick with that now-familiar static energy, my level of determination unwavering.

"What is your name?"

For a long moment, there was only silence.

Then, a whisper. A single word, spoken directly into my ear:

"Jonathan."

I shot to my feet, my entire body tense with adrenaline. The voice had been unmistakable—low, hoarse, and close enough that I had felt the breath of it against my skin. I turned sharply, expecting to see someone standing there. But the room was empty.

My hands were shaking. It was undeniable. Faint, but clear.

"Jonathan."

From that point on, the voices became more distinct. Some were hesitant, while others seemed almost desperate to be heard. Names, snippets of sentences, feelings—like waves of emotion washing over me—became part of my daily reality.

Even now, when asked by fellow seekers, I often compare mediumship to a love story. Especially the moments at the very beginning. It truly is the perfect analogy, if you think about it. At least, it has been for me. No wonder so many ancient writings and religious texts describe mediumship as consulting with "seducing spirits."

When one first begins to step into the world of mediumship, the connection to the spirit world often feels like the tender beginnings of a great romance. Much like the moment two souls meet for the very first time. There's an instant spark. A curiosity. An overwhelming desire to understand one another deeply. Just as two people falling in love can never seem to get enough of each other, a budding medium and the spirit realm begin a dance of discovery, drawn together by an invisible thread of mutual fascination and undeniable connection.

In the early days, it's not uncommon for the connection to feel intoxicating—like new lovers staying up until the early hours of the morning, talking about anything and everything and nothing, just basking in the presence of each other's energy. The spirit world, once distant and mysterious, then begins to whisper her secrets and her stories, as the medium leans in with an eager heart, craving every single detail. It's as if you're on a long phone call with a new love, and time loses all meaning. You hang on to every word, every pause, every shift in tone, learning how they communicate. Learning how they feel and how they move through your awareness.

There exists a sort of sweetness in that vulnerability—sweetness on both sides. The medium is learning to trust their senses, their feelings, and their intuition, while the spirit world is learning how best to communicate through this new and unique channel. It can be awkward and clumsy at times, just like every new romance. There are misunderstandings, missed signals, moments of doubt. But there's also magic in the trying.

Each small success, each message received and understood, feels like that very first "I love you" spoken out loud.

Over time, as in any true relationship, the connection only deepens. The initial excitement may soften into something steadier—but no less profound. What started as hours-long conversations turns into a silent knowing: a glance, a touch, an intuition that says everything without words. But those first moments—when the veil between worlds is drawn back and you realize you are not alone, when you find yourself in dialogue with something vast, compassionate, and wise—those moments are unforgettable. Like new love, they awaken something in you that can never go back to sleep.

As the relationship with the spirit world evolves, it begins to mirror the unfolding of an intimate partnership built on trust, patience, and the willingness to truly listen. In the beginning, I felt so insecure—just like a new lover wondering, *"Am I saying the right thing?" "Are they hearing me clearly?"* But over time, the nervousness faded into confidence, and the communication became much more natural. More fluid, if you will. I began to understand the subtle ways spirits reach out to me—the way a certain feeling in my chest always seemed to mean *pay attention,* or how an image would flash through my mind like a shared memory between lovers.

And just like a romantic connection that grows richer with every shared experience, so does the bond with the spirit world. You begin to recognize personalities in the energy that comes through—a grandmother with a gentle presence, a playful uncle with a loud, obnoxious laugh, a quiet soul who only communicates through symbols. They become familiar to you in this journey, just as a lover's moods and quirks do. You learn their rhythm and their pace—the way they lean in when the message matters most. And in return, they learn you as well—your sensitivities, your strengths, and the ways you best hear, feel, and see them. It becomes a sacred give-and-take, like a slow dance where both partners instinctively adjust to each other's steps.

There's also a deep emotional intimacy in mediumship that parallels the vulnerability of love. The spirit world shares its stories not just to inform, but to heal, to reconnect, and to remind the living that love never really ends. The love we feel —it never really ends. It never leaves. We take it with us, even when we go. And it reminds us, too, that we never really go anywhere.

The medium becomes the bridge, holding space for those deeply human moments of grief, joy, and release. It's a role that requires an open heart and a willingness to be changed by the connection. Just as falling in love transforms the way one sees the world, so too does communion with the spirits. You begin to understand that death is not the end—and that love transcends dimensions.

And maybe that, for me, has been the most beautiful part of this love story between medium and spirits: it's never been one-sided. I've never been just a receiver. I've been cherished, supported, and guided. I feel as if I've been chosen—again and again—to be part of something sacred. And in this partnership, I discover over and over again a depth of love that is eternal, beyond the limits of this world. The more they leaned in, the more I listened, the more I fell in love all over again.

I no longer tried to ignore it—the world that had not long before seemed so ominous and horrifying to me. Instead, I craved it. It was as if the spirit world had brought me to life. I had found not only peace in the experiences that once seemed more a curse than a blessing, but, even more so, I had found contentment. The spirits had followed me, always. They were never more than a thought away. And to this very day, all this time later, that is still the case.

I could never escape them—nor did I want to. Because somewhere along the way, I had become a part of their world, just as they had become a part of mine. I had spent so much time testing, questioning, pushing for proof and seeking answers, and somehow, in the midst of it all, I had found my greatest love. In a lifetime of horror, I had, somewhere along the way, inadvertently stumbled upon my reason.

The activity continued, but something shifted. The air became lighter—no longer heavy. The tension, once thick enough to strangle, loosened its grip. It was as if the spirits had been waiting for me to acknowledge them—not as a threat, but as something that had always been there by my side, as a trusted companion and friend. And so, I made peace with them. I no longer tested them or challenged their presence with fear or defiance. Instead, I accepted the simple truth: I was not alone, and I never had been.

Not all spirits are trapped. Some simply choose to linger. And some, for reasons I may never fully understand, choose to follow us.

As I began to accept the presence of the spirits around me, I found that my perception of them grew clearer as well. It was no longer just a vague awareness of whispers or flickering lights. There was something deeper—a sense of familiarity, as if I were no longer just sensing spirits but recognizing them.

And then, I met Artemis and Adrianne.

It started with dreams. Vivid, strikingly real dreams where I was not just an observer but an active participant, walking through spaces that felt both foreign and familiar. In these dreams, I saw a woman—tall, powerful, and radiant. Her presence was commanding and yet strangely comforting. She introduced herself as Artemis—not just a spirit, but a guide.

At first, I struggled with this. Could I really be communicating with something so ancient? So revered? But the signs were undeniable. Whenever I thought of her, I would see symbols: crescent moons, arrows, or the sudden appearance of a stag in places where none should be. Her presence was not subtle; it was immense, like a force woven into the very fabric of my mind. She was not just a spirit lingering in my space—she was something greater. A guide. A protector.

Then there was Adrianne. Unlike Artemis, Adrianne's presence was much more delicate. More human. She came to me in quiet moments, with her soft laughter echoing in my mind. The faint scent of oil paint and cigarettes would fill the air when nothing physical could have caused it.

She was an artist. A soul who had once lived, once dreamed, and once created. I learned more about her in fragments—in pieces of memories she allowed me to glimpse. She had lived in New York City, painting in a small apartment with floor-to-ceiling windows, chasing inspiration in the rush of the streets below. She had died in 1988, only 27 years old, though the details of how remained unclear. Sometimes, I sensed a sorrow in her presence—a sort of weight she carried even in death. But she wasn't lost. She had simply chosen to stay.

She was the first to truly speak to me—not in whispers or riddles, but in thoughts that entered my mind as clearly as if they were my own.

"You're not crazy," she told me once, her voice carrying a warmth I had never realized I needed. "You're just finally listening."

With Artemis and Adrianne beside me, I no longer felt haunted at all. I felt guided. They weren't just spirits lingering on the edges of my reality. They became my teachers, my protectors, my guides—companions on this strange path I had chosen.

I began to trust them. When Artemis sent me signs, I paid attention. When Adrianne's presence filled the room, I listened. And for the first time since all of it began, I stopped questioning whether I was meant to experience this. I knew without a doubt that I was.

As time passed, my ability to perceive the spirit world sharpened. The shadows that had once seemed to lurk at the edges of my vision took on form and detail. I could see them more clearly than ever—the curve of a face, the way the light bent around them, the subtle shifts in expression that revealed emotions as raw and complex as those of the living.

Artemis was always the most striking. When she appeared, she was a luminous presence that seemed too vast to be contained in a single form. Sometimes she looked like a huntress from mythology, clad in flowing robes. Other times, she was simply a flicker of energy—a force more than a figure. She filled the space with an undeniable presence.

She rarely spoke aloud, but when she did, her voice was a command, woven with the weight of the ages.

"You are listening now, Beautiful Soul," she would say. "But you have only begun to understand, and there is still much to see and to witness."

I remember the words as if they were spoken to me only moments ago.

Adrianne, in contrast, was almost casual in the way she appeared. She didn't seem to look like Artemis. She simply existed beside me, like an old friend dropping in for a visit. When I saw her, she was often perched on the edge of my couch, her legs crossed, dressed in an oversized sweater with paint smudges on the sleeves, her jeans tattered and aged. She had a mischievous smile, dirty blonde curls framing her sharp features, and a way of speaking that made it easy to forget she had died decades ago.

"The dead don't have to be sad, you know," she told me one night as I sat enjoying a glass of wine, struggling to put my thoughts into words. She seemed to enjoy my company as much as I enjoyed hers.

"We still feel, and we still think. It's just a little different now."

I couldn't help but ask aloud, "Different how?"

She tilted her head, as if considering.

"Like watching a movie you once starred in. You remember what it felt like, but you're not quite in it anymore."

It made perfect sense to me. Our conversations became frequent, like talking to old friends. Artemis would offer wisdom in brief, deliberate statements, her words carrying an undeniable authority. Adrianne, on the other hand, would ramble about art, about the way New York smelled after it rained, and about how she used to sit in Washington Square Park watching people pass by, capturing their faces in quick, frantic strokes of charcoal.

"The living forget how much we still see," she mused one evening, stretching out on my couch.

"You think death is an ending, but we still watch," she said. "We're just not as weighed down by things."

I had begun to see her as more than just a guide. She had quickly become a constant companion to me. So often, I found myself saying, "Tell me more about your art." She loves when I ask that.

I began to understand that the dead had so much more to share than the world gives them credit for. The dead aren't just lingering echoes or lost souls. They aren't simply spirits with unfinished business. They have wisdom, memories, and even humor. And most importantly, they have stories.

As I listened, I realized something profound: they had never wanted to frighten me. They had never even wanted to test me. They simply wanted to be heard. The more I listened in that season, the more the spirit world unfolded before my very eyes. No longer just flickers of movement in the periphery of my vision but fully realized presences, rich with thought, emotion, and history. I could see them more clearly now. Details I had once struggled to grasp sharpened into focus—the way Adrianne absentmindedly tapped her fingers on the arm of the couch when watching me with clients. The way Artemis's presence seemed to command the very air around her, like an ancient queen. Conversations with them became as natural as speaking with the living.

Sometimes, Adrianne would appear when I was lost in thought, slouched at my desk with a pen in my hand.

"You think too much," she would say with a smirk, lazily floating just above the chair across from me. "You should paint instead," she smiled. "You ever try painting? It's better than writing sometimes."

I began to take her advice.

Artemis, in stark contrast, was a presence that demanded stillness. When she arrived, the air would shift, becoming completely still—just like the silence before a storm. She never wasted words, but what she did say carried weight.

"You walk between worlds now," she told me one evening. "You must learn balance, or you will be consumed by what you do not understand."

"Consumed?" I asked hesitantly. "What do you mean?"

"The dead will always speak," she said. "But not all should be answered."

For the first time in what seemed like a long while, a cold chill ran through me, and I thought of how very ominous the warning seemed. Not every spirit was Adrianne, eager to reminisce about old paintings and lost cities. Not every entity was Artemis—ancient and powerful, yet guiding. Some are something else entirely. I still had much to learn. Even now, I still do.

But despite that warning, I didn't feel afraid. Instead, I felt more awake than ever before. More aware of the delicate thread that weaves between the living and the dead. I realized that wherever I went, the spirits would follow. Not because they were trapped, but because they had found someone willing to listen. Someone who could see them. Someone to carry their stories into the world of the living.

In that understanding, I seemed to come to life for the very first time.

Chapter 6

"The Beauty That's Been"

Often, a single song can encapsulate your entire journey —your struggles, your revelations, your growth. For me, in my experiences with mediumship, that song is *Listen to Your Heart* by Roxette. I can think of no other lyrics that more clearly reflect the path I've walked or more accurately echo the whispers that have guided me when the noise of the world tried to drown them out. The refrain, "Listen to your heart when he's calling for you," has taken on a profound, almost sacred meaning in my life.

In my work, that "he" isn't always a person, though. It's a presence—a calling, a spirit, or an intuition far too deep for words. And listening to that quiet voice has been the cornerstone of everything I've come to understand and trust in my life.

When I first began to sense things beyond the physical world, recognizing how desperately the spirits want to interact with the living, it wasn't some lightning-bolt moment. It was subtle, like hearing a song playing faintly in the background. During those early seasons, I doubted myself. I questioned my sanity. I tried to silence it. But the more I resisted, the more persistent it became.

I remember driving one night, thoughts swirling, emotions storming, and *Listen to Your Heart* came on the radio. Of course, I had heard it countless times before and had always loved it. But, for some reason, that night the lyrics seemed to take on an entirely different meaning. The lines, "There are voices that want to be heard, so much to mention but you can't find the words," pierced right through me.

That was exactly it. I wasn't imagining things. I was tuning in to voices that longed to be heard, and I simply hadn't found the courage to listen—or the words to express it publicly—yet. That moment helped me embrace what I had become. It helped me surrender even more.

Listen to Your Heart was released in 1988 by the Swedish pop duo Roxette, composed of Marie Fredriksson and Per Gessle. It was first included on their second studio album, *Look Sharp!*, and became their second number-one hit in the United States the following year. The song, with its emotive melody and heartfelt lyrics, quickly became a timeless ballad, often associated with love and loss. But for me, its meaning has gone far beyond romance. It's a sort of spiritual anthem. A reminder. A vow.

"The scent of magic." "The beauty that's been." Even now, all this time later, every time I hear those words, I find myself reminded not just of where I've been, but of how important it is to trust the spirits—even when they seem to beckon into the unknown. That is the message I carry forward with every reading, with every quiet moment of personal communion. In my life, I had stumbled upon the most beautiful of things, and I had become better because of it. Unknown to me at the time, a very real philosophy for life was beginning to take shape and reveal itself.

Looking back, even after all the physical encounters I'd had—those undeniable, visceral moments when spirit made themselves known in ways I could see, hear, and feel—I still had yet to fully grasp the greater, grander picture behind it all. There were times I'd leave a session overwhelmed, not just by the presence I had felt, but by the sheer magnitude of what seemed to be unfolding just beyond the veil. And still, trying to explain it felt like catching sunlight in my hands. My words always seemed to fail me. I constantly questioned what was appropriate or even possible to share with clients and audiences. Would they understand? Could they feel the weight of it the way I did? Or would it be misinterpreted, dismissed, or worse—sensationalized?

I wrestled with that boundary for a while, I must admit—always trying to honor the sacredness of the experiences while also doing my best to bring some part of it into the open. There were truths that felt far too vast and far too tender to be handed over lightly. And there were other pieces I wasn't even sure I was meant to speak of yet. It's one thing to experience the spirits, but translating it into language and context—framing it into something that helps others without diluting or distorting the overall essence—has been an ongoing journey.

In truth, it continues to be even now.

Some days, I felt like a translator for a language I was only just beginning to understand—a language not made of words, but of presence, energy, and deep emotions. The spirits would communicate in waves, in impressions that bypassed logic and struck something deep in the soul. I could feel their love. Their sense of urgency. Sometimes, even their pain. Yet putting that into coherent, earthly terms always felt like fumbling in the dark for a light switch that kept changing walls.

I remember sitting in my car after sessions, staring out at nothing, wondering what it all meant—not just the messages, but the mechanisms behind them. Why was I allowed to glimpse these things? Why did it come with such responsibility, and such profound silence around certain parts? There were moments of clarity where I thought I finally understood. And then, just as quickly, the vastness of it would slip through my fingers again. The truth is, the more I experienced, the more I realized how little I truly knew. And maybe that's the point.

Maybe mediumship wasn't supposed to be about having all the answers or painting a complete picture. Maybe it was more about holding the brush, adding strokes where I could, and learning to live in the mystery of it all. That seemed to be the hardest part for me—the part about learning to be okay with the mystery. Learning that I didn't need to explain everything. Realizing that some things are meant to be felt instead of told. But still, every time I stood in front of audiences, I tried to be as clear, as honest, and as respectful of that mystery as I could— all the while knowing that even fragments of truth could be life-changing if shared with care.

Looking back now, I often find myself returning to the same haunting question: What's the meaning of these experiences? After all the years, the sessions, the tears—both mine and theirs—I still don't have a complete answer. I've tried to make sense of it, to map out some spiritual architecture behind the moments that left me speechless or in awe. Sometimes, I wonder if the meaning lies not in the answers but in the asking itself, and in the deepening of the question each time I brush up against something I can't explain.

There were so many nights back then when I replayed the encounters in my mind, trying to extract something definitive —some rule, some specific pattern, the definitive purpose. But the spirits never seemed to work that way. It was much more like a dance, requiring far more surrender than certainty. And maybe that was the meaning: not to decode the mystery, but to live inside it somehow, to allow it to change me. To soften me. To teach me humility.

But those natural, human questions always lingered. "Why me?" "Why this?" "Why now?" I wrestled with the weight of that responsibility, dealing as best I could with the quiet pressure that comes with being trusted by something greater than myself. I realized I might never fully understand it all. I had seen healing take place in a moment—as words that came through me, not from me—restored peace to someone who hadn't felt it in decades. And I'd seen silence, too. Times when no words would come, and I had to sit with the discomfort of not knowing. Of not being able to reach into the invisible and pull out a tidy, coherent message. Still, even in that silence, something was happening. Something real.

So perhaps the meaning was layered. It was in the connection, the healing, and in the reminders that we are not as alone as we think. That love doesn't end. That life, in all its forms, continues. I realized I might never be able to explain how or why, but I kept showing up. I keep listening. I keep honoring the sacred thread that seems to weave through it all. Though not always gracefully, I did try.

What I did come to realize—slowly, and oftentimes in the most ungraceful of ways—was that mediumship had never been just about messages or proof of the afterlife. It had always been about healing. Deep, quiet, sometimes unexpected healing.

And not just for the living, but for the dead, too. I used to think the spirits who came through were already whole, already at peace—and many are. But over time, I began to encounter those who still carried echoes of sorrow, regret, and unfinished business. Their messages weren't always declarations of love or poetic closures. They were often apologies, confessions, or long-awaited acknowledgments.

And in those moments, I saw something shift—not just in the sitter receiving the message, but in the energy of the spirit itself. There was a sense of relief. A shared breath across the veil. It showed me that healing is not limited by death. Rather, it's a sort of continuum, stretching across lifetimes, anchored in love, and made possible through the fragile, often faltering and clumsy, but sacred act of communication.

Mediumship, then, became less about proving something and much more about serving something—serving that healing, that reconciliation. I'd seen people walk into a room with grief so heavy it changed the shape of their bodies, only to leave a little lighter because they'd heard something or felt something that reminded them their loved one was not gone. And I'd felt the presence of a spirit grow brighter—freer—after finally being able to say the words they couldn't in life.

In those moments, I came to understand that my role wasn't to perform or to impress, but to be present. To be available. To be a witness and a vessel for a process that's much greater than I am. And honestly, I came to learn that that's where the greater meaning really seemed to live—not in having all the answers, but in participating in the healing. In holding space where the living and the dead meet together, even if only for a moment, just to remind each other that love doesn't end where life does. It goes on. And so do we.

When I look back, I see how much I wrestled with the question of how to present mediumship to the world. Not because I didn't believe in it, and not because I lacked the experiences to back it up, but because I had never been entirely sure just how to frame it. Clients came to me for readings, and in those intimate, one-on-one sessions, the work felt natural. Organic. Sacred, even. There were quiet agreements in those spaces—spoken or unspoken—that we were stepping into something personal and transformative.

But when it came to standing on stages, facing rooms filled with people, or weaving the subject into broader talks or presentations, I hesitated. Not out of shame, but out of a deep reverence for what mediumship really meant to me—and a genuine concern for how easily it could be misunderstood, dismissed, or reduced to mere performance.

I never wanted to sensationalize it. I didn't want to stand under bright lights and turn something so delicate and so vulnerable into just entertainment. And at the same time, I knew there was power in sharing it. Power in giving voice to the invisible, and to the enduring presence of love after loss. The challenge for me wasn't whether it was real—I had no doubt about that. The challenge was how to translate the depth of those experiences into a language the world could receive, without losing the sense of sacredness that had transformed me.

I found myself asking the spirits, "How do I honor both the spirit world and the human audience in front of me?" "How do I speak to skeptics without shrinking the truth?" "How do I reach the curious without overpromising?" These weren't just logical questions; they were soul questions. And for a long time, I never had the answers.

So, I kept it close. For a time, I kept talk of my private experiences away from public audiences. It wasn't until I began to trust that the message never needed to be perfect that I began to open up more in public spaces. I began to speak less about the mechanics of mediumship and more about its greater impact—the healing, the peace, the beauty of realizing we are part of something so much larger than ourselves. And slowly, as I let go of the need to control the narrative, the work began to unfold in ways I had never expected.

Audiences, I began to find, weren't just curious—they were hungry for meaning. For connection. And when I met them with honesty and humility, the message landed perfectly. Not always with everyone, but always with the ones who needed it most. And that, I came to learn, was more than enough.

Looking back now, I can see that during that season—in those early, uncertain years of stepping into the work publicly—I wasn't just learning how to talk about mediumship. I was learning how to own it in a way that was unique to me. I was slowly crafting a message and a style, and discovering my own voice in the process. It wasn't something I could borrow from someone else, no matter how much I admired other speakers, teachers, or mediums. Their voices were their own, shaped by their stories, their lessons, and their truths. I had to find mine in the pauses between sessions, in the quiet car rides home, in the moments of doubt when I wondered if I was really cut out for a life on the stage.

Strangely enough, it was in the hesitations and in the discomfort where my voice began to form. Because it had to come from a place deeper than performance. It had to come from lived experiences. From vulnerability. From the grit of walking through the unknown and choosing to speak anyway.

At the time, I didn't recognize it for what it was. I thought I was just trying to figure out how to explain things better and more articulately—how to put language around the unseeable. But now I know, through it all, I was doing something much bigger. I was learning how to carry a message without shrinking it. I was learning how to make space for both reverence and relatability—to speak about spirits in a way that felt grounded, human, and real.

I tried a lot of things that didn't work. I stumbled. Sometimes, I spoke too much. Other times, I was far too cautious. I edited myself into confusion. But with each attempt, I got a little closer to the truth of what I needed to say—not just what would land, but what would last. And over time, I realized that finding my voice never meant needing to have all the answers or never wavering. It meant being willing to stand in front of people and speak honestly from where I was. Not from a place of certainty, but from a place of presence.

The real shift began to happen, though, when I stopped trying to be impressive and started trying to be present. When I trusted that the messages would come if I stayed connected to the moment, to the energy in the room, and to the spirits and people who brought us all together. I wasn't just developing a presentation; I was developing a relationship with the work. And maybe that's the part no one ever tells you about the early stages of this path—that it's not just about learning how to connect with the dead. It's more about learning how to live with the responsibility of what they teach you. It's about becoming a vessel, yes, and about learning how to deliver to the audience. But more so, it's also about becoming yourself in the process. For me, more than any message I've ever delivered, that's the most sacred gift mediumship has given me.

And as for fine-tuning my own personal philosophy where the work was concerned? Well, that came when I saw *her*. The one who helped put it all into even greater perspective for me. I can still see every detail of her beautiful face, even now. I vividly remember what she wore and can still see the way her dark blue blouse opened just enough to reveal her necklace. And her eyes—it felt like I had never seen anything more beautiful in my life.

It happened on one of those nights when dreams slip in with the weight of memories, where you wake up unsure of where the boundary lies between sleep and something else. Something deeper. I remember it so clearly, and more vividly than most days I've lived wide awake. I was sitting with my brother at our favorite restaurant in the city—a little Italian place on the corner with red leather booths and a chipped tile floor that always smelled faintly of garlic and old wine. The place was just how I had always remembered it. There was laughter in the air, clinking glasses, and the voice of Sinatra low on the speakers, like a ghost humming through the walls. My brother sat across from me, talking fast, with that fire in his eyes he only ever had when he was about to tell a story that made no sense and every sense all at once. I was smiling, warm with the buzz of wine and comfort and familiarity, thinking to myself, *God, it's good to be back here again.*

And then I noticed her.

She was sitting alone at a small table just behind me, close enough that I could feel her presence even before I turned. A young woman—mid-twenties, maybe—with a delicate frame and deep eyes that seemed to glow softly under the flickering candlelight. Her hair was long and dark, tucked behind one ear like she was trying not to draw attention, though everything about her drew mine. I tried not to look. I still don't know why. Maybe it was the way she kept glancing over at me, those eyes full of urgency, almost pleading. It was as if she wanted me to notice her. I smiled briefly, then looked away. I didn't want to be pulled away from that moment, from that meal with my brother. It felt like I hadn't seen him in so long, and I didn't want anything to break the spell.

At all the other tables, couples and families were enjoying their own conversations. I couldn't help but overhear them, even as I listened to my brother talk about a recent trip with his girl-friend to see his favorite band at one of our favorite venues in Atlanta. Across from us was a family having dinner, seemingly welcoming a daughter back from college. I heard the mother ask, "How was dorm life?" To our left, a man and woman were enjoying an evening meal, and the conversation seemed to be work-related. "I signed a new deal yesterday," he said. Everyone seemed to be in their own little world, enjoying themselves fully. A line had formed at the door, with others standing outside waiting for the next available table.

But the woman behind me still sat alone. There was no one at her table. When I had turned to briefly smile earlier, I couldn't help but notice she hadn't even ordered. I was trying to enjoy my own conversation, but I couldn't shake the sense of eyes on me. Then I heard a soft voice whisper, "Excuse me." It was coming from the table behind me. I turned, looked, and smiled again. She said nothing.

I couldn't help but wonder—had I known her? Had she been someone I'd met before? I tried to resume my conversation. My brother was just getting to the part of his story about how the band came back out for a second encore when I heard the voice again.

"Excuse me, could you listen to me, please?"

By now, the curiosity had turned into a sense of awkwardness. A specific kind of discomfort that no one else around me seemed to notice. I turned again and smiled at her in silence, waiting for her to say more. She never did. She just stared and smiled. I returned to my conversation.

My brother was telling me how the second encore included a song we had always both loved, and how the band had saved it for the very end, when I heard the voice again.

"I need you to listen."

She was trying to get my attention again. I turned quickly and said, as politely as I could, "Please don't interrupt our conversation."

As beautiful as she was, it felt rude to me—especially when she never seemed to say anything else when I turned to listen.

Trying to enjoy my conversation, I could hear her shifting in her seat. My brother glanced around me and motioned with his head, as if to get me to turn my attention back to her. Then her voice—quiet and almost musical, like a song I half-remembered from a dream—begged, "Please." I pretended not to hear. I kept my focus on my brother, nodding as he finished telling me his tale, even though I could feel the weight of her gaze pressing heavier upon me with every passing second.

"I need you to listen," she said.

I turned to her again and said as politely as I could, "Please leave me alone."

And then I heard it. The sound of sobbing. The sound of immense pain. It was as if I had hurt her in some way. As if my insistence on being left alone had not only wounded her, but had literally broken her heart. I turned to her again, this time leaning over in my seat, waiting for her to somehow, in some way, explain herself and share why she so desperately needed my attention. I can still see the tears in those beautiful eyes.

"I want to talk to my family, too," she sobbed.

And then, just like that, the scene began to unravel.

The strange thing is, everything felt so very real. So physically, viscerally real. The heat of the marinara, the chill of the wine glass in my hand, the rhythm of my brother's laugh. I could smell the basil, feel the softness of the bread in my fingers. It wasn't just a dream. It couldn't have been. It was real, in a way that dreams rarely are—the kind of real that leaves you shaken when you wake, unsure which side of the mirror you're really on.

Only when I came to my natural senses, finding myself sitting alone at my own dining table, did the cold sweep in. The chill that runs deeper than skin. The kind of coldness that moves through your bones like a memory you didn't know you had. I could still feel her with me, though, just beyond reach.

"Elizabeth."

I didn't know how I knew her name, but it came to me like a tide pulling in. Elizabeth.

She had been trying to tell me something. Something important. And I had ignored her. When I finally came to, my eyes blinking open, I was breathless. My heart was pounding, not with fear, but with the sudden, aching knowledge that I had missed something. Something vital. That Elizabeth wasn't just a dream or some random figment from an out-of-body experience. She had been there, with me, somehow, trying to reach me from a place just out of sight. A spirit, maybe. Or a soul in need. And I had turned away.

Throughout the remainder of the day, I couldn't get her out of my mind. The sight of those beautiful eyes. All day, she lingered just behind my eyes like an afterimage—quiet, still, and insistent. The way she looked at me, the way her lips parted like she was about to say something she'd rehearsed a thousand times but had never been able to speak. It stayed with me that day. I went through the motions like a sleepwalker. Coffee tasted like dust. The city moved around me, loud and fast, but none of it touched me. I kept replaying every second of that dream—or visitation, or whatever it was—trying to pick apart the details like they were clues.

"Come back to me," I found myself saying.

She never did.

But still, her name hovered in my thoughts with a strange sort of weight. Elizabeth. It wasn't just a name. It had gravity. I started to wonder if I'd met her before. Maybe in passing. A stranger on a train. Someone I saw once across a crowded room. Had I known her in some past life?

But the more I sat with it, the more I realized—no, I'd never seen her in life. I would've remembered. Her face had that kind of beauty that was less about symmetry and more about truth, like she wore her soul close to the surface. No. She wasn't from this world. Not anymore.

That night, I returned to bed with a strange sort of anticipation —like maybe if I surrendered to the spirit world just right, I could find my way back to her. Like maybe that moment in the restaurant still stood in some liminal place, just between dream and death, waiting for me.

But I didn't find her. Not that night. Not the next. She was gone.

I still see her in my mind's eye, but she never speaks. I see only the image of her in that restaurant, seated behind me, pleading for my attention. That image still haunts me.

Still, something had changed. It's difficult to explain unless you've felt it yourself—that thinness in the air, like the membrane between here and somewhere else has stretched tight, becoming almost translucent. Lights flickered more than usual. I started waking up at 3:33 every morning, heart pounding like I'd just been running. And I kept hearing her words again and again, burned into my mind. Soft and trembling and almost afraid, pleading: "I need you to listen."

I began to realize that the encounter served some greater purpose. Some lesson, of sorts. Hers wasn't the sort of message I'd typically been receiving up until that time. It was something else—some lesson I needed to learn in my own life, in this work. And it became crystal clear: the dead don't leave us yearning for closure or final goodbyes; they linger because they want to stay a part of our lives. They want to be in on the jokes, hear about our troubles, and celebrate our wins alongside us— just as they would have when they were alive.

I realized that the dead don't wish to be memorialized as something separate or distant; they want to be included, almost as if they had never really left at all. They crave to sit around the dinner table when we laugh about an inside joke they would have loved. They want to hear us mention their names, retell their old stories, and feel the warmth of being remembered— not just with sadness, but with life.

Since then, I've made a habit of inviting those moments in instead of pushing them away. When a memory or a strong, psychic emotion tugs at me out of nowhere, I treat it as a nudge from someone—a reminder that they're still around, still loving, and still wanting to be part of our messy, beautiful lives. I no longer think of the dead as silent watchers or distant echoes. I think of them as ongoing participants, sitting quietly in the corners of our rooms, nodding along to the rhythm of our days. It's a comforting thought, and more than that, it's a call to remember them not with hollow reverence, but with living, breathing love.

That experience—that realization—slowly started shaping something deeper in me, quite honestly. A kind of personal philosophy. I began to believe, in a way that went beyond simple hope or comfort, that the dead are always close. Not sometimes. Not only when we call out to them. Always. They weave themselves into the spaces between our breaths, into the pauses in our conversations, and into the heavy silences at night when we're too tired to pretend we're okay. They're with us—not as memories trapped in the past, but as living presences, still wanting, still needing, and still loving. And above all, they want to be heard.

This belief changed how I move through the world. I no longer dismiss the small things—the sudden feeling that someone is standing behind me when I know I'm alone, the flicker of a scent that reminds me of someone long gone, or the strange timing of a song that seems to answer a question I haven't even spoken aloud. I pay attention now. I listen. Because I truly believe that when the dead reach out, they aren't doing it to haunt us or to drag us backward into grief. Instead, they're reaching out to participate.

It feels almost sacred to me, this trust I place in them. Almost as if mediumship has become my personal religion. They want to be included. They want to be listened to. They want to share life with us—not be locked away in a corner of the past, where we only visit them on anniversaries and holidays. They want to be woven into our everyday lives, in ways as natural and necessary as breathing.

And so, I began to do my best to honor that. I began talking to them when I felt them near. I told them about my day, as if praying a prayer to Heaven. I began asking for their advice whenever I felt lost. Sometimes, I even found myself laughing out loud at a memory they stirred up—at their private jokes and their well-timed reminders of who they were and who they still are. The encounters became a living relationship, not a mourning. It became love, stretched across whatever unseen space lies between this world and whatever comes next. And it became a love that reminds me, over and over again, that the dead are never really gone. They are just waiting, patiently, to be let back into the conversations.

As I began to find my own personal philosophy and purpose, the messages began to sharpen. They began to resonate with larger audiences, seemingly more and more. What I found is that when you speak from a place of vulnerability, people feel it. They lean in. They listen—not with their ears, but with their hearts. And something inside them shifts, too. Those moments are the ones I still live for. The quiet, trembling pauses when the living realize the dead are not gone—they're simply changed. And that love doesn't disappear with the body; it expands. It finds new ways to speak.

I had never set out to be a messenger between worlds. I had simply been drawn to share my experiences with others having similar ones. But looking back now, it felt like everything in my life had been gently nudging me toward those very public demonstrations of mediumship. The visions weren't simply invitations—they were instructions. And every time I honored them by sharing them, I felt the presence of something greater.

So, I kept speaking. I kept showing up, night after night, room after room. Not because I had all the answers, but because I had learned that healing often begins with the courage to listen —to the whispers of the past, to the voices of spirits, and to the stories that refuse to be forgotten. My purpose became clearer. I had been tasked with helping those stories find their way back home.

With every story I shared, I felt a deepening sense of responsibility—not just to the spirits who entrusted me with their messages, but to the people sitting in front of me, often unsure of what they believed but hoping for something they could feel. Some came with skepticism, arms crossed and hearts guarded. Others came wide open, already knowing what I do: that this world and the next are not separated by some vast, unreachable distance, but by a veil so thin it can part with a single breath, a single word, or a single memory.

There is no script to what I do. No formula. No guarantees. Even now, I never know who will show up—on either side. But I trust it now. I trust the process, the timing, the symbols that arise. And over time, I've come to see these messages as more than just messages of comfort. They are invitations to live life more fully. To love without holding back. To forgive before it's too late. The dead don't come to us with bitterness or blame.

For as long as I live, I'll never forget that night in North Carolina. The auditorium was filled, the lights dimmed, and the familiar hum of anticipation buzzed in the room like electricity before a storm. I had already done countless events before that one, but something about the energy in the room told me that night would be different. I stepped onto the stage and, as I always do, took a moment to quiet myself. I never know who will show up, and I've learned not to force it. The spirits come when they're ready. But when they do, it's as if a floodgate opens and I'm simply the vessel.

That night, it happened so quickly. A man's presence came through with a force that nearly took my breath away. I could feel the weight of his energy—steady, grounded, weathered by years on the road. He showed me highways stretching out like veins across the country, the hum of wheels on asphalt, and truck stops glowing under neon lights. He was an over-the-road truck driver, and I felt the loneliness of those long nights. I felt the comfort he found in his routine. But I also felt the deep, unspoken love he carried for his daughters. He had passed, and that night, with a sense of urgency, he wanted to be heard.

"I wasn't always good at saying it," I heard him say clearly—just as clearly as if he were standing beside me. "But I loved them. I still do."

I repeated his words aloud, scanning the room as I did. He began to show me vivid details, one after another, like scenes flickering through an old film reel. I saw a diner where he always stopped. A torn photo of two little girls he kept tucked in the sun visor of his cab. A keychain shaped like a heart that he'd picked up from a roadside gift shop one lonely Valentine's Day. Then he showed me his passing. I saw the inside of his truck, the soft glow of the dashboard lights, the pain in his chest, and the suddenness of it all. I described what I saw. There was a calm in his passing, but a sorrow too—a sorrow that he hadn't been able to say goodbye.

And that's when I noticed them: two women sitting close together, hands gripping each other tightly, tears already falling before I had even finished the message. One of them raised her hand, trembling, and with a soft, cracked voice said, "That's our dad." The room went still. You could hear nothing but the sound of their quiet sobs and the occasional creak of a chair as others shifted to witness the moment unfolding. They confirmed every detail.

Their father had driven trucks most of his life. He had died of a heart attack in his rig, pulled off to the side of the road just as I had described. The photo, the keychain, the way he never said

"I love you" often but always showed it in his own quiet ways—it was all very real to them. It was him.

The man's spirit stood beside them as they cried, and I could feel his pride radiating through me like warmth. He hadn't come through to relive his death. He came to finish what he hadn't been able to in life—to tell them, in no uncertain terms, that they were loved. That he had seen them, always. That even from the road—and now from beyond it—he carried them in his heart.

I stood there, barely holding myself together, and let the message land. Those two women, in that moment in time, received something that night that no earthly words could manufacture. It wasn't just about the evidence of mediumship. And it most certainly wasn't about me or my abilities. It was about healing. It was about presence. It was about love surviving even the longest roads.

That moment reminded me why I did this work—why I faced the doubt, the fear, and the vulnerability of stepping into the unknown. Because when spirits speak like that, with such clarity and accuracy, there's no room left for skepticism. Only awe. Only gratitude. And the realization that our connections don't end when life does. They simply change lanes.

In the years that followed, there would be thousands of people. Faces in the crowds. Strangers at first, but each carrying a story waiting to be spoken into the light. Thousands of others would come, not always searching for answers, but for connection. And with them came thousands of spirits, each one with their own message, their own emotion, and their own presence that would slip into the space between silence and speech.

I didn't know then, standing on that stage in North Carolina, just how much this work would grow. I couldn't have imagined the miles I'd travel, the rooms I'd enter, the tears I'd witness, or the moments that would forever live etched in my heart. But it did grow. The calling deepened. And each time I stepped on a stage, I felt the sacredness of it all expand. Each time, it was as if the whole world stopped around me, and I glimpsed Heaven.

There were messages from lost sons, husbands, best friends, mothers who passed too soon, fathers who never said what they needed to say. Some spirits came through with joy, with laughter, and even with jokes they used to tell in life that only one person in the room would understand. Others came through in whispers, cautious and tender, sharing secrets that had waited years to be released. There were times the energy in the room was so strong it felt like the very air shimmered. Times when I felt the spirits not just beside me, but around everyone—weaving a net of connection so awe-inspiring it made the room feel smaller, as if the entire audience had stepped into a shared living room of the soul.

And through all of it, I found it still so unbelievable that I could have such an honor. Because these weren't simply messages. They were moments of transformation. I watched as people softened, broke open, forgave, and remembered. I saw strangers embrace after a shared message connected them. I saw healing take root where there had only been grief. And every single time, I was reminded that I was nothing but a translator of love between worlds. What made this real wasn't me. It was the undeniable truth of what happens when we open ourselves to something greater than what we can see.

As the years passed, the stories kept coming. The feeling of each one is something I'll never forget—the raw, aching beauty of a soul reaching across time to say, "I'm still here. I never left." And the living, hearing those words in their own language, in their own hearts, finally breathing a little easier. I've come to believe that we don't just carry our own lives; we carry legacies. And sometimes, spirits wait patiently for someone to be the voice for what was left unsaid.

I suppose that's who I became. A storyteller, in a sense. But more than that, a witness. A witness to the invisible thread that binds us to the truth that love cannot die, and to the miracle that—even in the wake of death—we are never truly alone. There are thousands of stories. Thousands of moments of encounter I will never forget.

Over the years, I've watched as skeptics became believers. Not because I convinced them, but because spirits did. There's a look people get when they hear something so personal, so specific, that it breaks through every wall they've built to protect themselves from hope. It's a kind of surrender—not to me, but to the possibility that there's more. That their loved one is still with them, guiding them. That life doesn't end with a final breath, but continues on in ways we're only beginning to understand.

I live for that moment. Not because it validates my gift, but because it reawakens theirs.

I never really got used to it. It's the sort of thing that can never become routine. The truth is, I feel every single story. I cry more now than I ever did before I started doing this publicly. Not out of sadness, but because I witness the depth of love that exists beyond this life. The beauty still takes my breath away. There's nothing ordinary about it. It still leaves me in awe every time.

So I became more determined than ever to continue doing the work. In big cities, in small towns, in quiet rooms, and in crowded halls. I kept opening my heart and my voice to whoever wanted to come through. Because I knew that each message—each connection—is more than just communication; it's communion. It's the spirit world saying, "I'm still here." And for the living, it's a chance to say, "I remember you."

Thousands of stories have passed through me, and thousands more are still waiting. And I will honor every single one. Because this work—it's not merely my purpose. It's my promise.

Chapter 7

Encountering the Darkness

For more than twenty-five years, one resounding question that continues to be asked, time and time again, is whether dark and malevolent entities truly exist. People often seem to lower their voices when they ask, as if merely speaking of such diabolical things might invite them in. I can always see the fear and curiosity warring in their eyes. The question is valid, and I feel I would be remiss if I did not address it in my own way when sharing the encounters of my life.

When one deals with the world unseen, it's only natural to wonder if every whisper in the dark is a friend—or something else. I have encountered more than my share of difficult energies over the years, and I will say that yes, they do exist. Not everything beyond the veil is benevolent. Some entities carry the heavy weight of malice, confusion, and even predatory hunger. They may not be common, but they are very real.

When speaking on this topic, I've always found myself thinking of a line from Shakespeare's *Hamlet*: "The devil hath power to assume a pleasing shape." A chilling reminder that darker entities don't always reveal themselves as monstrous or frightening in the beginning. Most often, they come cloaked in beauty and warmth, providing a false sense of comfort. They wear masks because fear is a powerful barrier, and manipulation requires lowering your defenses first. I've felt it firsthand—more times than I can even count. That strange dissonance when something feels far too sweet, far too eager to please. And then that subtle unease creeps in. A warning whispered by the soul that all is not as it seems.

When fellow seekers ask me how to protect themselves, I always say, "Above everything else, trust your feelings." The body knows what the mind might rationalize away. If something feels wrong, it is. It's as simple as that. Light and darkness exist side by side in the spirit world, just as they do here. But understanding this isn't cause for panic or alarm. It's a reason for empowerment. With knowledge, discernment, and a steady heart, we can walk among both realms without fear. After all, darkness only has power where light has not yet been claimed.

Over the years, I've learned that fear gives these entities more power than anything else. It's our own fear that feeds them, strengthens them, and gives them a foothold. When I was younger and less experienced, I made the mistake of meeting darkness with fear—always recoiling instinctively, trying to shut it out without taking the time to understand it. But the more I ran, the more it pursued. It wasn't until I stood still, faced it fully, and met it with calm certainty that things began to change. Darkness cannot survive long in the presence of unwavering light. And that light isn't something you have to borrow from anyone else. It's already inside you. It's always been there.

I often tell people that not every unpleasant spirit is malevolent. Some are simply lost, confused, or burdened by the heavy emotions they carried in life. Pain can twist a soul's energy until it feels harsh and frightening, but that doesn't always mean it's evil. In fact, I would add that "dark" does not always equate to "demonic" the way we so often believe it does. True malevolence—that real sort of conscious malice—is rare compared to the sheer number of spirits just trying to find their way. Still, it's important to acknowledge that darkness does exist, because pretending otherwise can leave us vulnerable.

What's even more important, though, is to recognize that you are never truly helpless in the face of it. Spiritual sovereignty is real. Boundaries are real. You can tell a spirit to leave, and it must obey. You can call on your own guides, on whatever higher power you believe in, and they will always stand with you. Faith—not in dogma, but in your own divine connection—is your greatest shield. Darkness may assume a pleasing shape, as *Hamlet* warned, but no mask can hide the truth from a spirit—or from a human being, for that matter—who is truly awake and aware.

At the end of the day, I don't share these things to scare people. In fact, I rarely share these things at all. I share them because facing reality is a kind of armor. If you know what exists in the spirit world, you can meet it without fear. And when you meet it without fear, it has no hold on you. Every encounter, even the unsettling or horrifying ones, has taught me more about courage, about discernment, and about the extraordinary resilience of the human spirit. Darkness exists. But so, too, does an even greater light.

The truth is, I love the spirit world far too much to ever truly be afraid of it. Fear is not the lens through which I view these encounters—even the unsettling ones. In my life, I made the decision long ago that I could never fully love something I feared. And I love the things of the spirit world. The spirit world, in all its complexity and marvelous wonder, has been a teacher, a guide, and a source of endless hope for me. I refuse to ever fear it again the way I once did at the beginning of my life.

It's so easy to focus on the stories of shadowy figures and deceptive, predatory entities, but that is only a small fraction of what exists beyond the veil. What I have found, most often, is an overwhelming presence of compassion, of healing, and of spirits who come with messages of hope, forgiveness, and deep, abiding love. Even when darkness crosses my path, it only strengthens my appreciation for the light that exists there as well—not in some naïve or willfully blind way, but with a clear-eyed understanding of the full tapestry of that realm.

To me, the spirit world is alive with purpose, with beauty, and with a kind of wisdom that humbles the mind and lifts the heart. This is the reason I always keep things lighthearted, even in readings involving very dark and shadowy things. The spirit world is a realm where truth sings louder than any lie, where connection endures beyond death, and where real love reveals itself as the ultimate guiding force. How could I fear a world that has shown me, again and again, that we are never truly alone? That the soul's journey is eternal, and that light is always stronger than shadow? My awestruck wonder for the spirit world is rooted in that truth. Because of this, I will never approach it with dread.

In fact, the more I work with the spirit world, the more I realize that love and immense wonder—not fear—is the true language that bridges the gap between their world and ours. Fear closes us off, isolates us within our own preconceived notions, and makes us small. But love—love expands our awareness, sharpens our intuition and sense of discernment, and invites a deeper communion with the unseen world. When I sit quietly and open myself to the spirits, it's no longer a trembling, fearful process. It's more like stepping into a familiar embrace—a remembering of something my soul has always known.

There is a sacredness to it, really. A transcendence. A gentle exchange that leaves me feeling more whole, more grounded, and more alive than ever before. Even when I encounter troubled spirits—those heavy with regret or confusion—my first instinct is now one of compassion and interest, not primal fear as it once was at the beginning of all this. Most spirits are seeking what they struggled to find in life: forgiveness, understanding, and peace.

That's not to say that caution shouldn't be exercised. Caution is vital. Just as I wouldn't invite a stranger into my home without careful discernment, I don't throw the doors of the spirit world wide open without careful intention. But that discernment comes from a place of deep self-trust and respect for the boundaries between worlds. It doesn't come from fear. I honor boundaries because I respect the sacredness of both realms—not because I fear what lies beyond the veil. Every encounter, every message, and yes, even every whisper from the other side feels like participating in something profoundly meaningful and far greater than myself.

When people ask me why I'm no longer afraid, I often find myself smiling as I tell them that fear has no home where love resides. I have seen too much beauty, too much grace, and too much evidence of a greater design to let the rare encounters with darkness overshadow the truth of what I know. The spirit world, in all its mystery and magnificence, continues to be one of the greatest loves of my life. It has taught me that courage doesn't mean the absence of fear. Instead, it means choosing to move with trust and reverence anyway. And so, every time I step into that space between worlds, I do so with an open heart, a clear mind, and the deep, unshakable knowing that I am part of something vast, beautiful, and utterly sacred.

I often hear others in the paranormal community—many of them dear and trusted friends and colleagues—say, sometimes with great urgency, that the Devil and evil exist whether we believe in them or not. And to that, I don't necessarily disagree. I've encountered enough to know that darkness is a reality woven into the fabric of both this world and the world of the unseen. There are forces that thrive on chaos, fear, and division —forces that can influence the living if they're given an opening. It would be foolish to pretend otherwise, just as it would be foolish to walk through the physical world pretending there's no such thing as danger.

But where I vehemently differ at times—differ completely—is in the premise that darkness holds greater power than we do. That it can seemingly just overtake us and consume us at will. That is a premise I reject with every fiber of my being. Darkness may be real, but it is not sovereign. It is not omnipotent. It is not the final word. Human beings, anchored in the light of their own souls, are far stronger than any shadow that tries to loom over them. I have seen people stand in the presence of overwhelming grief, fear, and loss, and yet still choose love. That's where spiritual power resides.

The narrative that darkness is somehow lurking around every corner, always waiting to consume us the moment we slip, is one created by fear—not by reality. It strips us of our agency and autonomy and paints us as helpless children in some cosmic war in which we have no say. But the reality I have seen, again and again, is that we are never helpless. We are powerful beings with the divine spark within us—a spark that darkness can threaten and try to cloud but can never fully extinguish without our permission. The spirit world has taught me this just as vividly as anything I have experienced on this side.

I have stood in places heavy with sorrow and anger, and I have watched how even a single act of love, a single memory, a single moment of pure, unwavering light—or even a song—can shift the entire atmosphere. Darkness recoils when faced with wonder. It thrives on fear, yes, but it withers in the presence of awestruck wonder. We are never powerless. In fact, we were never anything less than powerful to begin with. So, my advice when dealing with darker things? Stay in your sense of wonder, my darling.

I often hear people ask, "But what about poltergeists or demonic possession?" And honestly, my first reaction is: "What about them?" It's almost as if there's an expectation that the spiritual world should somehow be immune to the darkness we already accept in the world of the living. We walk this earth with murderers, abusers, tyrants, and monsters who've never once needed a whisper from beyond to commit terrible acts. Pain and cruelty are, sadly, not exclusive to the realm of spirit—they are part of existence itself.

If we know that awful, dangerous things exist among the living, why is it so hard to believe that some residue of that darkness might linger after death—or that some energies might be malevolent? To me, it's not a sign that the spiritual world is uniquely frightening. It's just a reflection—another mirror held up to what we already live alongside every day. Fear of the unknown is completely natural. As someone who lived most of his life battling agonizing terror, believe me. But sometimes that natural fear blinds us to a simple truth: danger doesn't start at death, and evil is not born in the grave. It walks among us right now.

That's not to say I take these things lightly or speak of them flippantly. I have encountered beings that cannot even be described in human language. I've seen objects move, heard voices growl words no human throat could easily form, and felt coldness that wasn't just a chill in the air—but a deep, gnawing cold that seemed to burrow into my very soul. Even then, I saw no proof that the spirit world is somehow worse or more terrifying than life itself. If anything, I saw proof that what is unresolved, what is broken, what is full of rage or grief—it doesn't simply vanish when the body dies. Sometimes, it lingers. Sometimes, it lashes out.

But just like in life, most of the spiritual world is not made of monsters. It's made of confused and seemingly lost souls—souls simply trying to communicate, trying to heal, trying to find peace. The truly dark forces—the ones people fear when they talk about poltergeists or possession—are rare. They are real, but they are rare. And often, they are not what Hollywood or horror stories would have you believe. They're more like emotional storms—wild, chaotic, and drawn to pain, anger, and fear. Very real emotions that are already present in the living. They feed off what we give them. They grow in the cracks of our own wounds.

I often tell people: if you're afraid of the spirit world, take a good look at the living first. Look at how much hurt we cause each other. Just look at how much hatred and violence we carry inside us every single day. That's where the real danger lies. Spirits—even angry ones—are simply echoes. They reflect us more than we realize. It's not about fearing them. It's about understanding them. Protect yourself, yes—but also recognize that most of the fear we project onto the spirit world is really fear of ourselves. Fear of our own darkness. Fear of the things we try to hide away but can never truly bury. The dead can be frightening, sure. But the living? The living is where the real caution is needed.

That seems to be the hardest truth for us to accept. Because it's easier, in a way, to imagine that some monstrous force from beyond is responsible for the things that scare us most. That's easier than admitting that evil is very much alive—here and now—wearing familiar faces and speaking in familiar voices. When people ask me about possession, they usually expect a story filled with terrifying visions, unholy growls, and levitations. And sometimes, yes, there are strange and chilling phenomena. But more often, the real "possession" I see is a person consumed by their own grief, rage, addiction, or despair —leaving them vulnerable to chaotic forces that only amplify what was already burning inside them.

Darkness, you see, doesn't create itself from nothing. It can't. It grows in wounds that are left untreated, and in pain that festers in silence. Spirits that seem malevolent are often those who died with their own deep scars, unable to find rest—still searching, still raging against a world they feel failed them. When I encounter these energies, I don't rush to battle them. I don't go in guns blazing like some paranormal warrior. Instead, I try to listen. Because just like in life, even the angriest, loudest, most frightening presence often just wants to be heard and acknowledged—to have someone understand their pain.

This life, this connection to the spirit world, has taught me a deep and sometimes uncomfortable compassion. Not all suffering ends with death. Not all wounds heal just because the body falls away. And it reminds me, over and over again, that our responsibility is not just to protect ourselves from darkness, but to bring more light into the world—for both the living and the dead.

So, usually when someone asks about demonic possession, I answer with another question: "What about the hurt we carry here and now?" "What about the healing we still refuse to do?" Because that's where it starts. That's where it has always started. Hell is here. But so is Heaven.

Most of the darker attachments I've encountered don't spring up out of nowhere. They aren't usually the result of some ancient curse or grand cosmic evil possessing us without warning. More often, they grow from the soil of unresolved trauma —deep emotional wounds that were never faced and never healed. Pain and guilt. Shame. Anger.

These emotions have weight. They have energy. And when someone carries them long enough—when they bury them deep enough—that energy doesn't just disappear when the body dies. It lingers. Sometimes it twists. Sometimes it even becomes something heavy enough to tether a soul to this world, or to create openings that draw in chaotic, even darker forces.

It's the same for the living, though. A person weighed down by years of emotional pain can feel almost haunted even while they're still alive. That's not some supernatural phenomenon. It's the natural consequence of carrying unprocessed suffering. Those energies, when left unchecked, can act as a beacon for troubled spirits. Or worse, they can amplify the negativity until it takes on a life all its own. This is why people who are going through intense grief, deep depression, or emotional breakdowns are often more vulnerable to attachments or spiritual disturbances. It's not that they're cursed or unlucky. It's that pain attracts pain, just like wounds draw flies.

When I step into a space that feels heavy—where objects have been thrown or strange disturbances are happening—I always find a story underneath. A history of violence. Some struggle with addiction. A tale of heartbreak or betrayal. The haunting isn't just a ghost making noise for fun. It's the imprint of real, lived human suffering that was never given a way to heal. In some cases, it's the spirits themselves struggling; in others, it's the living inhabitants unknowingly feeding the storm with their own pain. Houses hold trauma as well.

Healing, on both sides of the veil, is the key. Cleansing rituals, prayers, setting firm energetic boundaries—these things help, but the real work is much deeper. It's emotional. It's facing the things inside us we would much rather ignore. When someone begins to confront their own wounds, to work through their grief, their rage, and their fears, the disturbances often begin to fade. The attachments lose their grip because they no longer have fertile ground to cling to.

That's what so many miss when they chase after horror stories about possessions and hauntings: these events are never just random acts of spiritual terrorism. They're symptoms of deeper human wounds crying out for attention. The spiritual world, just like the physical one, is intimately connected to the emotional currents we carry within us. Where there is healing, the darkness retreats. Where there is light, the shadows dissolve.

And that's why, in my work, I always tell people: if you want to protect yourself from darkness, the first place you have to look is inward. Heal yourself. Face your pain. Clear the clutter of old grief and anger from your own soul. Because in doing so, you're not just safeguarding your own spirit—you're helping to heal the unseen world as well.

So, do terrible things exist in the spirit world? Of course. Are cases of poltergeist activity and demonic possession real? Absolutely. Does such darkness exist in the realm of the unseen, just beyond the veil, and can these things lead to horrifying and tragic encounters? Yes. But these things happen every day in our own world as well.

I remember years ago being a headlining speaker for a conference and checking into a hotel downtown in a large city. I was exhausted from the flight but restless in that strange, nervous way I always get before a big event. After tossing my bag onto the bed and flipping through a few local channels, I decided I needed to shake the tension. A run through the city seemed the perfect idea. It would also give me the chance to explore a city I'd never visited before. I laced up my shoes, threw on a light jacket, and headed down to the lobby. The place was elegant in that slightly over-the-top way—heavy marble floors, gold accents on everything, and a massive chandelier swinging gently in the lobby air currents.

As I pushed through the revolving doors, I was just about to take off down the sidewalk when the doorman, a kind, older gentleman in a sharp uniform, stopped me. He tipped his hat and said, "Sir, if you're going for a run, I'd strongly suggest you head that way," pointing right. "Stay away from the other side of town."

"That's the bad part of town," he added, motioning in the opposite direction. He said it in a low tone, almost confidentially, like he didn't want to scare me.

I paused for a second, completely caught off guard. I hadn't even thought about the idea that I might accidentally wander into a rough, dangerous neighborhood. I nodded, thanked him, and turned right, just as he suggested.

As I ran, I couldn't help but think about his words. *"Bad part of town."* What did that really mean? Poverty? Crime? A place where a guy like me would stand out too much? The streets I stuck to were busy and bright, full of coffee shops and boutique stores—the kind of place you imagine when you think "downtown." But every time I crossed an intersection, I caught myself glancing left, wondering what lay in the other direction. What would have happened if I'd just turned left instead? Was it truly dangerous? Or was it just different?

It made me think about how cities—and people—draw invisible lines all the time, carving places into "good" and "bad" based on a thousand little assumptions.

By the time I made it back to the hotel, sweat cooling on my skin and my head buzzing with thoughts, I realized I hadn't really run to clear my mind at all. I'd only filled it up more. And even as I thanked the doorman again on my way back in, I knew a part of me was still curious about the road not taken— that left turn I never made, and the stories waiting just beyond the boundary of someone else's warning.

Later, sitting by the window in my room with the city lights blinking like distant stars, I kept turning that moment over in my mind. As a psychic, it hit me just how much those casual warnings—those invisible lines we draw between "good" and "bad"—mirror the way most people view the spirit world. We're conditioned to fear what we don't see and to assume that if something is hidden from the physical eye, it must be dangerous.

Just like the doorman telling me not to run left because it was the "bad part of town," so many people are taught to believe that the unseen world is full of dark forces waiting to cause harm. It's almost automatic, really—the natural instinct to treat the unknown as a threat.

We hear it in other ways all the time, if you really think about it. We're told that Ouija boards are demonic by their very nature. That tarot cards open doorways to darkness. Or that listening to certain albums might inadvertently conjure unwanted spirits. The "Satanic Panic" of decades ago never really ended—not really.

The more I thought about it, the more I realized that fear of the spirit world isn't born from real experiences; it's fueled by stereotypes. By the stories we've been handed down about haunted houses and malevolent ghosts. It's fueled by movies that tell us every whisper in the dark is a threat and that every cold spot is a demon waiting to attack. It's the same fearful thinking that paints entire neighborhoods with a single brushstroke.

Unsafe.

Unwelcome.

"Bad."

When I connect with spirits, I don't find evil lurking around every corner. I find love, I find guidance, and I find souls that are just like us—complicated, imperfect, and yearning. But because we can't see it easily, because it exists just beyond the edge of our senses, we label it dangerous by default.

That night, I understood something even deeper: that **fear** will always shrink our world if we let it. It will close off whole streets, whole communities, whole dimensions of experience. It will convince us that staying safe means staying small and staying comfortable. But genuine connection and communion —whether it's with the living or with the spirit world— demands more of us. It asks for courage. It asks for curiosity. And maybe most of all, it asks for a willingness to step beyond the lines that other people have drawn, beckoning us to find out for ourselves what's really waiting there in unseen places.

I leaned my forehead against the cool glass of the window and watched a few late-night joggers pass by on the sidewalks below, their shadows stretching out long behind them. It struck me then that, just like in this physical world, the spirit world is made up of all kinds of souls. Some look familiar. And, admittedly, some do not. Some carry the energy of lives lived in places and cultures very different from ours. Their clothes might be strange to us, and their ways of speaking or showing themselves might feel foreign. But different doesn't mean dangerous. It doesn't mean malevolent. In fact, difference in the spirit world—just like here—is something that can be beautiful if we approach it with an open heart.

The more time I spent communing with the spirit world, the more convinced I became that it is not a place of automatic threat. It's a place of profound variety. A genuine reflection of humanity in all its many colors, shapes, and stories. It's easy to forget that when we cross into the spirit world, we don't shed our entire selves. We bring with us the imprint of the lives we lived, the cultures we loved, and the lessons we learned. To meet a spirit is to meet someone's history—and to encounter someone's journey.

And just like here, it's not about assuming the worst. It's about being open enough to recognize that every soul carries a piece of the great human tapestry.

Personally, I feel we should approach the spirit world the same way we approach this physical one—with a sense of adventure, a sense of wonder. It's not a haunted house we're trapped in. It's an endless garden of stories, of wisdom, and of connection. Sure, there might be times when caution is needed, just like here in the physical world. There are hurting souls in the spirit world, just as there are hurting souls walking the streets. But often, when we approach the unseen world with curiosity instead of fear, we are met with kindness, love, and unimaginable beauty.

So, allow me to say it more simply: fear builds walls. Wonder builds bridges. And every time we choose to lean into wonder —whether by exploring a new city or opening ourselves to the voice of a spirit who feels unfamiliar—we expand our world a little more. We become bigger, braver, and far more whole.

As I sat there watching the city breathe around me, I made myself a quiet promise: to always turn toward the unknown with open eyes and to honor every soul I meet, both seen and unseen, not with suspicion, but with the awe and respect every traveler on the great journey deserves.

I stayed there at the window for a long time that night, listening to the city hum like a living thing beneath me. The neon reflections of signs danced on the pavement, and somewhere far off, a siren wailed and then faded into the night. It reminded me how much life is happening all around us at every moment—so much we never even notice unless we make the conscious choice to pay attention. The spirit world is no different, really. It's pulsing, breathing, and alive in ways we're often too busy or too afraid to recognize. It's not tucked away in some dark corner waiting to frighten us. Instead, it's woven into everything we are and everything we touch, whispering like a river just beneath the noise of our lives.

When people ask me what it's like to commune with the spirit world, they usually expect some kind of eerie story—something dramatic, something frightening. But more often, it's profoundly ordinary in the most extraordinary way. It's the grandmother who shows up because she wants her family to know she's still part of their Sunday dinners. It's the best friend who just wants to say, "I'm so proud of you." It's the quiet, powerful reminders that love doesn't end just because the body does. When you strip away the fear, what you're left with isn't horror—though I admittedly do love a good horror story. It's connection. It's belonging. It's the understanding that we are never as alone as we sometimes feel.

I think that's the real tragedy of fear, too. It cuts us off from these moments. It convinces us to turn our heads, to tighten our hearts, and to stay safely on the "good" side of the street, where everything looks familiar. But real life never works that way. Life starts when we step out into the places we don't know yet—when we allow ourselves to believe that there might be something beautiful waiting for us where others told us not to go. This is the best analogy I know to make regarding journeys in the spirit world. It's not some haunted wasteland. It's a living, breathing continuation of the love, the lessons, and the messy, miraculous humanity we experience here.

As I finally pulled the curtains closed and got ready for bed, I felt a deep, steady peace settle over me. I wasn't afraid of the unknown. I had been—in fact, I had been for a long, long time. But I refused to fear any longer. Fear was exhausting even to think about. If anything, I was grateful. Grateful that there were still roads yet to be explored. Grateful that every day, in my work and in my own heart, I have the choice to meet the unknown not with fear, but with wonder. And maybe that's all the spirit world ever really asks of us—not to be fearless, but to simply be willing. To be willing to listen, to see, to believe in the beauty that lies just beyond what we think we know.

As I lay in bed, staring up at the ceiling, the city's distant sounds lulling me toward sleep, another truth rose to the surface—one I've seen proven again and again, both in my own life and in the lives of those who seek out the spirit world: what we bring into our spiritual exploration shapes what we find. It's not a neutral exchange. It's a mirror. Our intentions—whether rooted in fear, love, curiosity, or skepticism—act like tuning forks, vibrating out into the unseen world and calling back experiences that match our own beliefs.

If someone approaches the spirit world always armed for battle, constantly scanning for demons, convinced that every shadow hides a threat—then yes, they will encounter darkness. Not because the spirit world is inherently malevolent, but because they are feeding that energy through their own expectations and beliefs. They are projecting fear outward, and like calls to like. Their experiences become self-fulfilling prophecies—not because spirits are eager to harm them, but because their own energy demands a reflection of their internal landscape. We create much of our own darkness through our own beliefs, through our own preconceived notions. We will always find what we're looking for.

But when we enter spiritual exploration with a different mindset—armed instead with wonder, humility, and respect—we are met with a vastly different response. The spirit world, like this physical world, responds to the posture of our hearts. If you seek love, you find it. If you seek guidance, you find it. If you seek understanding, you find it. The spirit world is always more than willing to respond to us.

It's not about pretending that darkness doesn't exist. It's about recognizing that darkness is never the entire story—not here, and not there. Just like in the living world, the spirit world holds complexity: light and shadow, wisdom and confusion, peace and unrest. But we have the power to choose what we engage with. We have the power to set the tone for the conversation.

If you open the door with fear in your eyes and a weapon in your hand, don't be surprised when fear meets you on the other side. But if you open it with an open heart, a spirit of discovery, and a clear, calm mind, you'll find something far richer, far deeper, and infinitely more beautiful than any horror story ever told.

I say that as a self-described lover of horror.

We are not passive victims in this great dance between worlds. We are active participants. We are co-creators. And with every thought, every feeling, and every intention, we are shaping the bridge between here and there—not with fear, but with wonder, trust, and the unshakable belief that love, in all its many forms, is the truest force in any world.

Our preconceived notions not only color our experiences; they build our reality, brick by invisible brick. If we believe the spirit world is dangerous, we will see danger at every turn. If we believe the spirit world is dark and malevolent, then that is what will stare back at us from the shadows. It's not because spirits are out to get us; it's because we are carrying the fear so tightly inside of us that we can't imagine encountering anything else.

The reason so many people feel the need to "fight" darkness in the spirit world is because they haven't yet learned to face the darkness inside themselves. It's always easier to battle something external—something out there that we can point at and blame. It's much harder to sit with the uncomfortable truth that most of the fear, anger, and chaos we experience comes from within. That maybe the demons we think we're fighting aren't always malevolent beings lurking in the unseen corners of the world, but are crouching quietly in the places inside ourselves we've been too afraid to confront.

We create boogeymen because it's easier to fight shadows than it is to heal wounds. It's easier to wage war against some imagined evil than it is to look in the mirror and admit that we are still hurting, still afraid, and still carrying the heavy bags we packed long ago in childhood, trauma, heartbreak, and moments of betrayal.

It's human nature. When faced with pain, we want a villain. We want something to blame so we don't have to do the harder work of healing ourselves.

But the spirit world isn't some chaotic battleground where good and evil constantly clash for control of us. It's far more compassionate—and far more patient—than that. It reflects back to us what we carry, just like life does here. It asks us, gently but persistently: "Who are you?" "What are you bringing to this exchange?" "Are you ready to see yourself clearly?"

It gives us opportunities, not enemies. Lessons, not battles. And when we finally turn inward—when we are able to face and heal our own inner darkness—we find that the outer world, both seen and unseen, softens too. The monsters lose their claws. The shadows begin to look like doorways instead of threats.

I began to understand that true spiritual exploration isn't about conquering anything. It's about surrender. Surrendering the need to control, to label, and to defend ourselves against imaginary armies. It's about stepping into the unknown with the faith that what we encounter is simply a reflection of what we are ready to heal, love, and transform.

And in that space—free from fear—the spirit world isn't something to dread. It becomes what it was always meant to be: a beautiful continuation of our own beautiful, complicated, ever-evolving journey home.

In my time working within the psychic industry, I've come across every kind of marketing imaginable, often playing on fear to draw in potential clients. Ads promising to remove spells or curses, rid people of demonic possessions, or clear negative attachments are common. These types of ads work on the deeply ingrained fears that many people carry—fears that something dark or malicious may be holding them back in life.

It's a powerful form of marketing, and in many ways, it does tap into the reality of spiritual challenges. Negative energies, attachments, or even dark forces do exist in the world, and it's essential to acknowledge that these things can affect our lives in ways we may not always understand.

But despite all this, I've always preferred to keep things light-hearted, even when addressing serious topics.

It's not that I deny the existence of darkness or the necessity of addressing it—far from it. But I've learned, through my own experiences and through helping others, that the real power lies in our intentions: the energy we focus on, the thoughts we nurture, and the beliefs we hold. Those are what shape our reality.

I truly believe that darkness can only manifest in our lives if we feed it with fear and belief. It can only take root if we allow it to control our perspective. When we view the world through a lens of fear, we inadvertently invite negative energies to latch onto us. But when we choose to focus on love, light, and positivity, we create an environment where darkness struggles to survive.

For me, it's never about frightening people into submission or making them believe they are constantly under threat from unseen forces. Instead, it's about empowering individuals to take charge of their own lives and their own experiences. Yes, spell and curse removals are important, and there are times when intervention is necessary, but my approach has always been to help people reclaim their own sense of power. When people realize that their intention is the key to unlocking their experiences, they begin to see the world in a whole new light. Instead of worrying about what's lurking in the shadows, they focus on what they can create in the light.

I've found that when people embrace a more joyful, optimistic, and light-hearted perspective, they tend to attract more of the same. It's about setting boundaries, living consciously, and choosing to nurture the parts of ourselves that align with our highest good. Darkness can only survive where it's allowed to thrive. If we deny it the fuel of our fear, it's far less likely to have any lasting impact. So yes, the work is real, and the challenges that people face are real, but I prefer to approach them with a sense of lightness and empowerment. The universe, in my belief, is not inherently good or evil; it just reflects our energy. We create the world we live in. And when we step away from fear and into love, it's amazing how much brighter things become.

The entertainment industry, religion, and our own primal fear of the dark have long been sources that shape our preconceived notions of good and bad in the spirit world. From horror films that depict demons as grotesque, malevolent beings to religious teachings that frame the spiritual realm as a battleground between angels and demons, we've been conditioned to see the spirit world through a binary lens. We categorize things as either light or dark, good or bad, often missing the vast, nuanced tapestry of energies and experiences that lie in between. This stark division feeds into the fear that many people hold around the unknown, creating an almost mytho-logical narrative where everything must be either of the light or of the darkness. But what I've come to realize over the years is that this division often limits our understanding of what is truly happening in the unseen world.

I've seen how these constructs shape the way people approach their spiritual journeys. They come with a list of "dos" and "don'ts," convinced that certain spirits or energies are inherently evil simply because of how they've been portrayed in movies or in scripture. In this sense, we are trained to fear what we don't understand and to label it as "bad" simply because it's unfamiliar or doesn't fit into the box we've been told to believe in. This fear creates a wall between us and the deeper mysteries of the spiritual world. Instead of exploring with curiosity and openness, many approach it with trepidation, always on guard, as if the mere act of reaching out into the unknown is dangerous.

When we allow ourselves to be awestruck by the vastness of the unseen world, we open ourselves to a whole new level of spiritual growth. Instead of feeling burdened by the weight of what we've been told is "dangerous" or "evil," we can approach it with curiosity, ready to learn from every experience, no matter how it might appear on the surface. It's in this space of awe and open-hearted exploration that true transformation can happen. We learn that the spirit world is not a realm to be feared or controlled, but one to be respected and embraced, knowing that it reflects the energy we bring to it.

In the end, darkness will always exist, but it's not something to fear. It's simply another aspect of the whole—just another part of the journey. The more we face it with courage, curiosity, and a sense of wonder, the more we realize that we are not at its mercy. We are the creators of our own experiences. And with the right intention, even the darkest spaces can be transformed into opportunities for growth, healing, and ultimately, enlightenment. The spirit world is vast, complex, and beautiful in all its shades, and when we let go of our preconceived notions of good and bad where communion with the spirits is concerned, we can truly begin to explore its mysteries with a sense of joy and awe. I love the spirit world far too much to ever fear it again.

Chapter 8

"After the Glitter Fades"

I n the swirling, champagne-drenched chaos of the Roaring
Twenties—an age defined by jazz, flappers, and unbridled
ambition—Aimee Semple McPherson emerged like a comet
across the American spiritual landscape. While traditional religious institutions strained under the pressures of modernity,
McPherson seized the moment with an outlandish and
theatrical flair that was nothing short of revolutionary. She
reimagined what faith could look like in an era hungry for
spectacle and performance, wrapping the ancient Gospel
truths she believed in with the glittery garb of Hollywood
showmanship. With her magnetic presence, creamy blonde
waves, and a voice that could both soothe and electrify, she
transformed the religious experience in America from solemn
ritual into dazzling, unforgettable performance. Spirituality in
America would never again look quite the same.

Her Angelus Temple in Los Angeles became a luminous
beacon—a place where spirituality and entertainment inter-
mingled beneath its soaring dome. McPherson understood,
with razor-sharp instinct, that the new American religion was

one of images and emotions, and she made herself its high priestess. She employed elaborate stage sets, costumes, and even full orchestras to dramatize ancient stories, turning her sermons into technicolor productions that captivated audiences far beyond traditional pews. No one before her had so masterfully harnessed the tools of the nascent Hollywood machine—the glitz, the drama, the relentless appetite for stars—her presentations rivaling even the creations of Cecil B. DeMille. She courted the newspapers, whose cameras adored her, and crafted headlines with the same strategic finesse as a silver screen siren.

McPherson's genius was her ability to sense that faith and spirituality, in the new century, needed to be seen and experienced to be believed. She painted her message across the canvas of a modernizing America, using radio waves to beam her sermons into homes and tabloids to spread her name like wildfire. Every miracle healing, every dramatic disappearance and reappearance, every controversial court battle added to her mythos, drawing the curious and the devoted alike. She stood at the crossroads of celebrity and sanctity—a sort of living bridge between the fervent revivalism of the past and the mass-media spirituality that would define the future. By embracing the luminous allure of Hollywood rather than recoiling from it, Aimee Semple McPherson forever altered the face of American spirituality—making it louder, brighter, and, most of all, impossible to ignore.

Yet McPherson's brilliant embrace of the entertainment industry was a double-edged sword, one that often slashed deep into the very foundations of the Pentecostal community that had birthed her. The same fiery holiness movement that first nurtured her meteoric rise prized modesty, humility, and separation from the worldly amusements of theater and cinema—all things Aimee seemed not only to accept but to baptize in the name of some higher purpose. To her increasingly uncomfortable Pentecostal base, McPherson's shimmering costumes, dramatic altar calls, and breathless media spectacles began to look less like spiritual ministry and more like blasphemy in high heels. She was accused of diluting the sacred with the profane and of selling the Gospel like a commodity on the glimmering streets of Los Angeles—a city already notorious for its gilded sins.

This tension reached its scandalous apex in 1926, when Aimee Semple McPherson suddenly and mysteriously disappeared— vanished without a trace. Whispers of kidnapping, secret love affairs, and illicit rendezvous swirled through the hot California air like wildfire. After an anxious month, she resurfaced, claiming she had been abducted and held captive in Mexico. It was a story that thrilled the faithful and titillated the skeptical. But the details didn't quite add up. Footprints led away from the beach where she supposedly vanished. Hotel employees testified to seeing a woman matching her description during the time she was missing. And rumors of an affair with a married man—one of her radio engineers—darkened her once-pristine image. Some even claimed she had disappeared from the spotlight in order to recover from a facelift.

The media, which had once carried her on wings of adoration, now circled like vultures, pecking at the inconsistencies and suggesting lurid escapades behind her angelic façade. Courtrooms, newspapers, and pulpits alike became stages for the public trial of her virtue. Though no concrete evidence ever proved an affair and no charges stuck, the scandal marked a turning point. To many Pentecostals, Aimee had strayed too far into the shimmering fog of worldly fame—her halo tarnished by the very spotlight that had once crowned her. She would never fully recover in the press or in the courtroom of public opinion.

Still, McPherson remained undaunted—or at least she seemed to. Even amid scandal, she wielded controversy like a sword, using it to carve out an even larger legend in Hollywood. She understood, perhaps better than any preacher before her, that in the new America—the America of movies, motorcars, and mass communication—it was better to be notorious than to be forgotten. Her life became a living parable for a generation grappling with faith in a dizzyingly modern world: messy, electric, theatrical, and unforgettable.

Despite the relentless storms of scandal, Aimee Semple McPherson pressed forward with an almost supernatural determination—expanding her ministry, broadcasting her sermons across the nation, and solidifying herself as a household name. Yet beneath the glittering surface of her larger-than-life persona, cracks were beginning to form. Years of ceaseless work, mounting pressures from both the religious and secular worlds, and the heavy burden of maintaining her image as both saint and star took a toll on her spirit and body alike. Behind the dazzling smile and electrifying sermons, Aimee struggled with exhaustion, depression, and chronic pain—afflictions she fought in the same way many of her contemporaries did: with a growing dependence on prescription medications.

On September 27, 1944, in a lonely hotel room in Oakland, California, Aimee Semple McPherson's meteoric life came to a sudden and tragic end. She was found unresponsive, a half-empty bottle of sleeping pills nearby suggesting an accidental overdose. The news of her death swept across the country like a somber wave, leaving both devoted followers and lifelong critics stunned. Official reports ruled it an accidental overdose of barbiturates—a tragic but grimly fitting epilogue for a woman who had lived her life on the razor's edge between ecstasy and collapse.

In death, as in life, McPherson's story refused to settle neatly into any one box. To some, she remained a martyred saint and a tireless servant of God, worn down by the unbearable weight of her mission. To the more traditional, though, she was a cautionary tale—a woman who had played too freely with fame and paid the ultimate price. But regardless of perspective, one truth was undeniable: Aimee Semple McPherson had reshaped American spirituality forever. She had dragged it out of dusty revival tents and thrust it under the klieg lights, merging sacred tradition with modern spectacle and carving a path that future generations of televangelists, media-savvy pastors, and religious entrepreneurs would follow. Her life—a fever dream of faith and fame—still casts a long, flickering shadow over the American religious imagination, a reminder that in the world she helped create, salvation and celebrity often dance hand in hand.

And then there was Kathryn Kuhlman. In the swirling haze of the late 1960s, at a time when the world itself seemed caught between a yearning for renewal and the tremors of social unrest, Kathryn Kuhlman stood as a singular, radiant figure in the world of Christian faith. With her flowing gowns and ethereal presence, she swept into packed auditoriums, her voice trembling with emotion as she spoke of her Lord's power to heal. Her meetings were electric, tingling with expectancy. Crowds surged forward at the mere mention of miracles. It was said that as she moved across the stage, the very atmosphere changed—becoming thick with an almost tangible sense of the divine. People wept openly, arms outstretched, as afflictions both physical and spiritual seemed to dissolve under the weight of an unseen hand.

Yet, as her fame blossomed and testimonies of spontaneous healings filled the air, a growing chorus of voices from within the more traditional branches of Christianity began to murmur with unease. These critics, grounded in a more sober, cautious interpretation of Scripture, viewed Kathryn's focus on the miraculous with increasing suspicion. Where they prized doctrine and dogma, she prioritized experience. Where they insisted on the measured exposition of text, she invited the unpredictable flow of what she called the Holy Spirit. To them, her emotionally charged services, her reliance on personal revelations, and her frequent invocation of an unseen spiritual presence smacked of something dangerously close to Spiritualism.

Whispers grew louder, accusing Kuhlman of consorting with "spirit guides"—a term that, in more conservative circles, evoked images of occult practices and forbidden knowledge. Though Kathryn herself never used such language, always declaring her allegiance solely to the Holy Spirit she believed in, her detractors painted her as a woman dangerously adrift— one whose dazzling displays of power might be more deception than divine. To these guardians of orthodoxy, her ministry was not merely suspect; it was a dangerous enticement, leading the faithful away from the firm foundation of religious orthodoxy into the misty realms of subjective, mystical experience.

Despite the mounting criticism, Kathryn remained undeterred. Her message was simple and unwavering: miracles happen today just as they did two thousand years ago. She insisted that she was merely a vessel—a "nothing" through whom God chose to work. But the tension between her soaring, supernatural ministry and the cautious world of traditional Christianity never fully eased. To her admirers, she was a modern-day apostle of wonder, breathing life back into a faith grown dry with intellect alone. To her critics, she was a troubling reminder of how easily the pursuit of signs and wonders could slip into a dangerous and dark partnership with forces unknown. So Kathryn Kuhlman walked a narrow, glittering path—caught between heaven and earth, between acclaim and suspicion—forever embodying the breathtaking, bewildering promise of a God who still moves in ways beyond understanding.

Despite the criticisms swirling around her, Kathryn Kuhlman's ministry only grew, as if fed by the very controversy that sought to undo her. Her healing services became legendary, with people traveling hundreds, even thousands of miles, desperate for a touch of the miraculous. Auditoriums that once hosted the glittering stars of Hollywood and the rising icons of music now echoed with the sound of worship songs and weeping prayers. Among the grandest of these venues was the Shrine Auditorium in Los Angeles—a majestic structure whose ornate arches and vast, sweeping space became the backdrop for countless nights of divine encounter. Kathryn would glide across the stage, her arms lifted high, a silhouette framed in the golden spotlight, as testimonies of healings spilled across the room like wildfire.

The crowds were not small, nor were they made up only of the desperate and the simple. Doctors, lawyers, celebrities, and skeptics sat shoulder to shoulder with the impoverished and the afflicted, each drawn by a hope that defied the cynicism of the age. People collapsed under the power of what she called the Holy Spirit; wheelchairs were abandoned, crutches discarded, and cancerous growths reportedly vanished. The Shrine became, for a time, a modern Pool of Bethesda—where the sick and the broken clung to the hope that an angel, through Kathryn, might trouble the waters once again.

Her growing renown eventually spilled beyond the walls of faith-based gatherings and into the broader arena of American pop culture. Television came calling. Kathryn appeared on *The Dinah Shore Chevy Show*, where the gracious hostess—herself a symbol of sunny, mainstream Americana—welcomed her with warmth and curiosity. There, in the bright, polished studios, Kathryn spoke about the love of Jesus and the miraculous power of faith with the same emotional fervor she brought to her healing services. The audience, more accustomed to celebrity interviews and lighthearted banter, sat completely transfixed in awe.

Perhaps more astonishing was her appearance on *The Tonight Show Starring Johnny Carson*. Carson, a man of quick wit and skeptical humor, was known for his ability to poke gentle fun at even the most serious of guests. Yet, when Kathryn Kuhlman sat across from him, clad in one of her trademark flowing gowns, her presence softened the edge of even his sharp wit. She spoke not with the steeliness of a religious crusader, but with a girlish enthusiasm and almost childlike wonder, weaving tales of the miraculous that somehow disarmed rather than invited ridicule. Though the setting was secular and the audience largely secular-minded, there was an undeniable magnetism about her—a sense that, whether or not one believed, something extraordinary clung to the very air around her.

Through it all, Kathryn remained a paradox: deeply adored and sharply criticized, celebrated by the masses yet eyed warily by many within her own religious community. Yet she pressed forward, her life an unfolding testimony to her singular belief that the same Jesus who once walked the dusty roads of Galilee still moved among His people, still touched the sick, and still called the lost home. Her fame was never the goal; it was, in her mind, merely the byproduct of a simple, stubborn faith in a supernatural God who refused to be boxed in by tradition or skepticism.

The remarkable tapestry of Kathryn Kuhlman's life, with all its soaring triumphs and shadowed valleys, was eventually captured in vivid detail in the biography *Daughter of Destiny*, written by Jamie Buckingham. Published after her death, the book peeled back the glittering layers of public perception to reveal the complexities and contradictions that made Kathryn so unforgettable. It didn't paint her as a plaster saint, nor did it shy away from the imperfections that clung to her humanity. Instead, it offered a portrait of a woman whose extraordinary calling often warred with the frailties and struggles of an ordinary heart.

In *Daughter of Destiny*, readers discovered that Kathryn's road to ministry was anything but straight. Raised in the small, dusty town of Concordia, Missouri, she grew up with an early sense of faith but struggled to find her place in a world where female preachers were viewed with suspicion. Her early years in ministry were spent in obscurity, traveling the back roads of America, preaching in storefront churches and tiny, drafty halls —often to more empty seats than filled ones. Yet even then, there was something about her. The fervor in her voice. The almost otherworldly conviction in her eyes. She was set apart.

The book also touched with painful honesty on one of the most controversial chapters of her life: her relationship with Burroughs Waltrip, a married evangelist whom she eventually wed. It was both scandalous and salacious. The marriage, clouded from the beginning by public disapproval, haunted Kathryn for the rest of her life. *Daughter of Destiny* didn't shy away from the sorrow she carried over that decision or the anguish of a union she later admitted had been born more out of loneliness than divine guidance. She would go on to end the marriage, but the wounds remained, shaping the humility and brokenness that became so much a part of her public persona.

Buckingham's biography also captured the awe-inspiring moments of Kathryn's healing services, bringing readers behind the scenes into moments of trembling prayer, raw exhaustion, and deep, almost aching dependence on faith. Far from being a mere performer orchestrating miracles on command, Kathryn was portrayed as someone who lived in near-constant awareness that she was treading on holy ground —someone who, despite her flaws, truly believed she was nothing without the Spirit moving through her.

I'm sure by now you must be wondering why I share so much about these faith healers, Darling. Well, to be quite honest with you, I idolized them in my younger days. In many ways, I still do. They embody the sort of theatrical spectacle that, for me— growing up on the stages of Pentecostalism in the rural South —inspired me to no end. I first read *Daughter of Destiny* as a teenager and remember being completely transfixed. It changed me, even then. For a young kid who, at the time, saw only a life in church as his future, the idea that real, human, messy people could impact the world in remarkable ways more than inspired me.

When I say, even now, that I'm still a nobody from a nowhere town, I truly mean that. I grew up deep in the rural South, where faith ran thick in the air like the humidity we wore like second skin. Our church was the kind of place where our traditions weren't just respected—they were treated as if they had been carved by the very hand of God. Back then, before I found my way into Spiritualism, and long before I made peace with my own otherworldly experiences, the framework of my beliefs was narrow and strict—a reflection of the world around me.

I remember one particular time, so vivid in my mind even now, when a woman in our congregation felt a deep calling to start a local television ministry. She had been profoundly inspired by

Kathryn Kuhlman, whose broadcasts she described as full of a presence she said could only be the Holy Spirit. I still remember the light in her eyes when she spoke of it, her hands trembling just slightly as she explained her vision to the church leadership.

"I feel I'm supposed to do this," she said.

But that light dimmed quickly when she faced the reality of our community's beliefs—beliefs that said women had no place leading ministries, no matter how sincere their callings. There was an almost immediate wall put up against her: polite on the surface but firm underneath. Most of the church simply turned away, uncomfortable and unwilling to challenge the order that had kept things "proper" for generations.

But even then, even before my mind and spirit had stretched into the broader world of Spiritualism, something in me resisted the idea that her passion could be dismissed so easily. I was young, barely out of my teens, but I felt in my bones that what she was reaching for was real, and sacred, and worthy of support. But I was just a kid.

I've always had a thing for powerful women.

A few of us—just a handful—stood by her. We weren't the ones with clout or money, but we had willing hands and hearts, and sometimes that's more than enough to set a thing in motion. I volunteered at the small, somewhat ramshackle local television studio where she managed to buy a tiny slot of airtime. My job was to answer the prayer line when people called after watching her program.

It was humbling, really—hearing the brokenness and hope that came through those crackling lines. People didn't care that she was a woman; they didn't care about the traditions that tried to bind her. They just wanted someone to pray with them, to believe with them, to remind them that they weren't alone.

Looking back, I realize now that those long, quiet hours manning that phone were one of my first real steps away from the rigid faith of my upbringing and toward something much more expansive. I saw that Spirit moved where It willed—not according to the structures we tried to confine It within. It moved through her. It moved through those calls. And, in a way, it moved through me too, even before I knew it.

That experience planted a seed that eventually led me into Spiritualism, where the soul's calling is honored—wherever it may arise—and where the voice of Spirit is heard without regard for the body it speaks through.

It was in that small, run-down television studio, sitting on a cracked vinyl chair with a battered telephone pressed to my ear, that something else began to awaken in me too. In those quiet moments between calls, I would watch the little red "On Air" light flicker on and off in the dim control room, and I became entranced—not just by the power of prayer, but by the sheer magic of communication itself.

The way a single woman, whose voice would never have been given a pulpit in our hometown church, could still find her way into living rooms across the region, offering hope and healing to people she might never meet. It felt like witnessing a literal miracle of a different sort.

There was a hum to that place—a buzz of possibility that I hadn't ever felt before. The equipment was old and patched together. The air smelled faintly of dust and overheated wiring. But to me, it was electric with potential. I realized that media— even on a shoestring budget, even without the official blessing of powerful men—could reach the masses.

It could bypass the locked doors of tradition and speak directly to the human heart. I saw how a message, once captured by a camera lens or carried through a phone line, could ripple outward like stones dropped into a pond, touching people far beyond the walls of a single church or a single town.

I think that was when the first cracks really started to appear in the world I had always known. The smallness, the insularity of my upbringing, started to feel confining. Even claustrophobic. I began to imagine what it would be like to live beyond those boundaries. To step into a world where Spirit and creativity weren't held hostage by dogma and tradition—where you didn't have to ask permission to follow your calling.

That little studio, with its flickering lights and tired equipment, became my first glimpse of a bigger, freer life.

Even now, when I walk onto a soundstage or sit behind a microphone, there's a part of me that flashes back to those early days. To that scrappy television ministry of hers. To the prayers whispered into the night. To the sheer audacity of reaching out through static and darkness and believing that someone out there would hear you.

It was there, long before I found the language of Spiritualism, that I learned something sacred: that Spirit isn't bound by walls, or rules, or by who the world says you are. Spirit moves. And media, I realized, could move with It—carrying light and truth farther than any one voice could shout on its own.

So, suffice it to say, when Hollywood came calling for me, I was more than ready. After more than two years of crisscrossing the Southeast with my own lectures, presentations, and readings—and having developed a following that already far eclipsed any church I had ever been a part of—I was ready when life presented me with an even larger stage.

But it came packaged in a way I never would have imagined. In fact, to be quite honest, it came wrapped in something I had once vocally criticized. The actual word *psychic*, even then, seemed to conjure strange images and was considered taboo at best.

So when a woman met me after an event and handed me her card, telling me to call her the next day, I never expected I'd find myself thrust into the psychic industry in a way that would brand the rest of my life.

I can still remember it to this day. I called her, and her first words to me were, "I love your voice, and I want you." I was awkwardly silent. What did the words even mean? She then said, "I think I have a way for you to help a lot of people." She went on to ask if I'd ever considered providing readings on the phone to callers seeking advice and insight.

The truth is, I hadn't. In fact, the idea had never even crossed my mind until I heard her ask the question.

To understand the feeling a little better, one would need to remember that, in those days, there was no social media as we have it today. There was no way to advertise upcoming events with just the click of a button. In fact—and at the risk of seeming old—the events I had headlined up until that time had been advertised by taping printed flyers to the walls of coffee shops. I didn't even have a mailing list at the time. So, when the idea was proposed to me, and I was given the reassurance that I would have the freedom to share from my heart on each call, I accepted her recruitment—though not entirely sure what to expect.

When I first stumbled into the world of the psychic industry, it was like stepping into a swirling, neon dreamscape that never seemed to sleep. It was the mid-to-late '90s, and the air was thick with the scent of incense, late-night desperation, and the irresistible glow of psychic infomercials that ran for hours on end. I remember the first time I watched Kenny Kingston on TV, perched like a charming relic of another time. His soft, effusive voice cooed sweet reassurances through the screen. He would gently clutch a crystal or a velvet-draped phone, as if holding a direct line to the great beyond. With a twinkle in his eye, he promised guidance and comfort to anyone willing to dial in.

It was camp in its purest, most earnest form—a world where rhinestone-studded psychics smiled knowingly through Vaseline-smeared camera lenses, and every caller was just one reading away from a life-changing revelation.

Then, of course, there was Miss Cleo. Oh, Miss Cleo! She crashed into the scene like a tropical storm—vibrant and larger-than-life. Her Jamaican accent, whether real or otherwise, rang out across the airwaves with a kind of theatrical authority, demanding you "Call me now!" She was part oracle, part tough-love auntie, part soap opera diva. I can still see her, swathed in bright colors and clutching her tarot cards like sacred artifacts, delivering dramatic fortunes to callers with a mix of warmth, scolding, and pure, unfiltered showmanship. The world she inhabited felt like a carnival tent pitched at midnight, buzzing with energy, mystery, and a slightly mischievous wink.

That was the psychic entertainment industry I first knew. A glittery, over-the-top parade of mysticism, performance, and salesmanship, all bundled together under the forgiving glow of late-night television. It wasn't about clinical precision or scholarly seriousness. It was theater. It was spectacle. It was emotion packaged into thirty-second sound bites and "free" minutes that always, somehow, turned into hour-long sessions. And somehow—despite, or maybe because of, all the camp and chaos—it felt intoxicating. It welcomed me with open arms. A strange and dazzling invitation to dance on the edge of mystery. To play a part in a drama as old as humanity itself: the search for answers.

It was obvious to anyone really paying attention that this was a world of "for entertainment purposes only." Those four words were everywhere—tucked into the fine print at the bottom of the screen, murmured hurriedly at the end of a call by a recorded voice, and stitched into the very fabric of the whole psychic spectacle. It was an unspoken understanding, like a secret handshake between performer and audience. They came to the networks to feel something—to be swept up in a moment of magic—not necessarily to walk away with the secrets of the universe in their pocket.

The over-the-top pageantry made that perfectly clear. Or, at least, it did to me. Kenny Kingston's sweet reassurances, often delivered with a wink and a nod, weren't the declarations of a stern prophet; they were part of a show. A kind of spiritual cabaret. And Miss Cleo, with her dramatic gasps and knowing chuckles, was as much an actress as she was an intuitive. The world they created wasn't about sober, quiet reflection—far from it. It was a late-night soap opera that just happened to involve tarot cards, crystal balls, and neon-lit promises of destiny.

I owe a great debt to those people. They created a stage that I, along with countless other psychics over more than two decades, have walked upon.

For me, I had no misgivings about the fact that I was stepping into a world of pure entertainment. But having been given the assurance that I would never be asked to read from a script and that I could always speak from my heart when providing insight to callers—it felt good to me. In fact, it fit perfectly. I also still had the freedom and flexibility to continue with my own presentations and onstage performances. Looking back, when asked how I found myself thrust into the world of psychic entertainment, I can only say that the time and culture had created the perfect storm.

Even the aesthetic made it clear that the world around me was one of entertainment: gauzy scarves draped over lamps, giant costume jewelry rings flashing like lighthouses as hands waved dramatically over decks of cards, and studio sets that looked like they were built from the spare parts of a magician's garage sale. You weren't being asked to believe. Not really. You were being invited to suspend disbelief just long enough to let yourself be entertained—to indulge in a fantasy where someone on the other end of a glowing telephone line might just have the answers you were too afraid to ask for elsewhere.

I had never felt more at home.

As I found my footing in that world, I realized that the best psychics—the ones who truly thrived—were the ones who understood that delicate dance. They knew how to weave just enough wonder to pull you in, but they also respected the invisible boundary that said: this is a show—a beautiful, strange, emotional show. And like any good performer, they knew that the real magic wasn't necessarily in seeing the future—it was in making you feel, if only for a few minutes, like you were seen, heard, and somehow understood.

When I first ventured into the world of the psychic industry, I had one goal in mind: I wasn't going to be the type of spiritual teacher you'd find at some ashram or silent retreat. I wasn't going to sit cross-legged on a cushion, offering cryptic wisdom while basking in a glow of incense and chanting mantras. That was never my style. I wasn't interested in presenting myself as some mystical sage who spoke in riddles, encouraging others to transcend their everyday lives and find peace in the quietest corners of the universe.

Instead, I envisioned myself as something far more grounded. Something relatable. Someone people could connect with without feeling like they had to fit into some otherworldly mold.

I wanted to be the kind of psychic one might find on the Vegas Strip—the kind you could sit down with over a drink, maybe even laugh at yourself, and still have a mind-blowing reading that felt real, raw, and incredibly human. I wanted to break down the walls of what people typically expect from a spiritual advisor. To me, spirituality wasn't about distance or detachment. It was about living fully in the present—with all its messiness, its imperfections, and yes, its contradictions. People don't need another guru who floats above the chaos of life. They need someone who's been through it, who's felt the highs and lows, and who can stand beside them with authenticity.

I wanted to offer something that felt more approachable. Something that didn't require a lifetime of meditation or ascension into some higher plane. People were genuinely looking for answers, but they were also looking for connection. They wanted a guide who didn't condescend but rather met them where they were. They wanted someone who could offer insight with a wink and a smile—not a far-off stare and cryptic advice.

And while I was determined to embrace the role of the relatable psychic, it wasn't about being a clown or taking away the sacredness of what I do. It was about keeping it real. It was about speaking their language, understanding their struggles, and making the mystical feel a little more tangible and a little more accessible.

So, I steered clear of the typical "spiritual" archetype—no flowing robes and no esoteric jargon that would send people scrambling for a dictionary. I wasn't going to be the type who made people feel like they had to change who they were to fit into some idealized spiritual version of themselves. Instead, I became the type of psychic who could be found under the bright neon lights, talking about life and love and work in a way that felt grounded in reality.

Because for me, the true magic lies not in detachment from the world, but in navigating it with an open heart—unafraid to laugh at the absurdity, to learn from the unexpected, and to celebrate the beauty of being human.

As I immersed myself deeper into the world of psychic readings, I began to realize just how much people long for that authenticity. They don't want to feel like they're signing up for some divine performance or entering a space that feels stiff and clinical. They want someone who gets it. Who isn't afraid to embrace their own flaws and quirks while still tapping into something beyond the ordinary.

What I came to understand is that the most powerful insights often arise not from moments of stillness and serenity, but from the chaotic, everyday moments that we all experience—those messy, real parts of life that make us who we are.

And that's when the magic happens.

When I work with someone, I make it clear from the start that I'm not here to "fix" them. I'm not a healer in the traditional sense—not someone who holds the keys to unlocking your destiny. What I offer is a window into the possibilities that lie ahead, a mirror reflecting the parts of you that you might not yet see or acknowledge. But it's never about making you feel inferior or lacking in some way, as though you need to change or conform to some spiritual ideal. It's about empowering people to step into their own light. To embrace their own wisdom. To find strength in the knowledge that they already have everything they need within them.

I've learned to keep the sessions grounded in real life. I use humor, honesty, and relatability as tools to break down the usual barriers people put up when they're stepping into something new and unknown. I talk about everything from relationships and career struggles to personal growth and self-doubt. We're all human. We're all messy. And we're all trying to figure things out.

When you can talk about something as abstract as the future in terms that make sense in someone's day-to-day life, it stops feeling like a mystical guessing game and becomes an actual conversation—a sort of deep dialogue between two people who may have different perspectives but still speak the same language.

This is why I think my approach resonated so well. People came to me with real questions—sometimes about big, life-changing decisions, and sometimes about simple things like whether to take a vacation or switch careers. Questions about lovers. And while I relied on the voice of the spirits to guide them, I never forgot that, at the heart of it all, they were just like me. They were doing their best to navigate the complexities of life.

So, I made sure to stay connected to that raw, unfiltered human experience. I still do. I'm not here to pretend I have all the answers, and I certainly don't think I'm more "enlightened" than anyone else. I'm just someone who's learned to tap into a deeper level of understanding—and who's committed to sharing that knowledge in a way that's relatable, fun, and down-to-earth.

There's something incredibly powerful about creating a space where people can be themselves—without judgment, without pretense, and without feeling like they have to live up to some idealized version of what a "spiritual" person should be. The more I embraced this authentic approach, the more I realized that the best readings often happen in the spaces between all the cosmic information. When I'm laughing with someone, or sharing a moment of vulnerability, or simply being present as they unravel their thoughts—that's when the real magic happens.

It's not in some otherworldly realm; it's right here. It's in the raw, imperfect, often messy beauty of life itself.

And in those moments, when people walked away with a sense of clarity or peace, it didn't feel like I'd performed something magical. It felt like I had simply reminded them of something they already knew deep down: that we're never truly alone in this journey. We all struggle. We all question. We all have our own paths to walk. The beauty lies not in escaping our humanity, but in embracing it fully—with all its twists, turns, and unexpected joys.

That's the kind of "psychic" I wanted to be. I stayed true to myself, connected with people, and helped them navigate life's mysteries with grace and laughter.

It wasn't long after I settled into this more relatable approach to the psychic world that something unexpected began to happen. As my reputation grew, I found myself attracting a completely different clientele—celebrities, influencers, and people whose names I had only ever seen in magazines or on the big screen. I had no idea how it happened at first, but suddenly, I was being sought out by the very people I'd grown up idolizing. The same people I had watched on TV, admired from afar, and fantasized about meeting were now sitting across from me, asking for my insights.

It felt surreal, to say the least. All this time later, it still does.

At first, I was humbled and a bit starstruck. Here were these larger-than-life figures—people who seemed untouchable—suddenly turning to me for guidance. It was both thrilling and a little intimidating. But as soon as I shifted my focus to the work itself, the excitement faded, and the real connections began. I was no longer starry-eyed. I was listening to their fears, anxieties, and desires with the same openness and sincerity I brought to every reading.

The truth is, the deeper I got into this world, the more I realized that the things that made these celebrities "famous" were also the things that made them human—the struggles, the self-doubt, the loneliness. They didn't need an idolized figure. They needed someone real. Someone who could see through the surface and into the heart of what they were really seeking.

What I found fascinating was how much the world they inhabited mirrored my own. Behind the glitz and glamour, there were the same fears of failure, the same need for validation, and the same longing for purpose I'd seen in every other client. In many ways, their lives were even more complex—twisted in ways I couldn't have imagined. They were surrounded by people who constantly needed something from them—whether it was their time, their image, or their energy. I was amazed by how few had someone to turn to who wasn't part of that whirlwind.

I soon realized that my grounded, approachable way of reading and advising was exactly what many of them craved. They were so used to people telling them what they should do and what they should believe. But when they came to me, I wasn't offering empty praise or telling them what they wanted to hear. I was offering honesty. I was offering clarity. I wasn't there to tell them how to live their lives—I was there to help them understand the bigger picture, to give them a fresh perspective, and to remind them of their own strengths.

It wasn't about living up to the expectations of others. It was about finding their own truth.

I'll never forget the first time I sat across from a celebrity I had long admired. We spoke about everything—career decisions, personal struggles, and the emotional weight that comes with being constantly in the public eye. At first, I was a little unsure of myself. Would they think I was just another psychic looking to make a name? Would they be skeptical, thinking I was one of the countless people trying to get in with the "right crowd"?

But it didn't take long for that tension to dissipate. The moment we started talking about real things—the things that truly mattered to them—it became clear that we were sharing a meaningful moment in time. I wasn't a fanboy. I wasn't a sycophant. I was just someone offering an honest, intuitive perspective on their life.

As I worked with more celebrities, I realized how much the experience had changed me, too. I had always been the type to look up to these figures, placing them on pedestals and imagining that their lives were somehow more "important" than mine. But as I got to know them on a personal level, I came to understand that we were all just human. I didn't need to idolize anyone, because the magic of it all lay in the connections we made—in the shared understanding and in the mutual respect we gave each other.

There was something deeply empowering about sitting down with people who were, in many ways, at the top of their game and showing them that we were all equals in this crazy, unpredictable world.

Over time, word spread, and I found myself working with more and more people in the entertainment industry—actors, musicians, athletes, and business moguls. But no matter who sat across from me, the dynamic was always the same. They didn't need another "guru" or someone telling them what to do. They needed someone who would meet them where they were, helping them navigate their fears, reminding them that even the brightest stars still had their shadows.

It became clear that in this high-pressure world, they were just as in need of clarity and direction as I was. They, too, were searching for the same connection—the same sense of meaning that we all long for in one form or another.

And so, as I continued to evolve in this world, I came to appreciate the strange irony of it all. I had entered the psychic industry with the idea that I would be different—that I wouldn't be the kind of spiritual teacher who lived in the clouds, but someone who could stay grounded and relatable.

What I hadn't expected was that, through this journey, I would become the very thing I had once idolized. Not in a superficial way, of course, but in the sense that I became a guide to others—a person they turned to for clarity, insight, and direction. And the best part? I didn't have to lose who I was to do it. If anything, I found that the more I stayed true to myself, the more people I could reach—celebrities included.

Because in the end, we're all just trying to find our way in this vast, messy world. And sometimes, all it takes is a little guidance from someone who doesn't mind a bit of self-deprecating humor at his own expense.

As the months passed and I continued to work with some of the most influential figures in the entertainment world, I found myself completely immersed in a realm that was as larger-than-life as the personalities that inhabited it.

It wasn't just the people themselves, though—it was the world they lived in. A world where everything felt amplified, exaggerated, and yet strangely familiar in some way. Like being caught in a film where the drama never stops and every moment is filled with an energy that borders on the surreal.

One evening, I found myself at a posh Atlanta lounge, sipping a glass of wine after a long day of readings. The place was buzzing with the kind of electric energy only a big city can provide. Every corner was filled with polished conversation, laughter, and the clink of crystal glasses.

It was then that I saw her. A woman from Broadway—someone whose name was synonymous with talent and charisma. She was sitting at the bar, elegantly draped in a flowing black dress, her platinum blonde hair perfectly coiffed as she effortlessly twirled a martini in her hand.

She had an air of such effortless glamour that it almost felt as though she had just stepped out of a movie scene.

When she turned to speak to me, she raised an eyebrow and greeted me with a smile so dazzling it could light up the entire room.

"Darling," she purred, drawing out the word with the kind of flourish you'd expect from someone who had been playing leading roles on Broadway for decades.

"Dahhhling," she repeated, her voice dripping with the sort of sophisticated playfulness that only someone who had truly mastered the art of charm could pull off.

Her delivery was flawless—a perfect blend of self-assuredness and theatricality. She wasn't just speaking; she was performing, drawing me into a world where every word, every gesture, felt like part of the grand show that was her life.

As she sipped her martini and continued to regale me with stories of her latest performance, I couldn't help but marvel at how she navigated the world with such grace and poise.

The way she moved through space, the way she spoke, and the way she lived—everything was infused with this larger-than-life energy that left you no choice but to become captivated by her presence.

She was like a walking, breathing performance. Always on. Always entertaining the masses. Never once slipping into the ordinary.

But beneath that dazzling exterior, I sensed something deeper. As much as she seemed to embody the epitome of confidence, there were glimpses of vulnerability that peeked through the cracks. She spoke of her career with pride, but I could hear the undercurrent of anxiety in her voice—that pressure of always having to be "on," of never being allowed to let her guard down. In her eyes, I saw the weight of the expectations that came with being in the spotlight. It wasn't just about the applause; it was about staying relevant, staying adored, staying... perfect.

That's when I realized that being immersed in this world, surrounded by personalities as grand as Broadway stars and as dramatic as film moguls, was about so much more than the glitz and glamour. It was about the constant tension between who these individuals had to be in the public eye and who they truly were when the cameras were off. The public image was larger than life, but the personal experience often wasn't. The persona was an act—carefully curated and carefully maintained. And yet, even behind the flashbulbs and spotlights, they still sought something real.

As I sat there listening to her talk about her latest role—the pressure she felt to keep living up to the expectations of her audience—I realized just how much the world she inhabited mirrored the very essence of my own work and the industry I had found myself thrust into. In many ways, it was no different from what I had been doing as a psychic: offering clarity, offering a mirror, offering a safe space for someone to strip away their public persona and simply be. Because in the end, beneath all the drama, beneath all the "Darlings" and the glitter, we're all just searching for a little peace, a little understanding, and a little connection in a world that can feel more than a little lonely at times.

I could see it in her eyes as she paused mid-sentence and looked at me, her bright smile softening.

"I'm just tired," she admitted, her voice quieter now, the weight of her words settling between us like an unspoken truth.

"Tired of trying to be something I'm not."

And in that moment, I saw it all clearly—the larger-than-life personalities, the glitzy world of Broadway and film, the glamorous parties and photo ops. They were all part of a carefully constructed façade. What they really wanted, what they really needed, was a safe space to be real. To be human. It wasn't the martinis, the adoring fans, or the bright lights that they craved. It was the quiet, grounded moments where they could let their guard down and remember who they truly were, without the weight of the world watching them.

It was a lesson I had learned early on in my journey in the psychic industry. No matter how high someone might rise, no matter how bright their star might shine, we're all just trying to find our way—trying desperately to navigate the complexities of our lives. Just trying to make sense of it all. And in this world of larger-than-life personalities, I found my own place too—not as a star or a performer, but as a needed friend and confidante to so many. A reminder that beneath all the glam and grandeur, we all have the same fundamental needs: to be seen, heard, and understood.

And as I sat there with her, I realized that maybe—just maybe —the most important thing I could offer wasn't just a psychic reading, but the space for someone to simply be themselves, free from the expectations of the world. Because at the end of the day, that's what we're all searching for: a little more authenticity in a world where it seems we're all just performers on a stage.

Part Four

Echoes from the Beyond

Chapter 9

The Curse of the Medium

My days have always been filled with the voices of others —some living, and some long passed. As a medium in the psychic industry, I've spent more than twenty-five years of my life offering clarity, comfort, and connection to those who seek answers from the spirit world. People come to me with pain, with questions, and with hope that maybe I can reach across that mysterious divide and bring back something meaningful for them. And, more often than not, I can.

The spirits often speak so clearly, their messages flowing through me like water down a well-worn path. For others, the insight came easily. I could see the threads of their lives—the crossroads, the warnings, the blessings waiting just ahead. I felt deeply honored to serve in that way and to be a vessel for something so much greater than myself.

But looking back, I can admit now what I couldn't say out loud then, in the very beginning: I was often lost in my own life, even as I helped others find their way.

It's a strange kind of dissonance, really. I could hear the spirits so clearly when they spoke of someone else's purpose or healing, yet when I turned inward—when I tried to ask for myself—I was often met with silence or static. It felt like trying to tune into a station that kept slipping just out of reach.

I remember one day in particular, especially vivid in my memory, after a long session with a grieving mother whose son had passed unexpectedly. The reading was powerful. He came through immediately, full of love and validation. She left in tears—grateful and relieved. But as soon as the door closed behind her, I sat there in my chair, staring at the wall, feeling completely empty. I had just helped someone reconnect with their deepest loss, yet I couldn't even answer the most basic questions about where I was headed in my own journey.

Why was I here, really? Was I fulfilling my own calling? Or was I just getting lost in everyone else's?

As my work gained attention and my calendar filled up, that quiet inner confusion only grew louder. Success in this field brought more eyes, more praise, and more expectations—but not necessarily more peace. There were moments I would walk off a stage after a gallery reading, having just delivered messages that left people in awe, and all I wanted was to go home and cry without knowing exactly why.

It wasn't sadness, exactly. It was a kind of spiritual homesickness—like I was guiding others home but had forgotten how to get there myself.

I began to understand that being a medium didn't make me immune to doubt or displacement. Far from it, in fact. It simply meant I was carrying both my own questions and those of everyone who came to me. And sometimes, that weight blurred the path of my personal life.

I've learned, over time, that clarity for oneself doesn't always come in the same way it does for others. The spirits don't always speak to me in full sentences when I ask about my own direction. Sometimes, they send silence to force me to listen more deeply to my own soul. Other times, they let me wrestle in the darkness, knowing that what I find there will shape me more than any whispered guidance ever could.

I used to think I had to have all the answers. Now, I realize my power as a medium isn't in always knowing—but in staying present, even when I don't know. In being honest about the paradox of seeing so much for others and still searching for myself.

Because maybe that, too, is a kind of gift: the reminder that we're all human—even the ones who talk to the dead.

I gave so much of myself to the stage—to the lights, the stories, and to the energy of the crowd hanging on my every word. There's a rhythm to it. A momentum that pulls you in until you're moving too fast to realize how far you've drifted from your own center. City to city, client to client, voice after voice from beyond—all demanding to be heard.

I loved it all. The work was sacred, and the impact undeniable. But somewhere along the way, I stopped being fully present in my own life. I was always "on," so to speak. Always pouring out. It was like I was living in service to everyone else's healing while quietly ignoring the parts of myself that needed the same kind of care.

There were times I'd come home after a long tour and barely recognize the life I was returning to. Friends had moved on. Relationships had frayed. I'd missed birthdays, milestones, and the quiet, mundane moments that root a person in reality. I had become a visitor in my own life—a guest in the spaces I once called home.

Even in my private moments, I found it hard to just *be*. My mind would race with lingering energies from the last reading or anticipation of the next. I'd sit at dinner with a friend, but my spirit was still back in a theater in Boston or a hotel room in Atlanta—still carrying the sorrow of a stranger whose loved one never said goodbye.

The irony of it all wasn't lost on me. I was helping people become present with their pain, their love, and their memories —while I was slowly becoming a ghost in my own story.

I remember standing backstage once, minutes before stepping out to a packed auditorium, and feeling this overwhelming wave of emptiness. It wasn't fear or anxiety. It was this haunting question: *When was the last time I did something just for myself?* Not for the spirits, not for the audience, not for the brand—but for the person I am beneath it all?

I found myself unable to answer. I had been too preoccupied with being *the medium* to recall how to be an individual. That realization was more alarming to me than any supernatural entity.

And yet, those moments of disconnection became wake-up calls. They reminded me that no matter how gifted I am, and no matter how in tune I may be with other realms, I still have to live this life. *This* life. I still have to anchor myself in the present and nurture the relationships that matter. I still have to find joy in the quiet, messy, beautifully imperfect human experience.

I've started to carve out more space for that now. I'm learning to say no when I need to. Learning to just sit in silence without needing it to be filled with messages from the other side. I'm remembering what it means to be here—fully. Because if I can help others come home to themselves, I owe myself that same saving grace.

The journey back to presence hasn't been easy. It's required confronting parts of myself I'd rather avoid, honestly. Sitting with the loneliness I used to drown in work. Acknowledging that the very gift that connects me to others can also isolate me, if I'm not careful. But it's worth it. Because now, when I step onto a stage or sit with a client, I do so not just as a conduit for the spirit world, but as someone who has fought for his own grounding and his own peace. And that, I've found, makes the connection even stronger.

What I didn't realize back then was how easy it is to mistake movement for meaning. I was constantly in motion—always traveling, performing, or serving—thinking that the momentum itself was proof I was aligned with my path. But when the applause faded and the crowds dispersed, I was often left sitting in a quiet hotel room, surrounded by silence that echoed a truth I didn't want to face: that I had lost touch with my own life.

I knew the names of people's deceased loved ones better than I knew the needs of my own body. I could recall exact dates and memories from strangers' pasts, channeled through Spirit, but couldn't remember the last time I had a real, grounded conversation with someone I loved—where I wasn't reading their energy or subconsciously trying to heal them.

There's a subtle danger in making your life about everyone else's healing. It can feel noble, even holy, but it's also a hiding place. It gave me purpose, yes, but it also gave me something to throw myself into so I didn't have to sit with my own vulnerability.

That caught up with me on more than one occasion. It always does.

Burnout didn't come like a wave. It came like a slow leak. My joy started to seep out. My boundaries thinned. I became exhausted in ways that sleep couldn't fix. And still, I kept showing up—because that's what people expected. And what I expected of myself. I had become so identified with the role of "the medium" that I forgot how to simply be a person.

Eventually, life forced me to stop and to pull away from stages. Not dramatically, and not all at once, but in little moments that broke through my performance—a friend confronting me about how distant I'd become, a family member expressing that they didn't feel like they knew me anymore, a persistent feeling of numbness that followed me even into the most profound readings.

The spirits hadn't left me, but they were no longer shielding me from my own truth. If anything, they were guiding me back to myself—not through messages for others, but through the silence that asked me to finally listen to my own voice.

It was humbling to realize that the answers I had been searching for outside myself—through clients, through crowds, through work—had been waiting for me in the quiet corners of my own neglected soul.

I had to relearn the basics: how to rest, how to be alone without being lonely, and how to say "I don't know" without shame. I had to reconnect not just to Spirit, but to *my* spirit.

And in doing that, something unexpected happened.

I became a better medium. Not because I tried harder, but because I started living more honestly. The more present I became in my own life, the more deeply I could hold space for others. The readings became less about performance and more about presence. The messages flowed not just from a higher place, but from a more integrated one.

Now, I take time to go for walks in parks. To sit by the ocean without needing to channel. To enjoy a meal without scanning the room for spiritual impressions. I've found a new rhythm— one that honors both the gift and the giver.

I've learned that even those of us who walk between worlds need a place to land. We need to be held, just as we hold others.

And perhaps that's the most sacred lesson of all, really: the understanding that healing isn't something I deliver from the outside—it's something I, too, must receive.

I never married. It's a fact I often reflect on with a mixture of quiet contemplation and, if I'm brutally honest, a hint of resignation. Marriage, as a concept, has always seemed so distant to me—so far removed from the world I inhabit. I've never quite been able to reconcile the idea of a traditional partnership with the life I've chosen, and in some ways, it has always felt as though I've been moving in circles, orbiting a commitment I was never meant to make.

Instead, my life has been a series of long-term relationships. Some tender and sincere, others filled with fiery passion and fleeting connections—along with a sprinkling of lurid affairs that, at the time, seemed to offer something I didn't know I needed.

There's a reason for this, if I'm to be honest—one that is both deeply personal and intricately tied to my identity. You see, as a medium—someone who feels the pulse of the world in a way so unlike the everyday person—I give myself to the world. The stage, the art of performance, the interaction with an audience... it's where I've always given myself. Every fiber of my being is attuned to the rhythms of the theater and the magic that happens when you step out into the light, when you become part of something larger than yourself. This life has been my calling—the only one I've ever truly known—and it has always taken precedence over all else.

I was always so drawn to the stage. The way it consumed me. The way it made me feel alive in ways nothing else could. There was no room for the mundane commitments of a conventional relationship when there was always another performance to prepare for, another show to give my all to. I'd pour my heart into my work, into my presentations, into the stories I told. And when the curtains fell, I found myself torn between the longing for connection and the cold, hollow feeling of knowing the stage was the only place I ever truly belonged.

It's not that I didn't try, or that I never sought companionship. I've loved—deeply, at times. But my love was often fleeting, consumed by the demands of my craft. Relationships would come and go. Some built on genuine affection, others on the electrifying thrill of the unknown. I'd find myself entangled in passionate affairs and moments of lust and excitement that filled the voids my career couldn't. But those, too, were always temporary. The excitement would fade, as it always does, leaving me feeling restless and unsatisfied—as if I were searching for something just out of reach. Something that would never come while I was giving my life to the stage.

I've learned to accept that this is who I am—a man of passion and intense connections. And while I've never walked down the aisle or exchanged vows, I know that, in my own way, I have loved as fully as I'm capable. The stage has always been my partner, really—my mistress, my true love. And perhaps, in some way, I am married to it. Bound by its siren call.

Committed to its demands and its unyielding grip on my soul.

So yes, I've never married. I've had long-term relationships and my share of fiery, transitory affairs. But in the end, my life has been devoted to the art I was born to perform. It's not a path I regret, nor one I would change. The stage has been my life, my love—my everything. And though I've never exchanged vows with another person, in its own way, it has been the one constant in my life and the one commitment I've made that has never wavered.

In the world I've inhabited for so many years, marriage never seemed to fit into the equation. It's a space filled with such intense, raw emotion—a world where I'm called to connect with both the living and the departed, to offer clarity, comfort, and insight to those who seek guidance. This work is all-encompassing, requiring a sensitivity to energies that, I'll admit, can be overwhelming. Every session brings with it a flood of emotion—stories of love, loss, joy, and regret. The people who come to me—and in many ways, it's primarily women who seek me out—are often searching for answers to questions that are deeply personal. Questions often involving relationships and emotions. They come with their pain, their brokenness, their hopes for reconciliation or closure, and I'm the person through which these emotions flow.

I've always felt honored to be in this position—truly, I have. But I've also learned that this work doesn't leave much room for anything else. When you spend so much time delving into the emotions of others, guiding them through the complexities of their own lives, there's sometimes little left to offer in return. The world of mediumship, at least for me, has not been conducive to long-term, traditional partnerships like marriage. I've seen it in the way people react when they learn what I do—

their eyes widening with a mix of awe and hesitation, as if they understand this work is all-consuming and leaves little space for the kind of intimacy a marriage demands.

The energy it takes to guide someone through a personal revelation or a message from beyond is immense. It requires focus, deep empathy, and a constant shifting of one's own energies to accommodate the needs of the client. I've often found myself drained after a session—not because I don't care, but because my own emotional reserves are emptied in the act of providing clarity to others. It's hard to explain, but there's a quiet kind of isolation that comes with this work. While I connect with people on such an intimate, emotional level—sharing in their grief or their joy—I'm always somewhat removed from my own emotions. At least in those moments. It's as though my own life is put on pause while I help others navigate theirs.

And then there's the demographic that seeks me out. Most of the individuals who come to me are women—many of whom are at a crossroads in their lives, seeking guidance on their relationships, marriages, or family dynamics. They often turn to me for advice, looking for insight into their partnerships and their struggles with love or loss. It's both a privilege and a responsibility.

But over time, I've come to realize that, in this environment, marriage just never seemed to be in the cards for me. As I listen to their stories—their heartaches, their dreams of what a marriage should be—I find myself wondering if the idea of partnership has always felt too elusive for someone like me. Someone who lives in the space between the living and the departed. Someone who's always been more in tune with the energies around others than with their own personal desires.

In a way, the work I do has always created a kind of emotional distance between me and the concept of marriage. The intensity of the emotions I experience during sessions—the deep, sometimes overwhelming connections I form with those seeking answers—leaves little room for the kind of emotional investment a lifelong partnership would require. The energy I might otherwise devote to a partner is instead poured into the lives of those who seek my guidance. And I've often felt that there is simply not enough of me left to give to a long-term relationship in the traditional sense.

I've tried, in my own way, to create connections with others. But these relationships always seem to be fleeting. As if the more I try to establish something permanent, the more it slips through my fingers. The incredible people I've met along the way— those who have come into my life for short periods—have often shared my passion for the intangible and the unknown. But only a few have ever truly understood it. And those few who did—I admit—I most often pushed them away.

And so, despite the love and affection I've felt, I've found myself alone more often than not. But not because I didn't want a partner—rather, because my life has always pulled me away from the ordinary.

Maybe in another life, in another version of myself, I could have pursued it. Built a family. Embraced that kind of life. But in this life—where my soul is tied to the voices of the spirit world, to the stage, and to the spirits that call to me—marriage has always felt like something just beyond my reach.

And perhaps that's okay. Perhaps some of us are not meant for the same paths others walk. Perhaps my calling was always to walk alone. But to the many who, even for fleeting moments of passion, kept me tethered to the earth and kept me from floating away for good—I owe a debt I can never fully repay.

Over the years, I've come to realize that my voice has become something of a fantasy for many of the people who seek my guidance. There's a quality to it, some say. It was the reason I was recruited by the psychic industry, after all. Something sultry, I'm told. Something soothing—almost hypnotic.

My manager at the time, all those years ago, said it had a way of settling the minds and hearts of those who called on me. Maybe it does. If so, I'm glad. For many of my clients, I've become a voice of comfort in their times of need, offering clarity or solace when they're lost in the chaos of their own lives.

I've heard it before—the way they describe it, with a certain warmth in their tone, almost as if they're entranced by the way I speak. It's not something I've ever intentionally cultivated, though. In a world filled with uncertainty, where emotions often run high, I've become a steadying presence they turn to— a voice on the other end of the phone, or a voice on stage, that reassures them when their world feels shaken.

To some, this connection might take on a deeper, almost fantastical quality. I know that for some, it becomes something more than just a psychic reading. My voice—the words I speak— becomes the solace they crave. And for some, an intimacy they desire but can't have.

And yet, there are boundaries. Lines I've always been firm about never crossing. Despite the allure—and despite the way some clients might fantasize about something more than the work we do together—I've always drawn a clear line between the professional and the personal.

Crossing that line—becoming romantically entangled with a client—is something I've never once dared to do. It's a boundary I would never compromise. Not because I don't understand the appeal, or the emotions that can sometimes surface in the heat of the moment, but because I understand the delicate nature of what I do and the responsibility that comes with it.

I've seen it happen more times than I can count—how a client can get caught up in the energy of a reading. The way their emotions can become entangled with the insight I provide. The way they might begin to blur the lines between psychic guidance and personal desire.

But I've always made it clear—whether directly or through my actions—that this is not a space for that kind of intimacy. As intimate as those emotions may feel.

The connection between a medium and their client is one based on trust, vulnerability, and the genuine desire to offer guidance. To introduce anything beyond that would distort the very essence of what I do. I have no doubt I would lose everything should I ever cross that line.

I understand why it might be tempting for some. The energy that flows between us during a session is powerful. And it is intimate in its own way. I'm always acutely aware that the closeness I create with my clients can be mistaken for something more. But I know where the boundaries lie, and I've always been resolute in my commitment to keep those boundaries intact. To cross the line from psychic to lover—at least where a client is concerned—would be to taint the very essence of the connection. To move from a place of pure guidance to something far less pure.

There's also the simple fact that I have a deep respect for the people who seek my help. Many of them come to me in times of vulnerability, searching for something deeper than just a quick fix or temporary comfort. They come because they're in need—

whether of clarity or closure. It would be an abuse of that trust to blur the professional boundaries we share, and so I've always kept a respectful distance. Perhaps that's part of what has kept me distant from traditional relationships most of all. In this world of mediumship, I find myself engaged in deep, meaningful connections with people, yet always separated by the nature of the work. It's a paradox—a push and pull that defines my life. My clients come to me with their emotional burdens, seeking answers, and I give them that. Blurred lines, I find, are just an added, unnecessary burden.

In the end, I suppose the work I do—and the connection I share with the people who seek me out—has always remained above the personal. Above the romantic. It's a responsibility I've never taken lightly, and while I'm always flattered by the attention, I know that the sanctity of my role is far more important than any fleeting attraction. There are certain lines, certain boundaries, that must never be crossed, and the line between psychic and client is one I have always—and will always—respect.

It's possible that my reluctance toward traditional marriage also has something to do with my upbringing—that religious foundation that shaped so much of who I am. Growing up, there were certain ideals instilled in me. Beliefs about love, family, and the sanctity of marriage that carried with them a weight of responsibility. Marriage, in that context, wasn't just a union of two people; it was a solemn promise. A lifelong commitment that required sacrifice and devotion. And perhaps, somewhere deep within, I understood that such a commitment would always clash with the life I was destined to lead—a life in the entertainment industry.

Or maybe it wasn't just religion, but more the personal experiences I had growing up, watching the marriages within my own family unravel over time. I saw the cracks that formed, the subtle fissures in relationships that once seemed so solid. I saw the way love, once vibrant, could slowly fade into bitterness and resentment. How the promise of "forever" seemed increasingly fragile as the years went by. I watched as some marriages dissolved and as the people I loved walked away from the promises they had made to one another. Those endings, those heartaches, made me question not the validity of marriage itself, but my own ability to make such a promise to another person. Perhaps it was a mixture of both: the teachings of my childhood and the disappointments I witnessed in those I loved. Together, they formed a quiet but insistent voice in my head, warning me that marriage was a path that would only lead to heartache, to disappointment, to a life that didn't fit with my own.

So, instead of marriage, I chose relationships. Lots of them, if I'm being completely honest. Long-term, sometimes intense, sometimes complicated—but always temporary. These relationships, for all their passion or tenderness, were never meant to last forever. They were experiences. Chapters in my life, not lifelong commitments. And in their own way, they allowed me to avoid the heartbreak I feared while still experiencing the connection, intimacy, and passion I craved.

But I've never truly felt alone. This is something I've always known, even as I watched others form families, settle down, and create lives entwined with one another. I've always had an audience—a sea of beautiful people, both literal and metaphorical, who have come into my life through my work. As a medium, as a performer, there are always people around me. There are always souls to connect with. Always stories to share. The stage and my social circles are always active. Whether it's the audience I speak to during a performance or the people who seek my guidance, I've never been without company.

In fact, the idea of isolation has always seemed foreign to me. I've lived in a world where people are constantly reaching out, constantly searching for something—whether it's answers, comfort, or simply a connection with another soul. And I've always been the one to offer that connection, to bridge the gap between the living and the unseen. In the process, I've formed bonds that, while perhaps not the kind that lead to lifelong marriage, have still been deeply meaningful. These bonds have allowed me to feel connected, to feel loved in my own way, without the constraints of traditional relationships.

And then there are the audiences. The crowds of beautiful people who come to witness the work I do, who are moved by the stories I tell, who are drawn to the energy we create together. There is something incredibly fulfilling about standing before an audience and feeling the collective energy of so many people—their eyes focused, their hearts open to a moment in time we're creating together. It's a kind of intimacy that is unique—one that fills the void of solitude, one that makes me feel seen and understood without ever needing to become romantically involved.

I've come to realize that perhaps this is enough for me. That the connection I share with my audiences, with my clients, and with the people whose lives I touch has been my greatest love of all. I've never felt truly isolated because I've always been surrounded by beautiful people—people who come for something I can offer, and in turn, they offer me something in return: their trust, their vulnerability, and their energy. This exchange has been enough to sustain me and to make me feel like I'm never truly alone, even when the world around me may seem distant or indifferent.

So perhaps it was my upbringing, perhaps it was the example of marriages in my family, or perhaps it was simply my own path—but whatever the reason, I've never considered marriage in the traditional sense. But I've also never needed to. I've always felt I had enough. Something that, while it may not fit the mold of conventional love, has been more than enough to fill my life with meaning, connection, and purpose. But when there have been those times and seasons of connection in my life, the only word I know to describe those times is "intensity."

I've never felt alone—not in the way many might imagine loneliness to feel. Even when I've been by myself, there has always been a sense of presence—the echoes of conversations past, the faces of those I've connected with, the voices of the countless individuals who've entered my life in one way or another. But there is something special, something undeniably precious and passionate, about the women who have crossed my path. The women who allowed me into their lives and tolerated the madness that comes with my life. Every woman, every lover who has ever taken the time to step into my world, to understand the complexities of what I do and who I am, has offered me something that I can never fully repay. Their presence has been a tether, a grounding force that has kept me connected to the earth even as I've wandered through the ethereal spaces of psychic journeys and performances.

There is a kind of magic in the way women have appeared in my life, though—not as distractions, not as fleeting affairs, but as anchors in a world that can sometimes feel as if it is floating between the realms of the living and the dead. They offered me their love, their affection, their understanding, and in return, I've given them the depths of my heart, my energy, and my insight. Though I may not have married any of them, and though our relationships may have been brief or long-term, I've always seen the value in each of them. They were not just lovers to me; they were co-creators of the space I inhabited—

whether they realized it or not. This story of my life is just as much theirs as it is my own.

It's a curious thing, isn't it? To be a medium and to live in a world where your work requires you to navigate the unseen, to commune with spirits and energies that most people cannot even fathom. To do so and still remain tethered to the physical world, to the tangible reality that others live in. This is where the women in my life have made all the difference. They kept me grounded. They reminded me of the beauty and the challenges of being human—of living in a world that isn't always so focused on the unseen, but on the very real emotions that tie us together: love, passion, loss, joy.

They were the ones who brought me back to earth after long psychic journeys—who reminded me that while I could touch the heavens, I was also meant to be present here, on this plane, in this life. Each of them, in their own way, gave me a reason to stay. They taught me to look at the world through a clearer lens and to remember that there is beauty in the ordinary—that there are joys to be found even in the most mundane moments. In long car rides. In passionate weekend getaways. In moments spent in vacant parking lots listening to music. In their laughter, their warmth, and in their presence, I found solace. They brought me back to myself when the chaos of my psychic work threatened to overwhelm me.

I'm deeply thankful to every woman who took the time to try and enter my world. I know that it wasn't always easy. It couldn't have been. My life, by its very nature, is unpredictable —always consumed by the demands of my work and by the constant need to give so much of myself to others. And yet, these women, with their patience, their understanding, and their grace, chose to enter this space with me. They knew the life I led. They understood the commitment I had to my work.

Yet they chose to love me anyway—or at least attempted to. Even when, in my own moments of isolation, I refused to let them fully. It's no small feat to love someone whose world is so consumed by the intangible—by energies that can't be touched or fully understood. But they did it, and for that, I will forever be grateful.

I'm also grateful for the lovers who, even if our time together was brief, gave me the gift of their companionship, their passion, and their energy. These relationships, while transient, were not without meaning. Each one left a mark on my soul and taught me something about myself—something about the beauty of connection. They were the ones who reminded me that I'm human. That I'm capable of feeling and being felt, even as I exist in a world that often demands I be more of a channel than a person.

To the women who entered my life—whether as lovers, friends, or confidantes—I offer my deepest praise. You have given me so much more than you realize. You have kept me tethered, kept me present, and kept me from losing myself in the intensity of my work. You have shown me that despite my immersion in the world of spirits, the greatest gift of all is the love and connection we share in the physical world.

So, no, I've never felt alone. Not truly. Because I have had the privilege of the women who have loved me and who have taken the time to try and understand me—even when I didn't care to attempt to understand myself. Women who grounded me when I needed it most. I may not have married them, and I may not have been the partner they'd hoped for, but they were anchors to me. For that, I am eternally thankful. Those connections were always the reminder that while my work takes me far and wide, I'll always have a reason to return to this world—to the love, to the passion, and to the beauty that exists here.

Chapter 10

Babylon

I never thought I'd make it in Hollywood—at least not in the way I did. I didn't enter the world of the psychic industry with dreams of the silver screen, fame, or riches. I entered that world chasing the energy. The mystery. I had a gift—or at least that's what people said—and I knew how to read a room better than most read a book.

A psychic in the City of Angels sounds like a grifter's cliché, but somehow I carved a space for myself in the velvet shadows between truth and illusion. Word got around, and soon enough, the studio execs, starlets, and producers were calling. I'd do readings on the balconies of haunted estates, cleanse crystals under moonlight for some I'd grown up idolizing, and whisper spirit-guided warnings in hotel suites thick with Chanel No. 5 and desperation.

For a while, it was magic—whether real or not. I was flying private, dressing in couture, and dining with the kind of people whose secrets could ruin empires. I held the scandalous and salacious details of many of the most powerful people in the world. And their secrets were safe with me. They still are, in fact. They wanted answers, direction, and comfort. I gave it to them—or they believed I did—and belief was its own type of currency in the land of stars.

I told myself I was doing good, that I was helping people navigate the chaotic waters of fame and fortune. But somewhere along the way, I crossed an invisible line. I would be remiss if I didn't admit, in the most brutally honest way imaginable, that the allure seduced me for a season. I became entranced by the glamour of it all—the cars, the watches, the champagne chilled on call, and the mirrored rooms filled with nothing but smoke and gold.

It's strange how easily you can drown in opulence. How quickly you start to believe you were always meant for it. There was a time I began to lose track of the line between performance and prophecy. Lines blurred. The tarot stopped speaking to me—or maybe I just stopped listening. But the calls didn't stop, and neither did I.

Sometimes, late at night when the parties were over and the quiet was too loud, I'd hear Stevie Nicks in my head singing:

"Well I never thought I'd make it here in Hollywood. I never thought I'd ever want to stay. What I seem to touch these days has turned to gold. What I seem to want, well you know I'll find a way."

My enchantment had been replaced with disenchantment. My visions, with disillusion. I made it in Hollywood, yeah. But I wondered sometimes if I'd ever really arrived.

To explain my mindset as best I can: I had given my entire life to the things of the spirit world. For as long as I could remember, it had been the voice of the unseen guiding my every move, every thought, every decision. But I craved carnality. Raw, unbridled, pure, unadulterated carnality. The spiritual, for me, began to seem far less appealing than the hedonism of the world around me. I partook of the fruits I had long considered *forbidden*. And I have to admit—I loved the taste.

I used to tell myself that I was merely playing the game. Hollywood has always been a theater of masks, and I convinced myself that mine just happened to be a little more mystical. I wore the most expensive suits, lavish Art Deco rings stacked like armor, and moved through rooms like a specter. Half confidant, half spectacle. People praised me in whispers. I felt invincible, really.

And the life of extravagant excess didn't feel excessive—until it collapsed on me.

I remember the moment it started to shift. When the glitter began to peel, and I was left staring at my own reflection under the harsh white light of morning. It wasn't in a dramatic fall or some great scandal—not at first. No headlines, no lawsuits. Just a slow sort of erosion. Friends who stopped calling. Clients who moved on to fresher faces with newer tricks. My name dropped off the party lists. Invitations dried up like the roses on my altar.

That was when I realized I'd attempted to build my empire on soft sand. I'd sold magic like perfume—fleeting, fragrant, and ultimately forgettable. And worse, I'd begun to believe I was the persona I had created. That the velvet couches, the imported incense, the endless champagne flutes had actually meant something. But the spirits never stopped coming. Their voices, once distinct, had become mere whispers within my own crowded mind.

I can't say I regret it entirely. In fact, to be quite honest, I do feel I needed it. Those seasons served some purpose, in some way. There's a strange kind of beauty in living a life so extreme it becomes its own kind of mythology. I did things most people only dream of. I walked among stars and shadows, whispered secrets into ears worth billions, and spent weekends in hotel suites with actresses so famous I still can't say their names without signing an NDA. But there was a hollowness that crept in after the last toast, when the moon set and the candles burned low. That's the part few seem to write about. That's the part Stevie was singing about: "Well, I never thought I'd make it here in Hollywood. I never thought I'd ever want to stay."

But I stayed. I stayed long enough to watch the shine wear off. Long enough to realize that the real trick isn't seeing the future —it's surviving it. I began to learn to keep things much quieter. The clothing became simpler. The readings, when I did them, became a little slower, a little softer. The people who came to me were never really looking for magic. They were looking for truth. And so was I. Maybe that's the greatest lesson success gave me. After all the glitter fades, you're left with whatever truth you didn't sell. And if you're lucky—if you're really lucky —you find yourself again in the ashes of what you once pretended to be. Truth has a way of becoming its own sort of reckoning.

They used to call me the "bad boy" of the psychic industry, half in jest, half in warning. I honestly don't know if it was the *Los Angeles Tribune* or *New York Today* who first coined the term in relation to me. It started as a joke in some glossy magazine profile, but the name stuck—and mostly because I leaned into it. I wasn't the serene, candlelit type you'd find in a wellness center with pastel chakra charts and herbal tea. I smoked clove cigarettes on the balconies of penthouses, wore black leather jackets over vintage silk, and never shied away from saying exactly what I saw, no matter how dark. I had a sharp tongue, a sharp jaw, and a reputation for taking clients that no one else would touch.

My circle was a revolving door of the infamous and the fallen. I liked them that way—scraped raw, bruised by the world. People who didn't flinch when you spoke about death, betrayal, or the price of fame. They came from every corner of society's underbelly: a former senator with a private plane and a public sex scandal, a fading rock legend who kept his heart in a pill bottle, a disgraced televangelist who swore I was a messenger from God, and a porn actress with eyes so tired they looked prophetic. I loved those people. I still do. They trusted me because I didn't judge them. I didn't want redemption. I wanted revelation. And they gave it to me—in pieces, in confessions, in crumpled stacks of cash and late-night phone calls when they thought the world was ending.

To the mainstream, I was dangerous. Unorthodox. Maybe even corrupt. They couldn't understand why I wasn't chasing approval, why I didn't try to become the face of some clean-cut metaphysical brand. I didn't want a book deal then. I didn't want to sell essential oils or teach weekend workshops on "manifesting abundance." I wanted to sit in the dark with the misfits and pull the truth out of their veins, saying, "Tell me your secrets, darling." And that's just what I did. And that's just what they did, too. There was something honest in their chaos, and it matched my own.

It wasn't all glamour, though. Some nights I'd find myself in the back rooms of strip clubs reading palms, or on balconies holding séance while the Pacific roared beneath us like it knew our secrets. I once read tarot for a notorious club owner while his driver watched me from the hallway, hand in his jacket. Another time, I got high with a former boy band heartthrob who cried for two hours because he saw his dead mother in every card I flipped.

I lived on the edge of respectability, and that suited me just fine. The spiritual world always liked to pretend it was above the grit of reality. But I knew better. Spirit doesn't discriminate. Ghosts haunt penthouses and trailer parks the same as anywhere else. Energy clings to broken people—not because they're weak, but because they're wide open and yearning for something more. And I was drawn to that openness. I was addicted to it, even. It gave me something real to hold onto in an industry that constantly rearranged its face.

Of course, there were consequences. Mainstream psychics whispered that I was dangerous, unethical, a sellout to the darkness. And the religious community I had once given everything to? To most in those circles, I had become the Devil incarnate. But I never sold anything except the truth as I saw it. It's just that most people didn't like what that looked like when it wasn't dressed in white linen and soft mood lighting.

And yet, even now, in the quiet years, I miss it sometimes. The heat of it all. The neon-lit chaos, the late nights. The clients who reeked of sin and stories. They were messy, beautiful, and so achingly human. We were a coven of the outcast, pulling prophecy from the wreckage. That's the version of Hollywood entertainment I belonged to—not the one on postcards, but the one that howls under the surface, desperate for meaning in the madness.

I've never claimed to be a saint. If anything, I was always more sinner—drawn to the fire rather than the light. People love to imagine spiritual awakening as this gentle unfolding, some serene ascent into higher realms, all soft voices and lotus petals. That's not how it was for me. That's not how it is for most people, if they're being honest. Real awakening? It's brutal. It rips you open. It drags your darkness into the daylight and dares you to look at it. It doesn't care if you're ready. It doesn't care if you're comfortable. It doesn't give a damn if you'd rather it come at a more convenient time.

Mine came in fragments. Through a near overdose I wasn't supposed to survive. In hotel rooms with blackout curtains and ashtrays full of someone else's regret. In moments of collapse, when the silence became unbearable and all the glitter I'd drowned myself in turned to sand. Enlightenment didn't come on a yoga mat or during a meditation retreat in the desert. It came at 3 a.m., when I was pacing barefoot on cold tile, sweating out the lies I'd told and the truths I'd buried. It came when I was alone, drunk, terrified, and face-to-face with the part of myself I'd always tried to dress up in mysticism and myth.

I remember one night, I was supposed to do a reading for a pop star who had just fired half her team and thought her mansion was haunted by her childhood. I had to reschedule because the truth was, I just couldn't face anyone. I'd looked in the mirror that morning and didn't recognize the man staring back. My eyes were sunken. My aura—if such a thing even still clung to me—felt gray and collapsing. I sat on the floor of my house, lights off, holding a deck of tarot cards like they were going to save me.

They didn't.

That was the beginning of something. Not healing, not exactly. Just the recognition that I was lost—and not in the romantic, poetic way. Truly, deeply lost.

And that's what most people don't want to hear. They want transcendence without the torment. They want to rise without ever going under. But you can't fake your way into grace. Not really. You have to wade through the muck. You have to let yourself shatter. That's the real initiation into this life, I think.

I didn't float toward enlightenment on a cloud of incense. I crawled toward it on bleeding hands, dragging the wreckage of my choices behind me. And every so-called awakening left me raw, confused, and more human than before. That's the part that never makes it onto the self-help shelves—that being spiritual doesn't mean being pure. It doesn't mean being "good." Sometimes it just means being willing to keep looking at yourself, even when you hate what you see.

So no, I wasn't some peaceful prophet delivering messages in a halo of white light. I was a man who made a home in the shadows and found glimpses of truth in strip clubs, detox centers, and the penthouses of the broken elite. I was dirty. Flawed. Addicted to chaos. And I told the truth—as much as I could. That's the closest thing to holy I ever managed.

My vices in those days were as expensive as they were unhealthy. I didn't just dip a toe into temptation; I dove in, headfirst, without checking the depth. It wasn't enough for me to brush shoulders with the elite. I wanted to live like them, burn like them, ruin myself like them. The drugs weren't always recreational, and the drinks weren't just celebratory. I told myself it was all part of the lifestyle. That it was all part of the "energy exchange"—some warped justification that let me believe I could destroy my body as long as I was still delivering truth to others.

But truth warped too, on many of those nights.

Word travels fast in the spiritual community, especially when your name is already a loaded one. I wasn't the sage on the mountain. No, I was the guy passed out in the VIP booth at 4 a.m., sunglasses on inside, whispering about karma with a whiskey in one hand and a televangelist's daughter in the other. I became a punchline, an enigma, and, at times, a scandal. I'd show up in the entertainment sections of magazines—not for some profound prediction or act of compassion, but because I'd been photographed stumbling out of a bar at sunrise, flanked by a rock star three divorces deep and a former prosperity preacher still wearing diamond rings paid for by the desperate tithes of his faithful followers.

The cameras loved me in the worst possible ways. Unshaven, eyes glassy, shirt half-open, muttering something incoherent to a photographer I thought was a client. There were pictures of me drinking from a bottle of wine on a balcony while someone recognizable from adult films knelt beside me, laughing into a crystal. Another one—my personal favorite disaster—had me falling—literally falling—down the steps of a private club, caught mid-collapse while a guitarist from a once-revered band tried to hold me up with one hand and finish his champagne with the other. That photo made the rounds for weeks. My publicist called it "unflattering." I called it "Tuesday."

There was no graceful way to live the way I lived. I wore my chaos like a signature scent. Even when I tried to disappear into a room, I stood out—too loud, too intoxicated, too infamous. The spiritual community didn't know what to do with me in those days. I was too visible to ignore and too volatile to embrace. They condemned me in newsletters, in pamphlets, and behind closed doors, wringing their hands over how I was "giving the movement a bad name." Meanwhile, half of them were clients once removed, hiding their appointments and clearing their browser histories after each session.

The truth is, I wasn't trying to be a role model. I never wanted to be anyone's guru. I was just trying to survive my own fire while convincing others I could see through theirs. But in Hollywood, even survival gets twisted into performance. I played the bad-boy psychic like it was a role written just for me. And the worst part? I was good at it. Too good. So good, I started to believe the act was all I had. And maybe, for a while, it was.

With time—and age—I started to understand what none of the flashy parties, several-thousand-dollar readings, or celebrity friendships could teach me in the moment: you can't take any of it with you. The cars, the watches, the designer everything—it all fades. The hotel suites start to feel the same. The taste of expensive wine dulls. The endless parade of "connections" blurs into a long, lonely echo of people who wanted something but never stayed. I used to think I was building something permanent, something untouchable. But everything I thought I owned was on loan—from luck, from fame, from timing.

Money is fast. It doesn't like to linger. It comes in waves, crashing hard, then receding without notice. One minute I was booked six months out and charging enough for a single session to pay someone's mortgage for a year. Next, someone who once valued my insight stopped returning my calls. The universe has a way of humbling you when your ego's gotten too comfortable. I learned that lesson more than once. Fortunes can be quickly made—and just as quickly lost—only to be made again.

And success? It's not a foundation. It's a gust of wind. I chased it like a drug, thinking if I caught enough of it, I could finally breathe. But it never lasted. Not really. Not in any way that mattered. It gave me access, sure, but never peace. I confused being in demand with being valued, and when the phones stopped ringing and the invitations dried up, I had to sit with the silence. I had to look around and realize I had built my entire identity on applause and adrenaline.

That's the thing about getting older, though. You start to see through the glitter. You begin to notice what's missing instead of what's shining. The money didn't save me. The fame didn't fill the void. And all the clout in the world couldn't buy me back the time I spent chasing things I couldn't keep. There's an emptiness that comes after you've had it all and realized none of it kept you whole. It's not a dramatic fall. It's more like a quiet fading—a slow realization that the thing you built your life around can't hold you when everything else falls apart.

I don't resent the life I lived. I don't even mourn it. It had its moments of beauty, of madness, of transcendence. But now, as I look back from a quieter, hopefully humbler place, I understand the truth in that old adage—you can't take it with you. And more importantly, you probably wouldn't want to.

Somewhere along the way, the word "Babylon" started getting thrown around in hushed tones—first as a joke, then as a quiet admission, and finally as a kind of code. Babylon meant Hollywood, sure, but not the Hollywood on billboards or walking tours. It meant the underbelly and all those unspoken layers beneath the glitter: the back rooms, the endless parties, the velvet-draped dens where secrets were traded like currency. Babylon was characterized by excess and indulgence, involving elements such as sex, power, drugs, ambition, and illusion. It evolved from being merely a city into a broader concept—a state of mind that people either moved beyond or became deeply entangled in.

And I'll admit it: I had the time of my life in Babylon. There was a stretch of years—more than I care to name—when I fully leaned into it. The hedonism, the chaos, the freedom from rules. I let go of every ounce of shame and stepped into that dark glimmer with arms wide open. I danced until my feet were numb, talked in riddles under moonlight on rooftops, made love with strangers I felt I'd known in other lifetimes, and woke up in places I couldn't remember entering. There was something intoxicating about living with no restraint, no filters, and no endgame. Babylon gave me permission to be mythic and to blur the line between truth and fantasy until they became one and the same.

For a while, it worked. I wasn't just surviving in Babylon—I was thriving. My name carried weight in certain circles again. The kind that didn't care about your résumé, only your energy. I was the psychic who threw parties where actors cried in Jacuzzis and politicians confessed past lives between lines of coke. I wasn't just reading fortunes; I was writing my own, one wild night at a time.

But like any myth, Babylon extracts a cost. It seduces you into believing the fire won't burn you and that the rules don't apply in a place made entirely of illusions. And I went along with that fantasy for far too long. I thought I could stay in that golden chaos forever. I thought being needed, wanted, desired was the same thing as being grounded. But when the lights came up and the music faded, I started to see the cracks—in the people, in the places, and in myself.

Still, I don't deny it. I don't pretend I was dragged into that world kicking and screaming. I walked in with my eyes open. I embraced it. I let it shape me. And part of me will always love it for what it gave me—that taste of ecstasy, rebellion, and untethered freedom. Babylon, for all its madness, was a mirror. It showed me everything I was too afraid to face in the daylight. And even though I left it behind, it never really left me.

There's a strange nostalgia that comes with it now. I can look back and smile, even through the haze and the wreckage. I lived like few get to live. And while it may not have been sustainable, it was undeniably, spectacularly alive.

These days, I've mellowed. I don't wake up with strangers anymore or fall asleep with a bottle in my hand. My nights are quieter, my circles smaller, and the parties I attend now usually end before midnight. I drink tea instead of tequila. I light candles without an audience. I actually listen when people speak, rather than waiting for my turn to say something cryptic and dramatic. Age has a way of sanding down the sharp edges —even for someone like me, who used to wear his chaos like a badge of honor.

But even now, sitting in the stillness I used to run from, I can't bring myself to regret any of it. I had the time of my life. I mean that. Every wild, irresponsible, soul-bending moment—I lived it fully, and I loved it. Maybe more than I should have. But I've never believed life was meant to be neat and safe. I've always felt, deep in my bones, that we're going to be around for a very long time. Not just in this body, not just in this era, but over life-times—stretching through time like thread through fabric, showing up again and again in new forms, with new names, and with new lessons.

That belief—that we're eternal in ways we can't even begin to fathom—is what made the madness bearable. It gave me permission to screw up royally and still find meaning in the mess. Because this life? It's just one chapter in a much longer book. Maybe this was my chapter to burn things down, to test the limits, to taste every vice and walk every edge. Maybe in another life I'll be the ascetic monk or the mountain-dwelling mystic. But this time, I came to play. I came to feel everything— raw, unfiltered, and fully immersed.

In that season of my life, I owned it fully.

People talk a lot about "living without regrets," but most of them say it as a defense or a sort of justification. I say it as a surrender. I do have regrets—but I've made peace with them. I carry them with me not as baggage, but as bookmarks. Reminders of where I went too far, where I got lost, and where I mistook noise for purpose. They're part of my story. And my story isn't over yet—not by a long shot.

So yes, I've slowed down. But I haven't stopped. The fire's still there—just lower, more controlled. I still get flashes of that old energy, the Babylon thrill, when the moon's high, the right song plays, and I catch myself remembering how good it all felt. And I smile—not with regret, but with reverence. Because for better or worse, I lived a life that felt like more than just survival. It was hunger. It was beauty. It was chaos. It was real. And I know, in the long arc of our infinite becoming, that's exactly what I came here to do.

Looking back, what humbles me most isn't the chaos, or the fame, or even the crash—it's the patience. The almost unreasonable grace that the spirits and, perhaps more surprisingly, the people extended to me during my most ungraceful, unflattering seasons. I was a spectacle at times. A cautionary tale in expensive leather boots. There were nights I stood on stages, reeking of gin and arrogance, barely holding it together—and somehow, the audience still leaned in. Still listened. They gave me the benefit of the doubt long after I'd stopped giving it to myself.

And the spirits? God, the spirits were kind to me. That's not to say they didn't hold me accountable—because they did. In quiet ways, in gut-punch synchronicities, and in dreams that left me breathless and rattled. But they never turned their backs on me. Even in the dirtiest corners of my excess, they were there. Waiting. Whispering. Watching me stumble toward clarity with the patience of something that doesn't measure time the way we do. I'd like to think they understood—that they saw through the performance, the bravado, the need to escape the weight of my own sensitivity. They knew I was still listening, even when I was pretending not to.

And the people—my clients, my audiences, my followers and critics alike—they could've left. They could've dismissed me when the headlines got messy, or when I showed up in those photos looking wrecked and barely human. But they stayed. Maybe not all, but enough. Enough to keep the connection alive. Enough to remind me that, despite everything, there was still something worthwhile in what I was offering—even if I had to dig through a mountain of my own dysfunction to get to it.

I'm thankful for that patience in a way I can't fully articulate. It saved me. It gave me the space to evolve without demanding that I be polished or perfect. It let me unravel, fall apart, and still find my way back to something real. I think that's one of the great secrets of this work—and of life itself, really: that growth isn't linear, and grace doesn't always look the way we expect it to. Sometimes it shows up as someone staying in the room with you when you least deserve it. Sometimes it's just not being abandoned when you've made a mess of everything you touch.

I've learned a lot since those wild days. I've learned how to sit with myself without needing a distraction. I've learned how to listen more and speak less. And above all, I've learned that love —whether from spirit, stranger, or soul tribe—is most powerful when it's offered freely, without condition, in the ugliest, rawest moments of our lives. That kind of love is rare. That kind of love is holy. And I'm lucky. Because I got to feel it. I got to be held by it. Even when I didn't know how to ask for it.

I think that's the crux of it, really—the patience and the love. They're not things that can be bought, or forced, or even earned in the way we usually think about earning. It's not transactional. It's just given. In the messiness. In the imperfection. In the moments when you're at your lowest and most flawed. I had people who saw through all the bravado, all the theatrics, to the realness beneath. And they stuck around. Not because I was anointed or special, but because they recognized something familiar in me—the struggle, the yearning, the desperate search for something that made sense in a world that often didn't.

I think about how many people I've met over the years who were just like I was then—burning through their own Babylon, chasing highs, chasing experiences, chasing answers, all while ignoring the quiet voice inside that kept whispering for peace. How many of them, like me, were looking for meaning in the so-called wrong places, stumbling in darkness while pretending to have it all figured out? Maybe that's what binds us together, after all—the recognition that we're all, in some way, walking through this life blindfolded, doing our best to see.

And when I think about those days of hedonism, of spiraling, of living on the edge of what felt like everything, I don't just remember the chaos or the glory. I remember the grace that was given to me in those times—the moments when people believed in me more than I believed in myself. The spirits that stayed close, even when I treated them like props or distractions. That's what stands out now. Not the scandal, not the excess, not the pictures in magazines that painted me as something other than what I was, but the quiet, unseen hand that held me when I was most lost.

I've carried that with me into these quieter years. And though I may not live the same way anymore—though I don't indulge in the same excesses—I haven't abandoned that part of myself either. I've simply learned to balance it—to honor the wildness without letting it consume me. The recklessness is still there, somewhere deep inside, but it's tempered now with the wisdom of knowing that life is brief—too brief to burn out completely. I know now that I can be bold, but I can also be still. I can dive deep into the unknown, but I can also rest, trust, and let things unfold naturally.

As I reflect on all that came before, I realize it wasn't just the spirit world that was patient with me—it was the people around me, the ones who showed up even when I wasn't at my best. The ones who gave me space to grow, to mess up, and to find my way back. I'm grateful for that—grateful for every soul who believed in me when I wasn't sure if I believed in myself. It's a kind of love that transcends all the chaos, all the noise. And it's that love, I think, that will carry me through the rest of the story—whatever chapters come next.

Sometimes, in life, we just want to feel something—anything. We search for it in a thousand different ways, trying to fill a void we can't quite name. It's a hunger that's hard to explain. It's not about the material things, or the accolades, or even the approval of others. It's about the sensation of being alive—of knowing, in the deepest sense, that you exist, that you're here, in this moment, and that it matters.

For a long time, I chased that feeling through the highs and lows of excess—through the rush of new experiences and fleeting pleasures. I was looking for something to shake me awake, to break through the numbness I felt on the inside, to give me that spark of aliveness that felt real. I thought I could find it in the lights, in the applause, in the endless cycle of parties and late-night conversations with people who lived on the edge. And for a while, it worked. I felt something—exhilaration, joy, freedom—but it was always temporary. A flash, then it faded, leaving me with the same emptiness I was trying to escape.

The truth is, we all want to feel something because it's easier to live in the extremes than to sit with the quiet. The extremes numb the discomfort of being human. When you're caught in the whirlwind of pleasure or pain, the rush keeps you from having to confront the stillness—the space between the moments. But that's where the real feeling is, if you're brave enough to sit with it. The stillness is where you find yourself. It's where the truth rises from the depths, where you stop running and just breathe.

I see it in the people I meet now—the ones who come to me for readings or guidance. They're all searching for that something —some way to feel alive, to feel connected, to feel seen. We all are, whether we admit it or not. We just want to know that what we're doing matters—that who we are matters. Sometimes, we go to extremes to find that reassurance, to prove to ourselves that we're not invisible, that we're not alone.

But what I've come to understand, as I've gotten older and more introspective, is that the truest feelings come not from chasing the next high—not from the applause or the validation—but from being present with the quiet stillness. It's in the simple moments—the sunrise that makes you stop, the calm after the storm, the way the air feels in the morning before anyone else wakes up—that you truly feel your aliveness. It's not always loud or flashy, but it's real. And it's enough.

For a while, I didn't know that. I thought I had to be bigger, brighter, and more exciting to feel something worth feeling. But now I see that the most profound moments often happen in the spaces where we least expect them. Life doesn't always have to be an intense, breathless rush to prove you're living. Sometimes, just sitting quietly with yourself, breathing, and letting everything else fade away is the most honest feeling you can have.

And in that stillness, you realize that you were never really trying to fill a void. You were just trying to reconnect with the simple fact that you are here—and that, in itself, is enough.

When it comes to the doubters and skeptics, I've learned not to fight it. I no longer feel the need to prove myself or convince anyone that what I do is real, or that the truths I've discovered carry more weight than their own. I used to get caught up in those conversations—trying to defend my work, explain my process, or justify what I knew in my heart. But over time, I realized something fundamental: it's not my job to change anyone's mind or beliefs.

Everyone must find their own path. We all walk at our own pace, in our own time, and each of us must come to our understanding in our own way. Some people will need to question, to doubt, to challenge everything before they find the answers they're looking for. And that's okay. That's part of their journey. It's not mine to dictate, to rush, or to mold into something it's not.

For me, it's become about offering what I know and allowing people to take it or leave it. I don't need to convince them, and I don't need them to see things through my lens. What I do is about sharing—about opening space for others to have their own revelations, their own experiences. If they find resonance in what I offer, if it sparks something in them, then that's beautiful. If not, that's okay too. Each person is their own teacher, and no one should be pushed into a belief system or way of thinking that doesn't feel true to them.

I used to worry, especially in the beginning, about winning the approval of others—about being validated by those who doubted. I thought that if I could just explain it better, if I could just show them the truth the way I saw it, maybe they would come around. But the truth is, it doesn't work that way. People have to be ready to hear what you're offering. They have to be open to it in their own time. Trying to force a shift—pushing someone into a space they're not ready to enter—only creates resistance. It doesn't give them the room they need to find their own answers.

What I've come to accept—with a sense of peace and even gratitude—is that I don't need to win anyone over. The world is full of doubters, skeptics, and people who aren't ready to step into the unknown, and that's all right. They're not lost, they're not wrong, and they don't need fixing. They simply need their own time and space to discover what they need to discover. And if our paths cross along the way—if they come to me in a moment when they're ready to hear something different—then I'll be here, with open hands, ready to share.

But I'll never force it. I've learned that forcing something that isn't meant to be only leads to frustration and disappointment. Everyone has their own story to tell, their own lessons to learn. And all I can do is live mine authentically, with the hope that it might inspire someone, somewhere, to follow their own path in their own time.

In the end, I've come to see that belief—any belief—is a deeply personal thing. It's something that grows and evolves within each person, and it's not something that can be hurried or coerced. It's a plant that needs time, space, and the right conditions to sprout. And sometimes those conditions take years to cultivate, or they may come from unexpected places—like a quiet moment of reflection or a sudden, unexpected experience that shakes everything loose. The truth—whatever that may look like for each individual—reveals itself in layers. There's no universal schedule for when someone is ready to embrace it.

I've learned to trust that people will come to the truth they need when they're ready for it. Whether it's spiritual, philosophical, or emotional, we all have our unique timelines. And just because someone isn't where I am doesn't mean they're behind or lost. In fact, it often means they're on the right track. Their path is unfolding in the way it's meant to, and sometimes it's messier, more chaotic, or more uncertain than mine has been. But that's the beauty of it. That's the human experience in all its complexity and mystery.

As for me, I've stopped trying to convince anyone that my truth is their truth, or that they should follow the same path I walked. I know now that everyone's journey is different, and if I can offer something of value along the way—if my experiences can serve as a bridge for someone else to cross—then that's enough. If not, I'm at peace with that too. I no longer measure my worth by the number of people I convince or convert to my way of thinking.

Instead, I find meaning in the quieter, subtler things—in the moments of connection that don't require words, in the exchange of energy between kindred spirits who know, without needing to say it aloud, that they are in the right place at the right time. In the people who come to me when they're ready, and in the space I offer them to explore whatever it is they need to discover about themselves.

This shift—this letting go of the need to control how others experience their own spiritual journeys—has been one of the most liberating lessons of my life. It's given me a sense of freedom I didn't know I was missing—the freedom to just be and to offer what I can, without attachment to the outcome.

At the end of the day, all I can do is live my truth. I can be a reflection, a mirror for others, but I can't live their lives for them. I can't be the one to awaken them or push them into something they're not ready for. My job, as I see it now, is simply to be present, to hold space for others to have their own awakening when they're ready, and to remind them that wherever they are on their path, it's okay.

So, to the doubters and skeptics out there—wherever you are, and wherever your journey takes you—I don't need you to believe in my way or my work. You have your own truths to discover and your own path to walk. And I'll be here, quietly, waiting for the moment when we might cross paths again, when you're ready to hear whatever it is I might have to offer. Until then, I'll keep living my story, and you'll keep living yours. And that's enough. That's more than enough.

Even now, I'm still chasing certain pleasures, still trying to find the perfect Vesper martini recipe. It's become something of a personal quest, really—a little ritual I indulge in when I want to remember the good parts of those heady days without diving back into the excess. I've tried countless variations, tweaking the proportions of gin and vodka, testing the twist of lemon just the right way. I'm still on the hunt for the one that feels just like the first sip of something intoxicating and new—smooth, sharp, and just a little dangerous. It's a small thing, but it's a reminder of my old love for refinement, for the artistry of something well made. The search itself is satisfying, even if I haven't found perfection yet.

I still collect art, too—paintings, sculptures, little things that speak to me in ways words often can't. I've always had an eye for beauty, even when I was caught in the more chaotic moments of my life. I remember the way I used to walk through galleries late at night, just after the parties had died down, when the world was quieter and the art seemed to breathe with a life of its own. Those were the moments when I felt most grounded, when the art felt like the last tether to something authentic. It wasn't about impressing anyone or showing off my taste—it was about finding pieces that made me feel alive in ways I couldn't always articulate. And now, I still search for that same spark in the pieces I collect—something that moves me, something that reminds me of the beauty that exists in the messy, unpredictable parts of life.

But more than anything, I still enjoy myself. I've mellowed, sure, but I don't think I'll ever lose my love for the little pleasures—the small indulgences that remind me I'm human. I still find joy in a glass of wine shared with friends, in the sound of good music, or in a quiet evening spent curled up with a book. I've learned to enjoy without letting it consume me, without allowing those indulgences to destroy me the way they once did. There was a time when I thought I could only feel alive by drowning in excess—by pushing my limits in every possible way, by saying yes to every temptation. But now I know the difference between living fully and living recklessly. And I've come to appreciate that I don't have to live in extremes to feel the depth of life.

There's a balance now. The wildness is still there, simmering beneath the surface, but I've learned how to control it—how to channel it into moments that feel like the best kind of rebellion against the mundane. I don't need to destroy myself to enjoy life—I can savor it slowly, without rushing toward the edge. The trick, I suppose, is knowing when to step back, when to let go, and when to dive in. And in this stage of my life, I've learned the subtle art of doing just that. I'm no longer in a hurry to burn through everything, to consume it all. Now, I allow myself to simply experience it—whether it's a perfectly mixed martini or the joy of discovering a new piece of art that moves me. Life isn't about the extremes anymore. It's about the moments—the small things that add up to a whole that's more meaningful than I ever imagined when I was running wild.

So yes, I still enjoy the little luxuries. I still chase the perfect cocktail. I still collect beauty. And I still embrace the joy of living. But now I do it with the understanding that true enjoyment doesn't always come from excess or chaos. It comes from balance—and from finding the sweetness in the simplicity of what's right in front of me. And that, more than anything, feels like the kind of luxury I can hold on to.

Chapter 11

Haunted

I t was a cold, foggy evening when I received her call. The voice on the other end was soft, containing a subtle tremor of fear. I could sense the underlying strength in her voice, though. Her name was Margaret, and her husband, Thomas, had recently passed away. She'd reached out to me because, for weeks after his passing, she had been experiencing something she couldn't quite explain.

At night, in the stillness of her home, she was haunted by shadowy figures—tall, dark shapes that seemed to move with an unnatural grace through the rooms. Never fully seen but always felt, they lingered at the edges of her vision, darting in and out of the corners of her mind and leaving her feeling trapped in a place that was once her sanctuary with the love of her life. Desperate and unsure of where else to turn, Margaret contacted me for help.

I had worked in the Bridgewater Triangle before, so I knew the area well. For years, it had been a place of whispered rumors and more than a few unsettling tales—a region steeped in strange happenings, paranormal energy, and unexplained events. It's as if the land itself holds secrets: some ancient, some more recent, all tangled together like a knot that refuses to be unraveled.

The homes in this area often have their own stories, but something about Margaret's situation felt different. This wasn't just a haunting—it was personal. The connection between the spirits and the space felt deeply rooted in grief, and that made it even more intense.

When I arrived at Margaret's home, I felt it immediately. The energy in the house was heavy—oppressive, like the air was thick with something unresolved. The once-bright and welcoming rooms now felt shadowed, as if they were holding their breath. Margaret welcomed me inside with a tentative smile, offering me a cup of coffee, her eyes red from more than a few sleepless nights.

She led me through the house, recounting the strange occurrences—how she'd feel a cold brush of air, hear faint whispers, or see the unsettling flicker of movement in the corners of her vision. It was as though the house itself had become a stage for an ongoing nightmare, with the shadow figures as the ever-present actors.

I set to work immediately, walking through each room, speaking quietly to the space, feeling for any lingering traces of the otherworldly. I didn't need to see the shadows to know they were there. The energy was thick with sorrow and confusion, and it wasn't long before I realized these figures were not simply random spirits. They were tied to Thomas—to his life and to his passing. There was unfinished business. Something left unsaid and unresolved, and now it had manifested in these dark, shadowy forms.

They weren't malicious, but their presence was far from benign. They were the physical manifestation of grief—manifestations of a soul in limbo, unable to fully depart from this world without closure.

I sat with Margaret, guiding her through a process of communication, not just with her late husband but also with the energy that lingered in the house. I could feel Thomas's presence more clearly as we spoke. His messages were fragmented at first, like a puzzle with pieces scattered across the floor. But as we continued, the connection between us deepened. He was struggling, his soul not yet at peace, tethered by guilt and unfinished emotions that needed to be acknowledged.

The shadows, I realized, were his attempt to make his presence known—reaching out in the only way he knew how. But they weren't a threat; they were a cry for help.

Together, Margaret and I worked to release the energy that had been binding Thomas to the earth. I performed a clearing, walking through each room with a sense of reverence, calling upon the light to guide Thomas's spirit toward peace. Slowly, the oppressive weight in the house began to lift. The shadows, once so persistent, began to fade—their forms dissipating like mist in the morning sun.

When the process was complete, the change in Margaret's home was immediate. The air felt lighter and more open, as though the house itself had exhaled after holding its breath for too long. Margaret's face softened with relief, the tension in her shoulders easing for the first time in weeks.

It wasn't just the haunting that had lifted, but a burden she hadn't realized she was carrying. She had been trapped in a cycle of grief, unable to move forward, and in helping Thomas find peace, she had found a sense of closure as well.

Before I left, Margaret thanked me, her eyes filled with gratitude. But I knew the work we had done together wasn't just about clearing a house of spirits. It was about clearing the emotional and spiritual residue that had been left behind, allowing both the living and the dead to find their way toward healing.

As I stepped out into the foggy night, I couldn't help but feel that, in the Bridgewater Triangle, some stories are written into the land itself—stories that wait to be uncovered, understood, and released. And sometimes it takes a medium to help untangle the knots and let the spirits of the past rest in peace.

Hauntings, I've come to realize, are not just eerie occurrences or unsettling phenomena. They're stories—stories that have been left untold, suspended in the air like a heavy fog, waiting for someone to listen. Each one carries with it an unresolved narrative, an emotional echo that lingers in the spaces between the living and the dead. These spirits, these shadows—they're not malevolent entities seeking to torment. Instead, they're the manifestations of something deeper: cries for attention, for recognition, and for closure. They are stories trapped in a state of unrest, often buried beneath layers of grief, regret, or unfinished business. And like any good story, they yearn to be heard, understood, and ultimately allowed to unfold.

I've encountered countless hauntings over the years—each one unique, yet all woven from the same thread of unspoken words. In some cases, it's the unresolved trauma of a life cut short, like the sudden death of someone who wasn't ready to leave. In others, it's a lingering attachment to a place or a person, a soul unable to let go because it feels that something has been left behind. These entities—whether they take the form of shadow figures, disembodied voices, or fleeting glimpses in the corner of one's eye—aren't really intruders in the traditional sense.

They're simply spirits trying to tell their story, but their voices are muted by the very circumstances that bind them to this world.

I've often thought about what it means to be a medium in these situations. I'm not just a messenger; I'm an interpreter. A translator of sorts, trying to make sense of the fragmented pieces of a narrative that has been silenced by death or unresolved emotion. When I walk into a home, I don't just see dark shapes or hear whispers in the night—I feel the presence of the story that's waiting to be told. The shadows are the remnants of lives that still have meaning—of individuals who once had hopes, fears, loves, and regrets. People whose stories never had the chance to reach their conclusion. These people still matter, even in death. And in this way, hauntings are not so much a disruption as they are an invitation.

This is what I've come to understand: a haunting is an invitation to listen. To bear witness to a life that was lived, carefully acknowledging the emotions that are still hanging in the air long after the person has gone. Whether it's a home, a piece of land, or even a specific object, everything has its own story. And sometimes, those stories need help being told. When they finally are—when the spirits are acknowledged and their stories heard—the haunting ceases to be something to fear. It becomes a process of release. Of transformation. The stories can be allowed to finish, and the spirits can find peace, leaving behind only the faintest trace of their presence, like the last whisper of a dream fading with the dawn.

I've seen it time and time again, really. Once the story is told, the atmosphere in the space changes. The heaviness lifts. The shadows dissipate. And the house, once filled with a sense of dread or uncertainty, becomes just a house again—a place for the living to carry on their own stories. The spirits no longer need to hang around in the shadows because they've found a way to move on, to complete their own narrative arc. It's not about banishing them; it's about understanding them—helping them finish what was started.

Of course, not every haunting is as straightforward as Margaret's. Some are more complex, tangled in layers of history, of multiple lives and events that intertwine in ways that aren't always immediately clear. But that doesn't mean they can't be resolved. It simply means that sometimes, the story takes longer to uncover, and the energy requires more time and care to shift. But in the end, it's always the same: a story waiting to be told, a voice that has been silenced for too long, and a space that needs to be heard, understood, and healed.

As I walked away from Margaret's house that night, the fog still hanging thick in the air, I couldn't help but think about how many other stories were out there, waiting for someone to listen. Waiting for someone to help them find closure. The Bridgewater Triangle, with its rich history and mysterious energy, is a place teeming with untold narratives. But it isn't just there—it's everywhere. Every home, every street, every place that holds memories is a vessel for these stories. And as a medium, I'm honored to be someone who can help bring them to light, allowing them to rest, allowing the living to move forward, and allowing the dead to find peace.

Hauntings are not curses. They are invitations to listen—invocations to hear the echoes of lives that came before us, to acknowledge the past, and to help it find its way home. They're stories waiting for the right moment to be told, and I'm always ready to help tell them.

I'm not a ghost hunter; I'm a medium. People often confuse the two, and I can completely understand why. We both deal with the spirit world, after all. But the truth is, the paths we walk are very different. Ghost hunters go looking for evidence—for the thrill of the investigation, sometimes, and at other times in an attempt to bring healing, too. That EVP or cold spot that confirms a presence is vital information, and I respect that deeply. Some of my closest friends are in the paranormal investigation community, and I've been with them on countless occasions, watching them set up night vision cameras, pore over audio files, and ask all the right questions in all the right ways. Their dedication and courage impress me every time.

But that's not my calling.

For me, the spirit world isn't something I chase or try to capture in data. It comes to me—often uninvited—sometimes in quiet moments, other times like a tidal wave. Being a medium is less about seeking and more about listening. I don't walk into a haunted house looking for signs. I sit still and open myself to what's already there—to the voices that are ready to speak and to the messages meant for the living. It's an emotional, intimate experience.

When I connect with a spirit, it's not about validation through gadgets or readings. It's about being a bridge between two worlds and helping someone find peace—whether it's the soul that's passed on or the person left behind. Why would I hunt something that is already hunting me?

Ghost hunting has never been a passion of mine, even though I've been around it most of my life. The adrenaline rush of chasing shadows and analyzing evidence just doesn't stir anything in me. That's not to diminish it in any way. In fact, quite the opposite—I admire the scientific approach many investigators take. But while they're wiring up equipment and monitoring EMF levels, I'm often sitting quietly nearby, tuning into the energy in the room, letting the emotions and impressions come through.

It's less dramatic and not always something you can prove. But it's real to me. And it's where I feel most useful—and most myself.

So no, I'm not a ghost hunter. I've never claimed to be. I'm a medium, and that role brings its own challenges and rewards. We're all trying to understand what lies beyond the veil, each in our own way. And while our methods may differ, our shared curiosity and respect for the unseen bind us together. I'm grateful for that—and for every soul, living or departed, that's trusted me to listen.

I have the utmost respect for anyone in the field who takes an interest in the paranormal community—whether they're investigators, historians, researchers, or sensitives of any kind—because I truly believe that no one finds their way into this world by accident. If you're drawn to the dead, it's because, in some way, they've already found you. That's something I've always felt to my core.

Whether you're capturing a voice on a recorder, documenting a residual haunting, or simply trying to understand what's happening in an old house with a long history, you've been called—just like I was called, though in a different way.

The spirit world doesn't always call us with clarity or ceremony. Sometimes it starts with a gut feeling, a moment you can't explain, or a pull toward a place you've never been but somehow feel deeply connected to. But when that passion lights up inside someone—to start seeking answers, to explore the shadows, and ask the hard questions—that's proof positive in my eyes that something beyond this world is whispering to them.

You can't fake that kind of drive. You don't stay up all night in freezing temperatures with a camera and a recorder, or drive hours to a remote, abandoned location just for the fun of it. That's devotion. That's purpose. That's a genuine calling.

Ghost hunting, often perceived by outsiders as mere thrill-seeking or theatrical, demands a significant degree of dedication, discipline, and sensitivity. The experts I am familiar with pursue it with earnestness rather than for entertainment purposes. They're trying to give a voice to the voiceless and shine a light into places where stories have been forgotten—or buried under fear and time.

They want to understand the unexplained. To offer clarity to those who are frightened or grieving, and sometimes to bring resolution to spirits still lingering in confusion or pain. That's sacred work, whether you approach it with a recorder in hand or with open psychic senses.

So, while I might not walk through dark hallways with an EMF detector or comb through hours of static-laced audio, I stand shoulder to shoulder with those who do. We've all been called in our own way. Some of us are meant to hear the voices; others are meant to capture them. Some interpret the emotions, while others seek the evidence. But at the heart of it, we're all answering the same summons from a realm that's often misunderstood—but never silent.

And for that reason, I honor every single person who shows up —heart open, willing to listen, and ready to help tell the stories of the dead.

I think that's something the outside world doesn't always understand about this work—how deeply emotional it can be. Whether you're a medium like me or an investigator chasing shadows with a camera, you're dealing with real people. Real lives. Real loss.

The spirits we encounter aren't props or party tricks; they were someone's child, someone's parent, someone's friend. They carry memories, regrets, and sometimes, unfinished business. And the people on this side of the veil—the living who are grieving, confused, or afraid—deserve the same level of respect and compassion.

When we do this work, we become caretakers of these connections. That's not something to take lightly.

Over the years, I've come to realize that there's no hierarchy in this field. Being a medium doesn't make me more "in tune" than someone who uses equipment to make contact. It's just a different language. Spirit speaks in many voices, and not everyone hears the same way.

Some hear through emotion, others through sound, and others through patterns or physical responses. But we're all trying to translate the same message: "We are still here, and we still matter."

And whether someone's sharing that through a psychic impression or through a Class A EVP, it's still an echo from beyond—and it still deserves reverence.

I've sat in the dark with investigators as they asked their questions into the silence, and I've watched how careful and respectful they are—not just to the spirits, but to the space itself. That's what tells me they were called. You can't teach that kind of reverence; it's something that settles into your bones when you realize you're not just in a location—you're in someone's story. And when I see investigators pause, get quiet, and feel the energy shift in a room, I know they're experiencing the same awe and responsibility I feel when a spirit reaches out to me. We're on parallel paths, and both are valid.

Sometimes I wish more people understood that the paranormal community isn't just about ghosts and haunted houses. At its core, it's about remembrance. It's about storytelling. It's about healing. The dead don't always come back for vengeance or to scare us; they come back to be seen, to be heard, and to be understood. And whether you're sitting in a séance circle with me or reviewing hours of video footage with your favorite ghost hunter, if you're doing it with care and purpose, then you've accepted the role of storyteller for those who no longer have a voice of their own.

That's why I feel so deeply connected to this community, even though I'm not out investigating. I feel like we're all part of the same tapestry—each thread woven with the intent to make sense of what lies beyond this life. And no matter how we came to it—through grief, curiosity, a strange childhood experience, or a dream we couldn't shake—we're all here because the spirit world saw something in us and called us forward. That calling is not always easy. It can be heavy, confusing, even isolating at times. But it's also beautiful. It's humbling. And for those of us who answer it, in whatever form it takes, it becomes part of who we are. We carry their stories so they're never forgotten. And to me, that's sacred work—no matter how you do it.

When I've had the honor of being asked to join a paranormal team on an investigation, stepping in as a medium, I've always felt a quiet sense of reverence. Not just for the spirits present, but for the people around me—the investigators who are giving their time, their energy, and a piece of themselves to this process. It's not something I ever take lightly. While my role might be to tap into what can't be seen, to feel what lingers in the air and interpret the emotions that rise within a space, I know I'm only one part of a larger effort. And there's something incredibly beautiful about watching all the elements come together—the equipment, the research, the interviews, the audio clips, the personal impressions—all forming a complete picture. There's a kind of magic in the way it unfolds, really. How each person brings their own skill set to the table, each tool offering a different way to connect and to understand. It reminds me that no one can do this work alone, and that Spirit often chooses to reveal itself in layers, to multiple people, each receiving a different piece of the puzzle.

It's in the aftermath of these investigations, when everything is being pieced together—EVPs cleaned up, video reviewed, findings documented—that I find the most profound moments. That's where the heart of the work lies. Not in the thrill of hearing a knock or a whisper in real time, but in the reflection that follows. It's the same power I feel when walking onto a stage. When the dust settles, what remains is a story. A story that someone, somewhere, was desperate for the living to hear. Maybe it's a message to a family. Maybe it's validation for a tragedy long forgotten. Maybe it's simply a cry not to be erased from memory. Whatever the message, it's almost always rooted in the same universal human need: to be remembered, to be acknowledged, and to be understood. And when I see a team take all that raw experience—the fear, the curiosity, the evidence—and craft it into something coherent and respectful, I'm always moved. Because it's more than just paranormal investigation at that point. It becomes storytelling. It becomes advocacy for the dead.

Every finished case, every compiled report, every episode or write-up or presentation carries with it the weight of someone's experience beyond the grave. And when done with care, with integrity, and with heart, it gives that spirit a place in history again. It allows the living to feel connected to what was once invisible. That's a gift—not just for the spirit, but for the community, the family, and the future. So, while I may not be a ghost hunter, when I have the chance to work alongside those who are, and to witness their process unfold, I feel nothing but gratitude and admiration. Because I know that at the core of it all is a shared mission: to listen, to witness, and to give voice to the silent echoes that still linger in the spaces we call haunted. And what could be more sacred than that?

Over the years, I've also had the unique opportunity to serve as a consultant and advisor to various production teams and heads of networks in the creation of paranormal programming. It's a role I never imagined for myself when I first stepped into this strange and beautiful world of spirit communication, but it's one I've grown to deeply appreciate. Working behind the scenes in television helped give me a new perspective—not only on how the paranormal is presented to the public, but on how carefully and thoughtfully these programs can be shaped when the right people are involved. Because of my work in the psychic entertainment industry and my experience as a medium, I've been invited into countless creative conversations where my insights have helped shape narratives, refine investigations, and ensure that what makes it to the screen still honors the very real spiritual energy at the heart of it all.

There's a delicate balance between entertainment and authenticity. Paranormal television reaches millions of people, many of whom are experiencing unexplained things in their own lives, quietly, without any support or guidance. So, to me, the stories we tell and the way we tell them matter. I've consulted on episodes where I've helped define the tone, advised on how to ethically depict sensitive spiritual moments, and even helped teams understand how a spirit might communicate through a medium versus a piece of equipment. It's always been important to me that the finished product doesn't just sensationalize the paranormal, but that it also educates and uplifts the mystery with at least some degree of reverence. I've been fortunate to see some of my ideas come to life on screen—whether in the way a séance is presented, the structure of a spirit-led investigation, or how a psychic's role is integrated into the overall arc of a series.

To know that those contributions have found their way into some of the most widely recognized paranormal programs today is something I hold with quiet pride. It's not about credit or recognition; it's about knowing that a little more truth—and hopefully a little more heart—made it into the final cut. That somewhere, someone watching felt seen, or validated, or maybe even comforted because of the way the story was told. That's why I do it. Because I believe the paranormal isn't just spooky entertainment. It raises deeper questions about life, death, and enduring connections. If I can facilitate that understanding through television, then I've fulfilled my role effectively.

Whenever I was brought in to serve behind the scenes as a consultant—whether it was on a single episode or during the development of an entire series—I always preferred, and in most cases specifically asked, to remain uncredited in the final product. That's not out of modesty, and it's certainly not because I don't care about the work. On the contrary, I care about it deeply. But for me, the spotlight should never be on the consultant or the medium—or even the production team, really. The focus, always, should be on the stories themselves—on the families affected, the locations steeped in history, and most of all, the spirits reaching across the veil in the hope of being heard. When the credits roll, I want viewers to be thinking about them, not me.

I've always believed that the most powerful paranormal storytelling happens when the ego steps out of the way—when the work becomes about holding space for those who no longer have a voice and honoring the living, who are often carrying confusion, grief, or fear. If I've done my job well as a consultant, you'll never really know I was there. But you'll feel something resonate more clearly in the episode: a question asked with a little more compassion, a moment of silence held a few seconds longer, a decision made not to exploit a family's pain for the sake of drama. Those are the quiet fingerprints I hope to leave behind.

Remaining uncredited keeps me grounded in why I was called to this work in the first place. It keeps the focus where it belongs—on healing, on remembrance, and on truth. I didn't step into this field to build a brand or chase recognition. I stepped into it because spirits called me, and because I felt the ache of stories left untold and souls left unheard. Every time I lend my voice to a production from behind the scenes, it's with the intent to help tell those stories with at least some sense of integrity. And if doing that means stepping out of the frame entirely, then that's exactly where I belong—quietly behind the curtain, listening, guiding, and making sure the ones who should be seen and heard are given the space to do so.

Over the last twenty-five years, I've watched paranormal programming evolve in remarkable ways. It didn't happen overnight. It was a slow, steady shift shaped by the merging of entertainment, technology, and a growing public curiosity about what lies beyond. But part of that change, without a doubt, can be traced back even further—to the psychic boom of the early '90s. Back then, late-night TV was flooded with infomercials featuring psychic hotlines—neon-lit ads with mysterious music and charismatic readers with names like Miss Cleo or "Madame" something-or-other, promising answers to life's biggest questions for just a few dollars a minute. As gimmicky as it may seem now—and as problematic as some of it may have ended up being—that era cracked some-thing open in the collective consciousness. It gave people permission, perhaps for the first time in a very public and mass-consumed way, to admit that they were curious about the unseen. Suddenly, it wasn't as taboo to consult a psychic or admit that you believed in ghosts. Even if those hotlines didn't always offer the depth of true spiritual connection, they laid the groundwork for a broader cultural acceptance of psychic work.

And that laid the foundation for what would come next: a wave of paranormal television that moved beyond the carnival atmosphere of infomercials and into something more personal and immersive. Shows about haunted houses, spirit investigations, and psychic mediums became mainstream—and not just on niche networks. People who had quietly harbored their own unexplained experiences finally saw those experiences reflected back to them on screen. They saw ghost hunters enter spaces and take people's stories seriously. They saw mediums sitting with grieving families and delivering messages that brought tears, laughter, and closure. And slowly, something shifted. What had once been whispered about became dinner table conversation. The ghost stories passed down through families gained a new kind of legitimacy.

Of course, ghost hunting is nothing new. There have been investigators of the spirit world for centuries—scholars, mystics, Spiritualists, and even scientists more than a century ago, trying to prove the existence of life after death through séances and spirit photography. But now, we are in a unique cultural moment where the fascination with the paranormal has moved from the fringes to the mainstream. And I believe the psychic industry played a quiet but powerful role in that. While not all of its representations were accurate or honorable, it did spark the imagination of a generation. Now, thanks to a convergence of personal experience, media representation, and a collective yearning for connection, we're seeing more people than ever step into their curiosity. More people are visiting mediums, joining investigation teams, and openly discussing the possibility that death isn't the end of the story.

What's truly beautiful is that this cultural shift has inspired countless individuals to stop hiding their own spiritual experiences. They feel safer now—to consult with the dead, to seek meaning in the shadows, and to honor what they once feared. It's not just about chasing ghosts anymore; it's about understanding them. About listening. About healing the invisible threads that still bind the living and the dead.

And as someone who has walked alongside those spirits for decades—both in private readings and public work—I can say without hesitation that we are in a new era of spiritual engagement. One that's more open, more respectful, and more ready to hear the stories waiting just beyond the veil.

Whenever a young person approaches me at a convention— sometimes with a spark in their eye, a little nervous, sometimes bursting with excitement to share their first investigation or a strange experience they've had—I always take a moment to really listen. Because in that moment, I see myself. I remember what it felt like to be young and curious, feeling things I couldn't explain, drawn to spaces that gave me chills, sensing whispers in the dark before I even had the language to understand what they were.

I remember what it was like to feel both fascinated and afraid —eager to learn, but unsure if I'd be taken seriously. So when someone from the younger generation comes to me—whether they're an aspiring investigator, an intuitive still figuring it all out, or simply someone who had an experience they can't forget—I make it a point to encourage them. To let them know they're not imagining it, they're not alone, and most importantly, that they've been called.

I truly believe the spirit world chooses people in unique and deeply personal ways. It's not about age, experience, or credentials. It's not about how long you've been in the field, how many tools you own, or how many haunted places you've visited. It's about the openness of your heart, the sincerity of your intent, and the willingness to step into the unknown with respect.

The young people coming into this work today—whether through ghost hunting, psychic exploration, or a deep personal need to understand what lies beyond—have all been called, just as I was. Just as the generations before me were. They are part of this ever-evolving tapestry of seekers, each bringing something new and valuable to the conversation.

And what I always want to tell them is this: no matter your beliefs, your background, your upbringing, or your current understanding of the paranormal, the spirit world will meet you where you are. You don't have to fit a mold. You don't have to know all the answers. If you've felt something, seen something, or been drawn to this work with a pull you can't ignore, then you have something to offer. You belong in this space.

The paranormal community isn't meant to be an exclusive club; it's a gathering of people who've all heard the same quiet invitation. And if you've heard that call—even once—then you are already part of the work.

That's why I always try to make space for those conversations— at conventions, events, or even in passing. You never know what a single moment of encouragement can do for someone just starting to walk this path. So many of us begin with questions, with doubts, and with experiences that leave us more unsettled than enlightened. And it's easy—especially when you're young or just finding your footing in the paranormal world—to feel like you're not qualified enough or connected enough to have a seat at the table.

But the truth is: Spirit doesn't call the qualified; Spirit qualifies the called. If you've been drawn to this work, there's a reason. Spirit sees something in you. And that means you have something to offer the world—whether it's empathy, intuition, curiosity, or simply the willingness to listen where others won't.

What I love most about this younger generation stepping into the field is that they're not afraid to challenge old ways of thinking. They're asking deeper questions, blending science and spirituality in ways we never imagined twenty years ago. They're using technology—but also trusting their instincts. They're approaching investigations with sensitivity and inclusiveness, understanding that the dead, like the living, are diverse in culture, belief, and experience.

It gives me hope—not just for the future of the paranormal community, but for the spirits themselves, who finally have a wider range of voices ready to hear them.

The field is evolving, and that's a good thing—because the spirit world isn't static. It grows with us. It changes as we do. Every new generation brings a new language to communicate with the dead, and every person who chooses to engage with the unknown becomes a bridge—between past and present, between the seen and the unseen, and between what was and what still lingers.

That's why I always say: don't be afraid to step into your gift, even if it doesn't look like anyone else's. Whether you're a skeptic who's had an experience you can't shake, an empath who feels too much, or someone who simply wants to understand the energy of a place, you have a place here.

We need your voice. We need your perspective. The spirit world called you for a reason. Listen to that call. Honor it. Let it guide you into the kind of work that not only helps the dead be seen, but helps the living feel a little less alone. That's the heart of what we do. And no matter where or how you begin, you are part of something sacred.

The stories we tell in the paranormal community matter more than most people realize. Every EVP captured, every personal account shared, every investigation documented is more than just a strange event or eerie occurrence—it's a piece of a larger narrative. One that ties the living and the dead together in ways that are deeply human and profoundly moving.

When we do this work with care and intention, we're not just chasing shadows or trying to prove that ghosts exist. We are, in very real ways, bearing witness to the lives that came before us. And in doing so, we're allowing those lives to continue influencing the present. Because the truth is, the dead have something to say—not just about how they died, but about how they lived, what they valued, what they regretted, and what they still hold onto.

There is a belief that the deceased want the living to learn from their experiences. They want us to understand what truly matters and to pay attention to the things we often ignore in our day-to-day lives. I can't tell you how many times I've encountered spirits who are desperate to communicate—not just because they're trapped or unsettled, but because they have something to teach. Sometimes it's about forgiveness. Sometimes it's about love that went unspoken. Sometimes it's about acknowledging pain or injustice so it won't be repeated. The lessons vary, but the intent is often the same: to help the living grow, heal, and remember.

That's why our investigations matter. That's why telling these stories matters. We are helping to complete a conversation that didn't get to finish in life. We are allowing the past to speak into the present, and we're giving space for those who were forgotten or silenced to finally be heard.

The stories we uncover, even in the darkest or most tragic hauntings, carry threads of wisdom. They offer us perspective. They remind us of the fragility of life and the strength of legacy. And sometimes, they even help us course-correct—individually or collectively—by shining a light on what's been hidden or buried.

Whether we're capturing a voice in the static of a spirit box, feeling the energy shift in an old building, or receiving a message through mediumship that brings a family to tears, we're doing more than just exploring the unknown. We're participating in something ancient and sacred: the act of listening—to our ancestors, to our spiritual neighbors, to those who walked this earth before us.

And in that listening, we're reminded that the veil is not a wall at all; it's a doorway. One that the dead continue to walk through. Not to haunt us, but to help us. To guide us. To make sure their stories—and the lessons within them—are not lost to time.

Part Five

Beyond the Veil

Chapter 12

Philosophy of the Spirits

When I look back on my younger years, I realize how deeply ingrained my upbringing was in a traditional, conservative religious environment. My faith—the foundation of my world—became the lens through which I viewed everything. It wasn't just something I practiced or believed; it was the ultimate truth for everyone, as far as I was concerned. Or at least, that's what I had been told.

I remember feeling as though I had discovered the most precious gift in existence, and it became my mission—no, my duty—to share this gift with everyone I encountered. Evangelizing wasn't just a choice; it felt like an essential part of my purpose. I believed, wholeheartedly, that it was not only my right but my obligation to lead others to the same understanding of the world and to convert them to the faith I had embraced so fervently.

In my mind, the stakes were incredibly high. To me, the world was full of people wandering in the dark, oblivious to the salvation I had found, and it was my responsibility to shine a light on their ignorance. I spent hours memorizing Scripture, practicing how to approach conversations, and rehearsing the ideal ways to express my beliefs. There was a certain urgency to it all —a sense that every missed opportunity could mean the loss of someone's eternal soul. I wasn't just advocating for a set of practices or beliefs; I was advocating for what I believed was the path to eternal life. I often pictured myself as a sort of spiritual soldier, marching into the world with the sole purpose of expanding the reach of what I thought was divine truth.

At the time, this sense of mission felt both natural and righteous. I thought I was doing something noble—something that transcended the mundane concerns of daily life. Every person I met, no matter their background, seemed like a potential convert, someone who might one day see the light and join our fold. I wanted to save them. I wanted them to experience the same profound sense of purpose and peace that I had found in my faith. I couldn't fathom why anyone wouldn't want that for themselves. It was, in my mind, the most selfless thing I could do.

Looking back, it was ego—and the height of folly.

I now realize that my perspective was rooted in a very narrow and, perhaps, naive understanding of the world. I believed that if only people were exposed to the "right" teachings, they would see the truth as clearly as I did. But what I failed to recognize was the incredible diversity of beliefs, experiences, and worldviews that people hold. I didn't understand then that the very essence of faith is personal and deeply connected to one's culture, history, and inner experiences. To impose my beliefs on others—to view them as "lost" simply because they didn't adhere to the same doctrines—was a fundamental misunderstanding of the very concept of faith itself.

In those years, my focus was on numbers—on building a following, on winning souls. It was about spreading a message, but not necessarily understanding the individuals I was trying to reach. The idea of "mission" became about the outcome—about conversion—rather than about engaging with others with respect, empathy, and an open heart. I didn't see the richness of the diversity around me, and I didn't yet grasp the value in listening to and learning from others, rather than trying to convert them.

As I've grown older and expanded my horizons, my views have shifted significantly. I no longer see it as my mission to change the beliefs of others. Instead, I've come to understand that true connection and understanding are built on respect, compassion, and mutual growth. Faith is no longer something I feel compelled to push on others, but something I hold with quiet conviction—hoping that those who seek to share in it will find their own path to it, just as I did.

It's a humbling realization, really—one that has shaped my journey and continues to do so. I still hold my beliefs close, but I've learned that the world is far richer than I could have imagined in those early days. And in embracing the diversity of thought and belief around me, I've found a more profound sense of peace than I ever thought possible in my younger, more zealous years.

Now, as I stand on the other side of that journey, I find myself walking a different path—one that feels deeply personal and entirely unique to my own experiences. I have come to embrace the philosophy of Spiritualism, a way of life that has given me a deeper understanding of myself and the world around me. Mediumship has become the very core of my beliefs, and in many ways, it is the only religion I truly know now. Unlike the rigid doctrines of my earlier faith, Spiritualism is fluid and grounded in the belief that there is more to existence than what we see in the physical world. It speaks to the interconnectedness of all beings, the continuity of life beyond death, and the communication with the spirit world that can guide us on our earthly journey. This philosophy, with its emphasis on personal experience and inner growth, has resonated with me in ways I never imagined possible. It has become the lens through which I now interpret the mysteries of existence.

But the simple truth is, I no longer feel the need to convince others to walk this path with me. Unlike my younger self, who believed it was my duty to evangelize and "save" others, I now understand that each person must find their own way and discover their own truth. The philosophy of Spiritualism is not something that can—or should—be imposed on others; it is a deeply individual journey. One that requires self-exploration, reflection, and, above all, personal experience. I've come to see that everyone's path is different, and the beauty of the world is found in that diversity of thought and belief.

When I reflect on my past attempts to change the minds of others, I now realize how misplaced that desire was. I cannot walk anyone else's spiritual journey for them, just as no one can walk mine. Spiritualism teaches me that we all have our own unique relationship with the Spirit, with the universe, and with our own inner truth. Mediumship, in its essence, is not about convincing others of a particular way of thinking but about offering a space where one can connect with the unseen and the unknown—where we can find our own answers to the great questions of life. The wisdom that the spirits offer is personal and intimate, and it's meant for those who seek it, not for those who are coerced into it. In this sense, Spiritualism is not a message of conversion but a message of demonstration.

In this shift, I've come to appreciate the concept of spiritual sovereignty—the idea that each person has the right to choose their own path. There is no "one-size-fits-all" when it comes to matters of the spirit world. I no longer feel the pressure to preach or to convince others of my beliefs. Instead, I focus on living my truth—on embodying the principles of love, respect, and understanding that are at the heart of Spiritualism. I have found peace in knowing that my beliefs are mine to hold, and others have the same right to follow the paths that resonate with their own hearts and souls.

I no longer feel the need to have the answers for everyone or to impose my beliefs upon others. Instead, I'm content in the knowledge that each person's spiritual journey is sacred, and that it's their right to find the philosophy that speaks to them. Spiritualism, for me, is not about converting others; it is about living authentically, connecting with the unseen realms, and offering love and light to the world in whatever way I can. For me, that is through the demonstration of mediumship. Everyone must find their own philosophy to live by, and I'm learning that in doing so, we can create a world that honors the diversity of thought and belief that exists within us all.

I often find myself sharing with people that it's entirely possible to be a follower of any religion—or even have no religion at all—and still consider oneself a Spiritualist. Spiritualism, though it can be embraced as a religion, is, at its core, much more than that. It's a philosophy—a way of approaching life, death, and everything in between. It's not confined to a set of rituals or dogmas but is instead a mindset and a perspective on the world that encourages us to live with openness, love, and understanding. It's simply a recognition that the material world is not the entirety of existence, and that there are unseen forces and spiritual truths that can guide and uplift us. What I love most about Spiritualism is its inclusivity. It doesn't demand that you abandon your current beliefs; instead, it invites you to integrate its teachings into your life in a way that feels authentic to you.

For me, this philosophy has been a beacon of hope. In the most trying moments of my life, it's helped me to see beyond the challenges of the present and recognize that there is always a possibility for growth, healing, and transformation. Spiritualism has taught me that life is far more than the physical world we navigate every day. It's about understanding that we are part of a greater whole—a vast universe that operates on principles of love, interconnectedness, and growth. It's reminded me that even in our darkest times, there is hope—not just for the individual, but for humanity as a collective. The philosophy of Spiritualism helps me to see that no matter the pain or hardship we face, there is always the potential for light to emerge. There is always a chance for us to heal, to evolve, and to move closer to understanding the true essence of who we are.

Through mediumship, I've come to witness the continued existence of those who have passed—not just in memory, but in a tangible sense, through the messages and guidance they offer from the spirit world. This has reinforced for me the idea that there is something greater than us at work in this world—a greater force of love and wisdom that transcends time and space. It is a philosophy that nurtures the belief in the continuation of the soul, in the ongoing journey of growth and learning. And for anyone who feels lost, or who struggles with grief, or who is uncertain about what comes after this life, Spiritualism offers a sense of comfort and possibility. It doesn't provide all the answers, but it offers a framework to live by—one that nurtures the belief that there is more to existence than what we can see, and that death is not the end, but a transition.

In my own life, the philosophy of Spiritualism has provided a foundation for resilience. It has helped me understand that the challenges I face are not simply random or punitive, but part of a larger, meaningful process of growth. When I struggle with uncertainty, I turn to the understanding that I'm never alone—that there are unseen forces, whether you call them spirits, guides, or simply the energy of the universe, that support me on my path. It has taught me that even in the most difficult moments, I am part of something much larger, and that there is always the potential for healing and redemption.

Perhaps most importantly, mediumship has given me the profound realization that there is always hope for us all. The struggles we face, the losses we endure, and the hardships that seem insurmountable are all part of the human experience. But they are not the end of the story. There is always the potential for a new chapter—for a new beginning. Whether it's through the guidance of loved ones who have passed, the wisdom of the universe, or simply through our own inner strength, Spiritualism reminds me that we're never truly alone, and that there is always the possibility for us to heal, to grow, and to find peace.

When I speak to others about Spiritualism at appearances, I don't seek to convince them to adopt my beliefs or follow my path. I simply share the philosophy that has given me so much hope and strength, and I encourage others to explore it for themselves—to see how it might resonate with their own experiences and how it might offer them comfort and guidance. Whether one subscribes to a specific religion or none at all, the core message of Spiritualism is universal: that there is a greater connection between us all, that there is hope for the future, and that we are all part of a larger spiritual journey. And in that, there is something truly beautiful.

One of the most significant developments in the history of Spiritualism occurred during the height of the movement in the nineteenth century, when the channeling of principles became central to the philosophy. In England, Spiritualism was in full bloom, and in 1871, the "Seven Principles of Spiritualism" were publicly outlined. These principles were channeled through mediums and encapsulated the core beliefs of the movement at that time. They emphasized the inherent divinity within all people, the ongoing existence of the spirit after death, the power of personal responsibility, and the importance of spiritual development. These principles became the foundation of Spiritualism in England and are still regarded as guiding tenets today. The Seven Principles speak of fundamental truths—truth, love, and understanding—as the cornerstones of living a life that is in harmony with spiritual law.

In the United States, the movement took a slightly different shape, though its essence remained rooted in the same universal themes. In the early twentieth century, the National Spiritualist Association of Churches (NSAC) formalized what is known as the "Nine Principles of Spiritualism." These nine principles were crafted to provide a clear and cohesive framework for practitioners of mediumship and churches across the United States, further clarifying the philosophy for a rapidly growing movement. Like the Seven Principles in England, the Nine Principles emphasized the continuing existence of the soul after death, the personal responsibility we each have for our spiritual development, and the interconnectedness of all life.

There are significant overlaps between the two sets of principles, but the American version also highlights the importance of mediums as conduits of spiritual communication, the role of healing through spiritual energies, and the belief that all individuals are capable of accessing spiritual wisdom. These principles are more than simply doctrines to be followed; they are guideposts that help individuals navigate the challenges of life while maintaining a connection to something greater than themselves—no matter their beliefs.

For me, these principles have offered a lens through which I can frame my own experiences and growth. As someone who struggled for years to put context to his psychic experiences, these principles have inspired me to understand that the messages have always served a purpose. They provide a framework for living with integrity, for honoring the sacredness of life, and for understanding that our time in this world is but one part of a much larger, ongoing journey.

As I reflect on my own path, I've come to realize that while these principles offer guidance, they are not set in stone. Just as Spiritualism, as a philosophy, is dynamic, so too is the personal application of its principles. Each individual must take them in, reflect on them, and adapt them in a way that fits their own understanding and experience. That, to me, is one of the greatest gifts of Spiritualism — its flexibility and openness to personal exploration.

It's easy to see how the principles of Spiritualism can be embraced by individuals of various religious backgrounds, or even by those with no religious affiliation at all. At their core, these principles emphasize universal truths: that we are all connected, that we are all responsible for our actions, and that we all have the capacity to grow and evolve. They speak to the deepest parts of our humanity, offering hope, comfort, and a sense of belonging in a world that can sometimes feel chaotic or uncertain. That's why I often encourage people to explore these ideas, whether or not they identify as Spiritualists. These principles offer a framework for living with purpose, compassion, and awareness, and they are as relevant today as they were more than a century ago.

I share all of this not to convince anyone to adopt a particular set of beliefs, but rather to invite contemplation and reflection. As I've walked my own path within the philosophy of Spiritualism, I've found that it provides a sense of hope when I need it most — a reminder that we are all part of a much larger, interconnected whole. Whether one embraces all of the principles or none at all, the underlying message of Spiritualism remains the same: that life is precious, that love is a powerful force, and that we are all capable of transformation. For me, it's not about adhering to a particular set of rules or dogmas — those days ended for me a long, long time ago. Instead, it's about finding a philosophy that resonates with the heart. One that can help guide us through life's struggles and offer a sense of peace and purpose. And in that, there is a powerful and universal truth: that no matter where we are in our lives, there is always room for growth, healing, and hope.

The principles of Spiritualism, at their core, are rooted in two foundational beliefs: the continuity of life and personal responsibility. These ideas are not just abstract concepts but are deeply interwoven into the philosophy of Spiritualism in a way that shapes how I strive to live my life today. For me, these principles have provided clarity and purpose, helping me navigate the complexities of existence with a deeper sense of understanding and connection to the world around me.

The belief in the continuity of life is one of the most powerful and transformative aspects. It offers reassurance that life doesn't end with the physical death of the body — that the soul, the essence of who we are, continues to exist beyond the confines of the material world. This belief was revolutionary for me when I first encountered it, especially coming from a background that taught me to fear death or view it as the final, insurmountable boundary. But mediumship has shown me that death is not an end, but rather a transition — a passage from one state of existence to another. Our souls are eternal, and while the body may die, the spirit lives on, continuing its journey in a realm that is often unseen but no less real. This knowledge has given me comfort in times of loss and a sense of peace in the face of grief. I no longer view death as something to be feared, but as part of the natural rhythm of life — a rhythm that connects us all in ways that transcend time and space.

This understanding of continuity also reshapes how I view life itself. If we are eternal beings, living multiple lifetimes or existing beyond the physical, it implies that every moment in this world carries significance. Each life is not merely a fleeting experience, but part of a larger, ongoing journey. The decisions we make, the actions we take, the relationships we form — all of these are meaningful because they are part of something far greater than the physical life we live today. We are part of an ongoing process of growth and learning, and every experience contributes to the evolution of the soul. This belief has given me a profound sense of meaning and purpose, even in the most mundane or challenging moments. It reminds me that I am never truly alone, and that the journey I am on is part of something much larger than I can fully comprehend.

But the belief in the continuity of life isn't just about what happens after death; it also shapes how I live now. Mediumship teaches that we are constantly evolving, constantly moving toward a higher state of being, and that our actions today have a ripple effect on our future experiences — both in this life and the next.

This brings me to the second cornerstone of mediumship: personal responsibility. If we embrace the idea that we are eternal, evolving souls, then we must take responsibility for our choices, our actions, and our thoughts. Spiritualism emphasizes that we are not victims of circumstance but active participants in our own lives and spiritual growth. Each decision we make, no matter how small, has consequences — not just for ourselves, but for those around us and for our broader spiritual journey.

For me, this idea of personal responsibility has been incredibly empowering. It means that I'm not simply reacting to the world around me, but that I have the ability to shape my own path—even in my messy moments. God knows I've had more than a few of those! I can choose how I respond to challenges, how I treat others, and how I continue to evolve spiritually. It places the power back in my hands, reminding me that I have the agency to create change—not only in my own life but in the world around me.

If I encounter hardship, I know that it is not something that has happened to me by chance, but something that I am being asked to face, to learn from, and to grow through. This philosophy encourages me to take responsibility for my emotional, mental, and spiritual state, and to recognize that I have the ability to make positive changes in my life at any given moment. It also teaches me that I'm not simply here to passively experience life but to actively participate in the unfolding of my own soul's evolution.

Personal responsibility, as taught in Spiritualism, also extends to how we treat others. It teaches that we are all interconnected, and that the energy we put into the world—whether it's love, kindness, or negativity—comes back to us in one form or another. It asks us to consider how our actions affect the collective, the world, and the greater good. Spiritualism challenges us to be accountable for the ways in which we engage with others, to act with integrity, and to approach life with an awareness of the impact we have on those around us. This is not a philosophy that encourages passivity or detachment; rather, it urges active participation in the healing of ourselves and of the world.

In many ways, these two principles—the continuity of life and personal responsibility—are intertwined. The continuity of life reminds me that I'm part of something greater, something eternal. It gives me a broader perspective on life's challenges and a deeper sense of compassion for the struggles of others, knowing that we're all part of this ongoing journey together. And personal responsibility ensures that I engage with that journey intentionally, with mindfulness and purpose. It encourages me to take ownership of my actions and their consequences, constantly seeking growth. Together, these principles form the foundation of Spiritualism in my life through my mediumship, guiding me in my day-to-day life and providing a framework through which I can navigate the complexities of existence with both humility and strength.

As I continue to walk this path, I find that these principles offer a clarity and direction that I never had before. They remind me that life is not simply about surviving but about thriving—about becoming the best version of myself and contributing to the greater good of all. And in doing so, I come to see that there's always hope, always the potential for transformation, and always the possibility for a deeper connection with the divine, the universe, and with each other. This, for me, is the true essence of mediumship: a philosophy that not only offers comfort and guidance but also empowers us to live with purpose, to take responsibility for our actions, and to embrace the eternal nature of the soul with open arms.

Another philosophy of Spiritualism that has deeply resonated with me over the years is the belief that, as souls, we are always growing, always evolving, and always changing—not just in this lifetime, but even after we pass from the physical world. This idea was initially difficult for me to fully grasp, especially coming from a background that often viewed the soul's journey as finite, with an ultimate end goal or a final destination. But in embracing my mediumship, I've come to understand that the journey of the soul is truly never-ending, and that growth is a continuous process that spans beyond the physical plane, extending into the spiritual realms.

Life in the physical world offers us countless opportunities to learn, to heal, and to evolve. But death, far from being an end to this journey, is merely a transition—a stepping stone into another phase of existence where growth continues. Just as we evolve while living in the material world, we do the same in the spiritual realms. The soul, it seems, never really "arrives" at a place of perfection or finality. Instead, it is always in motion, always learning, always expanding. This is a concept that I've come to cherish because it speaks to the infinite potential within each of us—the potential for growth that exists beyond the limitations of our physical bodies, beyond the constraints of this lifetime.

The idea that the soul continues to evolve after death brings with it a sense of comfort, especially when faced with the loss of loved ones. I no longer view death as a static moment, a place where everything stops, but rather as a continuation—a passage to a different phase of life where the soul continues to refine itself, learning lessons, making progress, and growing toward greater wisdom and understanding. I believe that the spirits of those who have passed are not frozen in time, nor do they exist in a state of stagnation. Instead, they are active participants in their own spiritual journey, continuing to evolve as they move through different planes of existence, learning and growing as they did when they were embodied in physical form.

In fact, one of the most profound lessons Spiritualism has taught me is that the journey of the soul is not linear. It's not confined to the boundaries of a single lifetime or even a single incarnation. The soul is timeless, and as such, it experiences growth in many different ways, across many different lives. Each lifetime, each experience, is an opportunity for the soul to refine itself, to face challenges, and to learn deeper truths. But even once we pass from this life, we are not simply "done" or complete. The soul continues to evolve in the afterlife as well. There is always more to learn, more to discover, and more to experience.

This has made me realize that we are never truly finished with our growth. There is always the opportunity for us to expand, to change, and to reach new levels of understanding—no matter where we are in the journey, whether in the physical world or beyond.

This belief in the ongoing evolution of the soul offers profound meaning to every experience we face, every challenge we encounter, and every success we achieve. It reminds me that no moment in life is wasted. Every challenge, every difficult period, is an opportunity for growth, learning, and transformation. It helps me approach life now with a sense of curiosity rather than resignation—a curiosity about what each experience can teach me and how it might serve as a stepping stone on my soul's journey. It also encourages me to release judgment to the best of my ability—not to view any part of my life or anyone else's as final or absolute. Instead, I'm learning to see everything as part of an ongoing process of becoming, evolving, and reaching toward a greater, more expansive state of being.

Even on the other side, those who have passed are still part of this great evolution. They continue to grow, to learn, and to evolve alongside us. The spirits I communicate with through mediumship are not static or finished with their growth. Instead, they are living proof that evolution continues after death. They continue to experience growth in the spiritual realms—guiding us, sharing wisdom, and assisting us as we navigate our own lives. In many ways, their presence—their messages, their guidance, their support—reflects the ongoing process of growth and evolution that Spiritualism teaches us to embrace.

In this way, through mediumship, I've come to understand that the soul's journey never really ends. There is no final destination and no real "end" to our spiritual development. We are always in motion, always evolving, and always moving toward greater understanding, wisdom, and connection. And this idea brings me a sense of peace and excitement. Peace, because it reminds me that there is always room for growth, even in moments of struggle. And excitement, because it means that no matter where we are in life, there is always something more to learn and something more to become. It is a philosophy that embraces the infinite potential of the soul—a philosophy that encourages us to never stop growing, to never stop evolving, and to always keep moving toward the light.

In the early days of Spiritualism, particularly during its peak in the late nineteenth and early twentieth centuries, there was a strong emphasis on the inclusion of various psychic phenomena as part of the practice and belief system. Some of the most remarkable and awe-inspiring manifestations—such as levitation, speaking in tongues, and prophecy—were not just accepted but were formally recognized in the bylaws of the National Spiritualist Association of Churches (NSAC). These phenomena were not considered fringe elements or mere curiosities but were regarded as legitimate and integral aspects of the Spiritualist movement. In fact, they became the cornerstone of much of the movement's public appeal and helped bring psychic phenomena into the mainstream, capturing the imaginations of both adherents and skeptics alike.

Levitation—the ability of a person or object to be lifted off the ground without any physical means of support—was one of the most dramatic phenomena associated with Spiritualism. This phenomenon was often witnessed during séances, where mediumistic abilities were at their peak. Objects, chairs, and even people were said to float in the air, defying the laws of gravity. This kind of physical manifestation was seen as a clear demonstration of the power of the spirit world and the ability of mediums to connect with unseen forces. It was a powerful expression of the belief that the material world could be influenced by spiritual forces, and it contributed to the public fascination with Spiritualism.

Similarly, apports—objects that seemingly materialized out of nowhere, often through the medium's efforts—also became a prominent part of Spiritualist practice. These objects, which could range from flowers to coins to larger items, were thought to be brought from the spirit world, appearing in the séance room as a form of evidence that the spirit world was real and accessible. The appearance of apports was often regarded as proof of the continuity of life and the possibility that the spirits of the departed could interact with the physical world in tangible ways. The inclusion of these phenomena in the bylaws of the NSAC solidified their place within the movement as legitimate and integral expressions of Spiritualist beliefs.

Speaking in tongues, or glossolalia, was another phenomenon that gained significant attention in the Spiritualist community. During spiritual gatherings, some individuals would enter a trance-like state and begin speaking in languages unknown to them. This was interpreted as a form of spiritual communication, where the medium or the person in the trance was believed to be channeling messages from spirits or even divine beings. It was often seen as a demonstration of the power of the spirit world to work through the human body in mysterious

273

ways, and it became a hallmark of Spiritualist practices. For many followers, speaking in tongues was a profound sign of spiritual connection and a manifestation of the divine that could not be easily explained by conventional logic.

Prophecy—the ability to foretell future events—was perhaps the most widely recognized and anticipated psychic phenomenon within the Spiritualist movement. Mediums who were capable of prophetic insight were highly revered, and their ability to communicate with spirits was often seen as a gift that allowed them to access knowledge of future events. Prophecy, like other psychic phenomena, was not only a source of spiritual inspiration but also a form of practical guidance. For followers of Spiritualism, prophecy offered hope and direction, providing reassurance that the future could be understood and navigated with the help of spirit guides and mediums. The presence of prophecy within the NSAC bylaws helped to cement its role as an essential feature of Spiritualist practice, emphasizing the belief that the spiritual realm was not only a source of wisdom but also a guide for the future.

These extraordinary phenomena were not just curiosities to be observed; they were integrated into the core belief system of Spiritualism, serving as tangible evidence of the power of the spirit world and the existence of psychic abilities. The inclusion of these phenomena in the bylaws of the National Spiritualist Association of Churches was a bold declaration that these experiences were real, meaningful, and deserving of respect. Recognizing such phenomena helped to legitimize Spiritualism in the eyes of the public, making it a movement that could not easily be dismissed or overlooked. It gave Spiritualism a sense of credibility it needed to compete with other religious and spiritual movements of the time, many of which were deeply rooted in traditional doctrines.

Moreover, the widespread acceptance and documentation of these phenomena helped to bring psychic phenomena into the mainstream in a way that had not been seen before. The scientific community, for example, began to take an interest in Spiritualism, with some psychologists, physicists, and parapsychologists conducting experiments to explore and measure the validity of these occurrences. While many of these scientists remained skeptical, the very fact that such experiments were being conducted signaled a shift in public perception. Psychic phenomena, once considered fringe or superstitious, were now being examined with a level of seriousness and curiosity that had been absent in earlier centuries.

This mainstreaming of psychic phenomena was not limited to academics or skeptics. It also reached popular culture, with mediums, clairvoyants, and psychics gaining widespread fame. The public's fascination with figures like Edgar Cayce, the "sleeping prophet," and the Fox Sisters, who were among the first to bring attention to Spiritualist practices in the United States, helped to popularize the movement. These individuals became celebrities, and their psychic abilities were treated with a mix of awe and skepticism—but their prominence ensured that Spiritualism, and the psychic phenomena associated with it, remained part of the cultural conversation. The inclusion of these phenomena in official guidelines, such as the bylaws of the NSAC, contributed to the movement's legitimacy, making it easier for people to openly explore and embrace these experiences without fear of ridicule.

In this way, the inclusion of psychic phenomena in the bylaws of the National Spiritualist Association of Churches helped to bridge the gap between the mystical and the mainstream. It validated the experiences of those who had encountered such phenomena and allowed Spiritualism to carve out a unique place in the spiritual and religious landscape of the time. These phenomena became symbols not only of the power of the spirit world but also of humanity's potential to tap into unseen forces, to transcend the limitations of the material world, and to access higher realms of knowledge. For many, they were proof that the world was far more complex and mysterious than it appeared, and that the spiritual realm was a real and powerful force that could guide and uplift those willing to open themselves to its influence.

As I continue to reflect on my journey, I find it important to encourage you, Darling, to explore your own beliefs and philosophies with an open heart and a curious mind. Spiritualism, for me, has been a path of profound growth, but I understand that your journey may look very different. What I've learned over the years is that each person must find their own way, their own truth, and their own philosophy for living. What works for me may not resonate with you in the same way —and that's okay. The beauty of life is that we all have the freedom to explore, to question, and to discover what brings us peace, purpose, and a sense of connection to something greater than ourselves. Whether you embrace a particular spiritual tradition, choose no religion at all, or find your path somewhere in between, it is your right to follow your own compass.

However, one thing I urge you to remember is to never be afraid of experiencing the spirit world. There is so much more to this universe than what we can see, touch, or measure. The spirit world—whether you choose to believe in it as a physical place or as a metaphor for the unseen forces that shape our lives—is a realm of mystery, wonder, and infinite possibility. It is easy to become skeptical or fearful when encountering things beyond our usual understanding. But I have found that it is precisely that sense of wonder—the childlike curiosity that invites us to look beyond the surface and ask questions—that makes the exploration of the spirit world such a rich and mean-ingful experience.

When I was younger, it was that sense of wonder that first drew me into the world of Spiritualism. I remember the excitement of my first encounters with mediums and my first experiences of what I believed were messages from the other side. I didn't know what to expect, and I certainly didn't have all the answers, but I approached everything with openness—a sense of awe at the possibility that there were dimensions to existence I had yet to understand. That childlike wonder, that willingness to accept the mysteries of life as something to be explored rather than feared, shaped my entire approach to spirituality. It wasn't about having all the answers or understanding everything—it was about being willing to experience, to feel, and to learn. It was about allowing myself to be open to the unknown, to trust that there was something greater at work, even if I couldn't always comprehend it.

This sense of wonder is something I try to carry with me every day. Whether I'm engaged in a spiritual practice, connecting with the spirit world, or simply living my daily life, I remind myself that there is always more to learn, always more to discover, and always more to experience. I encourage you to embrace that same sense of curiosity in your own journey. Approach the spirit world with reverence and openness, not with fear or trepidation. There is a beauty and a depth to be found in the unseen realms, and it is in that exploration that we can find profound insights, healing, and connection.

But as I mentioned before, it's important to find your own way. I don't wish to impose my beliefs on you, but rather to share the understanding that the spirit world—in whatever form it takes —is an integral part of our existence. Whether you encounter it through dreams, meditation, prayer, or through your own unique experiences, it is a realm that can offer great wisdom and guidance. And even if you never engage with it in the ways I have, I hope that you can still embrace the mystery of life with the same sense of wonder that first guided me all those years ago.

In the end, the most important thing is to approach life—and the spirit world—with a heart full of openness, curiosity, and reverence. The journey is yours to shape, and whatever path you choose to walk, remember that the universe is vast and full of wonder. Approach it with the same awe and excitement you felt as a child discovering something new for the very first time, and let that sense of wonder guide you toward the wisdom and truth that lie just beyond the horizon.

For me, mediumship is not just a practice or an occasional endeavor; it is my religion, my path, and my way of life. It has become as integral to who I am as any other belief or spiritual discipline I've ever known. Communing with the dead—connecting with spirits on the other side—is as natural to me now as prayer is to someone who prays daily, or as natural as breathing itself. Over the years, I've come to view it not as something extraordinary or outside the realm of normal human experience, but as a fundamental aspect of how I relate to the world around me. Just as people seek out prayer to connect with the divine or find moments of silence to reflect, I have found that engaging with the spirit world is a natural and deeply meaningful form of connection—one that has shaped my life in profound ways.

Mediumship is often viewed by many as a mysterious or even supernatural ability, but for me, it has become a part of my everyday spiritual practice. It isn't something that requires a grand ceremony or exceptional effort. It's simply a part of my daily existence—an ongoing conversation with those who have passed, an exchange of energy and insight that helps me navigate this world. Just as one might speak to a loved one in prayer, asking for guidance, comfort, or support, I find myself speaking to those who have crossed over, seeking their wisdom, their understanding, or simply their presence. The boundaries between the physical and spiritual worlds blur in those moments, and the connection feels as real and immediate as any earthly conversation.

For me, mediumship is a living, breathing dialogue. It isn't about performing rituals or invoking spirits in grandiose ways. It's about being open to receiving messages, insights, and comfort from those who have passed—just as I would listen for guidance from within my own soul or from a higher power. There's a simplicity to it that I have grown to cherish. It is a quiet knowing that the energy of those who once lived still persists—that their love, their wisdom, and their energy are not lost, but continue to exist in a form that is accessible to us, if only we know how to listen. When I connect with the spirit world, it doesn't feel like a dramatic event or a one-off occurrence. It feels like an ongoing relationship, where communication flows freely, where presence is felt, and where the connection between the living and the departed is as continuous and intimate as any earthly bond.

Ultimately, mediumship is my way of experiencing the sacred. It is not separate from life; it is woven into the very fabric of my existence. The dead, to me, are not a distant memory or something to be mourned only in sadness. They are present, they are near, and they continue to offer their love, their wisdom, and their support in ways that enrich my life. Just as prayer connects someone with their God or their higher self, mediumship connects me with the energies of the departed. And through this connection, I feel that my life has a deeper meaning and purpose. It is my religion, my practice, and the very air I breathe.

Chapter 13

The Spirits Remain

I t was Halloween weekend, 2022, and I was in the green room of a small, historic theater tucked somewhere in the winding veins of Boston. The kind of place where the walls seemed to breathe with stories and where the very air hummed with ghosts—some figurative and some, in my case, more literal. It was billed as my farewell performance and the final evening of my twenty-fifth anniversary tour. The closing night of years spent walking the tightrope between worlds, offering voices to the voiceless, the passed-on, and the lingering. *Cali-Post* and *New York Today* had described the tour as my "love letter" to fans who had been with me since the beginning.

I had a glass of wine in my hand—red, dry, a Cabernet, I'm sure. Though in that moment, the specifics mattered less than the warmth it spread through my chest. It was a chill night, the kind that curled its fingers around your bones and whispered of endings.

The room around me was dim—lamplit and quiet, save for the occasional muffled crackle of the audience settling in on the other side of the curtain. My tools were laid out on the table—

nothing theatrical, nothing that screamed showman. Just the things that had always helped me center: a palm stone, an old silver ring I never wore but always brought, and a single taper candle I never lit but liked to look at. Ritual, more than anything.

And then she was there. Adrianne.

She never made a sound when she came in. Never needed to. She simply appeared, the way a memory suddenly sharpens into focus—vivid and insistent. She leaned casually against the doorframe, arms folded, one knee cocked slightly in that way she always did when she wanted to look both bored and deeply amused. Her hair was pulled back tonight, coiled up to expose the sharp, elegant curve of her neck. She wore a fitted leather jacket over a low-cut blouse, and somehow she still made it look ethereal. Or maybe it was just that I knew what she was. Or rather, what she wasn't.

"Nice wine," she said, raising an eyebrow and stepping farther into the room, her heels clicking like punctuation marks against the hardwood floor. She asked, "Like what I'm wearing? I chose it for our big night." Her oversized sweater, typically covered in paint, had been replaced. And I did like it very much.

"You look beautiful," I whispered.

"A little early to toast your own funeral, don't you think?"

I laughed—dryly, nervously. "I thought you only showed up when I was already on stage."

Adrianne smiled. *That* smile. Coy, knowing, the corners of her lips lifting like she was in on a secret I hadn't earned yet. There was something both magnetic and maddening about it. She crossed the room slowly, perched herself on the edge of the old makeup counter, and tilted her head just enough to catch my eye.

"So," she said, voice low and teasing, "what are we doing after this?"

It hit me harder than I expected. The question. Not because of what it implied—but because it came from her. After all the years, all the séances, all the cold nights of candles flickering in half-empty halls and whispered names barely audible in the static, she had never asked something so... human.

I'd never wanted to make love to a ghost as much as I did in that moment, quite frankly. However, the last thing I needed in my already jaded life at the time was a torrid tryst with a non-corporeal entity.

But she had always been with me every step of the way. I looked at her. Really looked. And for a second, the wine and the nerves and the weight of the evening all melted away. It was just me and her. Me, the fading medium. Her, the guide I'd never quite understood but always trusted.

"I don't know," I said quietly. "Maybe... something normal. Maybe I'll disappear for a while. Be anonymous. Let someone else carry the torch."

She reached over and touched my hand, her fingers impossibly warm for someone who wasn't flesh and blood.

"You never could disappear," she said. "But you can try."

Then the stage manager knocked gently—a signal. Time.

I stood, drained the last of my glass, and met her eyes one last time before heading toward the door. She winked—damn her —and said, "I'll be watching."

And just like that, I stepped into the light, and into my ending.

There really are never any goodbyes. Not for the dead, and not for the living, either, really. We tell ourselves otherwise because the illusion helps us grieve and helps us draw a line in the sand and pretend it won't shift with the tide. But over the years, I've learned that nothing ends cleanly. Spirits linger. Conversations never truly finish. We leave rooms, we part ways, but threads stay connected, pulled taut through time, memory, and intense emotion.

And that night, standing in the wings with the lights spilling golden across the dust-flecked stage, I realized I didn't really believe in farewell performances any more than I believed in permanent silence from the dead.

I've often thought of my life like one of those old rock bands that keeps announcing a farewell tour, always swearing it's the last time, the final bow, the big curtain call—only to be back six months later, playing the same cities under a slightly different name. "Back for one more night," they'll say, and everyone chuckles, because no one really expected them to stay gone to begin with.

That's how it's been for me. I've walked away from this work more times than I can count. I've boxed up the crystals, the notebooks full of names and messages, even burned sage ceremonially, as if I could smoke out the parts of me that still craved the connection. I've said, *This is the last reading. This is the last session. I need to live among the living again.*

Yet, the phone rings. A message comes in. A dream unsettles me. And before long, I'm sitting across from someone with hollow eyes and a heavy heart, reaching again into that space between worlds.

So that night, as I prepared to walk out and tell a packed theater this was it—my final mediumship performance—I said it knowing, deep down, that I was probably lying to myself. Not out of malice. Just out of truth. Because once you've heard the voices of the dead, once you've held their stories like delicate glass in your hands, you don't forget how. And even when you try, they have a way of finding you again, reminding you that the work is never really done. That there's always someone else who needs a message, a sign, a glimpse of something greater.

And maybe that's what Adrianne meant, with her coy smile and that loaded question. *"What are we doing after this?"* Not just *Where are we going for drinks?* Not just *How do we celebrate the end?* But what happens after the end that isn't really the final ending at all?

What do we become when we think we've laid our old selves to rest, only to feel them stir again? Maybe that's the real question. Maybe that's the one I'm still trying to answer.

When I finally stepped onto that stage, it was like walking into the heartbeat of something ancient and intimate. The theater lights were warm and blinding, but I could feel the crowd out there—hundreds of souls pressed together in reverent silence, their anticipation almost physical.

There was something sacred about that moment, about standing at the edge of the known and the unknown, a foot in both worlds, and knowing this could be the last time I'd let myself be the bridge.

I took a breath, steady and deep, and let the quiet stretch for just a moment longer.

Then I spoke.

My voice, clear and measured, carried the way it always had when the message wasn't just mine.

That night, I gave the performance of my life—not in some dramatic, theatrical way, not with grand gestures or staged tricks. No, it was different. It was raw. Pure. The air seemed to crackle with presence, as though every spirit I'd ever channeled, every name I'd ever whispered through tears, had gathered in the rafters to witness this final act. The energy was thick, potent, almost heavy. It pressed against my chest, but not in a way that choked. It filled me.

For two full hours, I stood there and let the veil thin. I gave voices to the voiceless, handed messages to weeping strangers in the front row who clutched their hands to their mouths in stunned relief. I described husbands, mothers, children, war buddies, forgotten lovers. Details poured through me with startling precision—dates, phrases, inside jokes no one but the recipient could've known. It felt effortless, as if the years of doubt and discipline had finally burned away, leaving nothing but clarity and channel.

At one point, I caught sight of Adrianne again, standing just behind the curtain in the wing, her arms crossed, watching with that same half-smirk she always wore when she was proud of me but wouldn't say it out loud. It grounded me. Reminded me that I wasn't alone in this. That I'd never been. Even at my most exhausted, even in the quiet years when I thought I had turned away from it all, she had never left.

The audience cried that night. They laughed, too—real, full laughs when I passed along some of the more irreverent remarks from the dead, who, in my experience, never lost their sense of humor just because they'd crossed over. There was something healing in that room, something ancient and deeply human. A shared sense that, for just a little while, the world had gotten smaller, the distances shorter, and we had all touched something real.

And when it was done, when I finally stepped back and took my bow, the applause came not like a roar but like a wave—sweeping, long, heartfelt. I stood there for a moment, taking it in, my hand pressed to my chest. Not because I was proud in the way performers often are, but because I felt grateful. Grateful that I had said yes to this life. Grateful that I had listened, even when it terrified me. Grateful that, after all the years and all the spirits, I could still be surprised by the beauty of it all.

It may have been my farewell, but it didn't feel like an ending. Not really. More like an ellipsis at the end of a sentence. A breath before whatever comes next.

Though that night in Boston marked the end of what had been billed, somewhat dramatically, I'll admit, as my 25th Anniversary Farewell Tour, life had other plans. I'd envisioned that performance as a final punctuation mark. A full stop at the end of a long, intense, and often beautiful sentence. But the truth is, the moment I stepped off that stage and the applause faded into memory, the real work began anew. I had expected silence—peace, even. Instead, I was met with a flood. Messages, calls, invitations, quiet requests written in shaking hands. People came out of the woodwork: old clients who hadn't spoken to me in years, organizers from cities I hadn't visited since my earliest tours, and those who had only just discovered my work and were desperate to see me in person before the opportunity truly vanished. It was as if retiring—or at least pretending to—had cast some kind of spell. Suddenly, everyone wanted one last moment, one final message, one chance to bridge the space between loss and closure.

I found myself busier than ever. My calendar filled overnight with private sittings, charity events, radio interviews, and podcast invitations. I traveled less, yes—gone were the grueling weeks of hotel rooms and endless flights—but my days were full. People didn't care about the fanfare anymore. They weren't drawn to me for the spectacle of a theater show; they came for the connection, the stillness, and the honesty. And that suited me just fine. The work deepened, becoming more intimate and more rooted in compassion than performance. I spent afternoons sitting in sunlit parlors and quiet libraries, holding the hands of grieving parents, listening carefully for the soft voices of loved ones beyond the veil. It was slower work, quieter. But it was also more real.

In a strange way, announcing the end of my touring career gave me permission to evolve. To let go of the part of myself that always had to prove something—prove that I was genuine, that this connection was real, that I wasn't another showman with a trick up his sleeve. That hunger to be understood, to be taken seriously, softened. What remained was a devotion to the people, to the stories, to the healing. I still had Adrianne at my side, of course. Her presence became less of a guide and more of a companion then. Sometimes appearing only when I least expected her, other times sitting beside me during a session, watching with a tenderness that surprised even me.

And so, the tour ended. But the journey, as ever, continued. No farewell is ever final. We leave stages, yes, but we never really leave the calling. It's part of the agreement, I think, when you first open that door between worlds. You don't just become a messenger—you become a steward. And that responsibility never really lets you go.

It took stepping away—or at least saying I was stepping away—for me to finally understand the true weight of what I had been doing all those years. For so long, I was consumed by the rhythm of the work: the travel, the preparation, the performances, the emotional labor of channeling the dead and holding space for the living. I never really had time to stop and take in what it all meant beyond the immediate moment. But after that farewell night in Boston, as messages poured in— some handwritten, some emailed, some passed to me in quiet moments after small gatherings—I started to see it differently.

People were telling me stories—not just about the readings they'd received, but about how those moments had altered the course of their lives. A woman wrote to say that hearing her son's voice through me had kept her from ending her own life. A man shared how a message from his late father had given him the courage to forgive after decades of bitterness. Others spoke of relief, clarity, closure—of being able to sleep again, to laugh again, to live again.

And I had no idea. Truly, I didn't. I had always thought of myself as a facilitator, a hollow bone the message traveled through, someone who was simply doing a job he'd been called to. I never saw myself as a healer. Never let myself imagine that I might be needed. But hearing those stories, feeling the raw gratitude in people's voices and letters, forced me to finally let that truth in. The work had mattered. It had changed lives. Not because of me—not because of anything extraordinary I had done—but because of the connection. Because I'd been willing to stand in that mysterious in-between space, to listen without judgment, and to pass along what I could as honestly and clearly as possible.

To realize that you've been part of the most intimate, transformative moments of people's lives without even knowing it—it's humbling in a way that shakes you to your core. I remembered the tears, the trembling hands, the moments of laughter through grief, and finally understood them for what they were: sacred. These weren't performances. They were ceremonies. And I'd been invited into those ceremonies again and again, often without realizing the full depth of the honor. Looking back now, I carry that awareness with a kind of reverence. I see the past not as a blur of tours and bookings, but as a tapestry of human moments—raw, beautiful, unforgettable. I didn't just deliver messages. I bore witness to resilience, to love stretching beyond death, to people healing in real time. And for that, I am deeply, quietly honored.

There's a kind of stillness that settles in once you've come to terms with what your life has really meant to others. Not the noise of applause, not the fleeting attention of press or crowds, but the quiet, enduring impact of having been present when it counted. That stillness began to take root in me after Boston. It wasn't peace exactly—more like a hum, a grounding frequency that I hadn't been attuned to before. I started to carry the memories of those moments differently. Not like weight, but like warmth. I'd be standing in line for coffee or walking through the park on a crisp morning, and suddenly I'd remember the way a woman once clutched a photo to her chest and sobbed when I spoke her sister's name, or how a teenage boy looked up in shocked wonder when I repeated the pet name only his grandfather had used. Those moments began to live in me not as burdens, but as blessings—proof that I had spent my life doing something that mattered.

And maybe it took getting older, slowing down, to really see that. In my twenties and thirties, I was chasing the next booking, the next breakthrough, trying to prove to the world—and maybe to myself—that I wasn't a fraud, that I belonged here, doing this strange and sacred work. But in this new chapter, without the pressure of the tour schedule or the relentless need to produce, I finally had room to feel the legacy of it. I realized I had been invited into people's pain, their questions, their hopes—and I had met them there, in that delicate space, again and again. That's not something most people get to say about their life: that they were present for the moments that mattered most to others. That they helped someone see the light in the dark, even just for a breath of time.

It changed how I viewed myself. I no longer saw the past as a blur of stages and hotel keys, but as a long, continuous act of service. Yes, there were times I'd questioned it—times I wanted to walk away, times I felt hollow and burnt out. But the love always pulled me back. Not just the love from the spirits, but from the living. The people. The ones who waited patiently, who placed their trust in me with trembling hands and tear-bright eyes. I had the immense privilege of being part of those stories—of stepping into the quiet rooms of grief and offering —if nothing else—proof that they weren't alone.

And now, every time I'm invited to do just one more session, just one more private circle, I no longer think of it as a return to the stage. I think of it as a continuation of something timeless. Not a job, not a show, but a calling. And callings, I've learned, don't really end—they just shift form. The messages keep coming, the love keeps reaching across the divide, and I keep saying yes—not because I have to, but because I get to. And because, more than ever before, I understand just how sacred that *yes* truly is.

Even as I stepped away from the performance side of things, I never fully left the world I helped shape. I still serve, in many ways, as a spokesperson for the psychic and spiritual community—not out of some sense of obligation, but because I know how far we've come, and I remember how hard-won that progress was. When I first started doing this work publicly, the idea of a medium being taken seriously in mainstream media was almost laughable. We were caricatures, punchlines, late-night filler for skeptics to roll their eyes at. But some of us pushed back. We stood firm. We spoke clearly. We held our ground with dignity. I was one of them, and I'm proud of that.

Twenty-five years ago, I contributed my name, face, and voice to a subtle shift in public awareness. I helped design the branding for spiritual television specials, co-wrote language for ethical guidelines in professional associations, and consulted on everything from book covers to psychic hotline scripts. I didn't realize it then, but I was helping to build a foundation that others would one day stand on.

To this day, I still receive royalties from some of those early ventures—payments that arrive like ghostly echoes from the past. A percentage from a syndicated television appearance that still airs in late-night reruns overseas. A residual from the first training video I ever produced, which somehow found new life on online streaming platforms. A licensing agreement for a phrase I coined that wound up on mugs, journals, and affirmation decks. It's surreal, really. Things I created in a cramped studio with a ring light and a borrowed camera now circulate the globe, still carrying my fingerprint. I'm not getting rich off it —at least not anymore—but the checks are enough to remind me that the work mattered. That what we did had staying power.

More than that, I've become a kind of elder voice in this world —one of the few who's still around from that first wave of modern spiritual branding, when we were trying to walk the line between authenticity and accessibility, intuition and professionalism. People reach out now not just for readings, but for advice. Young mediums, podcast hosts, authors trying to find their footing. They want to know how to navigate this strange landscape without losing themselves. I tell them what I wish someone had told me at the start: stay honest, stay curious, and don't ever pretend you have all the answers. Because this work, at its core, isn't about certainty. It's about humility. It's about standing in mystery with open hands and a willing heart.

So no, I'm not on the stage anymore. But I'm still here. Still speaking. Still guiding where I can. And as long as there's a place for that voice—mine, or anyone's who speaks from a place of integrity—I'll keep using it. Not to be seen, not to stay relevant, but to ensure the path we cleared stays open for those who come next.

I never imagined that easing off the public stage would lead to being more in demand than ever, but that's exactly what happened. Though I no longer tour in the grand, theatrical way I once did, my days are filled—sometimes even more intensely than before. I still speak at conventions—quietly, without fanfare, often unlisted on the official programs, just a whispered name on a private schedule for those who know where to look. I never charge for those. These days, I prefer the smaller breakout rooms over keynote stages. The energy is more grounded, more real. I also still take personal clients in my private practice, often from referrals or long-standing connections. These sessions aren't flashy; they're intimate, sincere. People arrive with real needs, real longing, and I meet them there—as I always have, but now with a different kind of presence. A slower, steadier rhythm. Less urgency. More intention.

On rare occasions, I still teach. Spiritualism. Séance. The old ways. I do it quietly, with small groups—usually in person, sometimes over private Zoom calls with the screen candle-lit and soft music playing in the background. These classes are never advertised. I don't need to. Word travels. The people who are meant to find me, do. And when I teach, it's not just about mechanics anymore. It's about the soul of the work. The reverence. The silence between words. I remind my students that the dead don't come to entertain us—they come to remind us of who we are, and who we still could be.

Celebrities reach out now more than ever. Some come with genuine hearts and old wounds. Others come searching for peace or for answers they can't find in the spotlight. I meet them the same way I meet everyone else—no velvet ropes, no special treatment—just the deep human ache of wanting to know that death isn't the end. They confide in me, trust me, because they know I'm not here to exploit them or sell their grief. I've earned that trust over decades, and I hold it close. That kind of access, that kind of honesty—it's sacred.

And somehow, despite the fact that I swore I was retiring, I find myself busier than ever, moving through each day with a full calendar, a full heart, and a quiet, knowing smile.

Because now I finally understand: there really are no endings. We tell ourselves otherwise because it's comforting. Finality feels neat—it makes things manageable. But real life, true connection, never ends cleanly. Not with death, and not with career. I tried to close the curtain, but it blew open again with the first breeze. And maybe that's the point. Maybe this work was never meant to be something I stepped away from entirely. Maybe it was never mine to end.

I am part of a continuum, a thread that winds through generations of seekers and sensitives and soul-whisperers. I just happened to be loud enough, visible enough, to help bring it into the light of the modern day. And now, I move with it differently—not as a performer, not as a face on a billboard, but as a keeper of the flame. And as long as that flame burns, I'll be here—still listening, still guiding, still answering the call.

That's how you know it's a calling—when you no longer have to do it, but you still can't quite walk away. When the pressure eases, the applause dies down, the wealth exceeds all need, and the ego settles—yet the work still calls to you each morning. That's when you know it's something profound. It's not a job. It's not even a passion, not really. It's a thread woven through your soul, tugging at you in ways that defy logic.

There were days after that farewell tour when I could have just turned it all off—no more readings, no more interviews, no more being "on." I told myself I'd earned the right to rest, to retreat, to slip into a quieter life. But then someone would write to me—just a few heartfelt lines about a sister who died too young or a father taken suddenly—and I'd feel it again, that familiar pulse in my chest. That pull. And I knew: I had to say yes. Not because I owed it to anyone. Not out of habit. But because this is who I am.

It's not glamorous, this kind of calling. It doesn't let you disappear. It doesn't grant you clean endings or neat conclusions. It follows you. It wakes you up in the middle of the night with a whisper, or a name, or the scent of someone's grandmother's perfume. It waits patiently at the edge of your quiet moments. And when you turn toward it, it meets you with open arms—like it always has, like it always will.

I used to think that when you completed your purpose, you'd feel finished, satisfied, released. But now I understand—it's not about finishing. It's about becoming. Over and over again. Every reading, every message, every soul I sit with shapes me a little more. Softens me. Grounds me. Reminds me why I began this journey in the first place.

And the truth is, I wouldn't want it any other way. I'm not looking for an exit anymore. I'm not chasing a final curtain. I've made peace with the fact that I'll likely do this work, in some form, until the day I join the very souls I've spent my life listening to. That's the nature of a calling—it's not something you retire from. It's something you are.

Financially, I could have retired years ago. If I'm being honest, I had the means to walk away comfortably well before that 25th anniversary tour ever began. The early branding I helped create—those deals, the media appearances, the spiritual content that somehow took root in pop culture—left me with a steady stream of royalties and a name that still opens doors, even now. I could have disappeared into a quiet life somewhere by the ocean, built a home filled with books and silence, spent my days in the garden and my nights under the stars.

But the truth is, the work never really let me go. Not even when I tried. Not even when I thought I wanted it to. Because long ago—so long ago now that it feels like a dream within another life—I was marked. Branded by spirit. And that kind of mark, that kind of sacred claim, doesn't fade with time or comfort or success.

It didn't come with fire and trumpets. There was no dramatic lightning strike, no cinematic moment. It was quieter than that —deeper. It happened in the stillness, in the first undeniable knowing, in the trembling breath I took when I first realized someone was standing in the room who wasn't alive anymore.

And ever since then, I've belonged to something larger than myself. Not in a way that strips me of free will, but in a way that connects me to a responsibility I could never ignore.

The call of the dead is not like any other call. It doesn't come once and vanish—it echoes. It weaves through the fabric of your life. It becomes the beat behind your heartbeat, the silence between your thoughts. And when it calls—no matter how much money you have in the bank, or how many times you've said you're done—you answer. Because once you've made that agreement with spirit—once you've said, "Yes, I will carry your messages. I will walk between the worlds"—you carry that commitment like a seal across your soul.

I was branded by spirits all those years ago, and it changed me.

People sometimes ask me why I still do this work when I could be living in ease, detached from all of it. I smile, and I tell them the truth: I *am* living in ease—because I am living in alignment. There is no peace greater than doing what you were meant to do, even when it challenges you, even when it exhausts you, even when it demands everything.

The spirits claimed me not out of force, but out of trust. And I have never wanted to betray that trust. So yes, I could have walked away. But every time I tried, I heard the whisper again. Felt the tap on my shoulder. Saw the name, the face, the message waiting to be spoken.

And in those moments, I remember: this isn't a job. It's a covenant. One I intend to honor for as long as I draw breath.

In the beginning, everything about my psychic experiences felt dark—terrifying, even. The first few times I connected with the spirit world, it wasn't the peaceful, radiant scene I had imagined. No—it was raw. It was shadowed. At times, it felt as though I was stepping into a vast expanse of blackness, thick and oppressive, with no clear path ahead.

I remember the sensation of being swallowed up by it—the overwhelming silence, the weight of unseen eyes, the creeping chill that made my heart race and my hands shake. There were moments I thought I had made a grave mistake, when I wondered if I was losing my mind—or if I had somehow opened a door that could never be closed.

The dead weren't always gentle or welcoming. There were miscommunications, angry spirits, confusion, and pain. I had no guide, no teacher to help me navigate the chaos. In those early years, I often found myself questioning everything I thought I knew about the afterlife, about spirit communication, and about my own sanity.

But slowly, as the years passed and my skills deepened, something began to shift. The darkness I once encountered began to clear, like fog lifting over water at dawn. I learned that what had felt so ominous was simply a reflection of my own fear—a fear of the unknown, a fear of stepping too close to something that felt too vast for the human mind to comprehend.

And as I learned to trust the process—to surrender to it—the nature of my experiences changed. Instead of blackness, I began to see blinding light: pure, overwhelming, unearthly light. At first, it felt like too much, as if I were staring into the heart of the sun. But then I realized it wasn't a force that would blind me. It was a presence that illuminated.

And what came with that light was beauty—beauty so profound and so pure that it took my breath away every time I encountered it.

Now, when I connect with the spirit world, it's no longer about darkness or shadows. It's about the radiance of souls who have transcended the limitations of earthly existence. It's the golden glow that suffuses the space around me, the shimmering colors that dance in the air like an aurora borealis, the warmth that fills the room even when no light is physically present.

I've seen the faces of loved ones who have passed, bathed in a glow so gentle and loving it could never be mistaken for anything other than peace. The clarity I now experience is nothing short of miraculous—it's as if the veil between worlds has lifted just enough to allow the beauty of the other side to pour through. And with it, the most profound sense of love.

Not the love we feel here on Earth, but a love that is expansive, timeless, unconditional. It's the kind of love that transcends everything—pain, distance, even death itself.

There are still moments when the work challenges me, when I find myself standing at the edge of that darkness again. But now, I know that darkness is just another layer of understanding—something to be embraced, not feared.

Because once you've glimpsed the light—once you've felt the beauty of that connection—you realize that the darkness is just a necessary part of the journey. It's through that contrast that we come to truly appreciate the radiance that surrounds us, the sacredness of the messages we receive, and the profound truth that death, in all its forms, is not an end.

It is simply another beginning.

And every time I connect with the spirit world now, I am reminded of that: the light is always there, just beyond the veil, waiting to be seen.

And once you see it, you can never unsee it.

It is eternal.

It still takes my breath away.

About the Author

For more than twenty-five years, Celebrity Psychic Medium Kenneth Drake has connected audiences throughout the world to the Other Side. Called "iconic" by *New York Today*, the psychic commonly referred to as *"Hollywood's Psychic"* has been credited with more than 50,000 readings in the psychic entertainment industry, serving as personal advisor to Hollywood's most elite. Beginning his career after what he describes as a "terrifying encounter" at an early age, Kenneth Drake began to surrender to the gift of mediumship, becoming a staunch advocate for the philosophy and religion of Spiritualism. A former member of the Spiritualists' National Union of Great Britain, the governing Body which oversees the prestigious Arthur Findlay College, Kenneth Drake continues to study and teach psychic phenomena. The information gleaned from his private sessions in séance have been published internationally in

Sedona Journal of Emergence. Though largely retired from public performances, Kenneth Drake maintains a private practice and on rare occasions makes appearances at paranormal and horror conventions, connecting with a new generation of haunted seekers.

For more information
www.hollywoodspsychic.com

instagram.com/hollywoodspsychic